Studies in discourse analysis

Studies in discourse analysis

Edited by Malcolm Coulthard and Martin Montgomery

Y 10 5

Routledge & Kegan Paul
London, Boston and Henley

First published in 1981
by Routledge & Kegan Paul Ltd
39 Store Street,
London WC1E 7DD,
9 Park Street,
Boston, Mass. 12108, USA and
Broadway House,
Newtown Road,
Henley-on-Thames,
Oxon RG9 1EN
Printed in Great Britain by
Thomson Litho Ltd, East Kilbride, Scotland
© Malcolm Coulthard and Martin Montgomery 1981

British Library Cataloguing in Publication Data

Studies in discourse analysis.
  1. Discourse analysis
  I. Coulthard, Malcolm
  II. Montgomery, Martin
  415   P302   80-41907

  ISBN 0-7100-0510-5

For John Sinclair

Contents

Transcription conventions

H	High Key
M	Mid Key
L	Low Key
p	falling tone
p+	rising–falling tone
r	falling–rising tone
r+	rising tone
o	level tone
// //	tone unit boundaries
....	incomplete tone unit
( )	utterances with intonation not ascertainable because of recording conditions
YES	tonic syllable underlined
CAPITALS	prominent syllables
// ..	no tonic syllable, therefore no tone choice

NOTE

(i) Tone unit boundaries // are always on Mid Key line.
(ii) Tone choice symbols p, r, etc. are on same Key line as tonic syllable.
(iii) Where a tone unit is incomplete, there is no tonic syllable and therefore no tone choice.

Chapter 1

Developing a description of spoken discourse

Malcolm Coulthard, Martin Montgomery and David Brazil

Scientific articles and books are typically concerned with presenting findings rather than the stages through which the research progressed and the false trails hopefully followed. However, we think it is occasionally useful to see some of the initial confusion and be party to some of the arguments and decisions which culminated in the polished production for the paying public, particularly when a discipline is, in Kuhn's (1970) terms, in a state of revolution, and when the way forward is by no means clear. The aim of this chapter, therefore, is not to present in detail our model for describing the structure of verbal interaction – the original version is already available in Sinclair and Coulthard (1975) and our present ideas are discussed in subsequent chapters. Our intention is rather to give the reader an insight into the way the problems were faced and solved, these solutions questioned in turn and new ones proposed. In so doing we hope also to give the reader criteria for evaluating alternative descriptions of verbal interaction.

SECTION 1 ORIGINATING A DESCRIPTION
SSRC Project 'The English used by teachers and pupils' 1970-2

It is now quite hard to realise that, when this project began a decade ago with the aim of producing a linguistic description of interaction in the classroom, there was virtually no relevant published research. Within linguistics it was the height of the conflict between generative and interpretive semantics and Robin Lakoff's paper arguing for the importance of context was two years away. Indeed all the articles which we now consider seminal were yet to come: Hymes was arguing for a broader definition of the scope of linguistics, but the paper outlining the concept of 'communicative competence' had not been published; the work by Labov on sequencing and A–B events and the Sacks lecture notes were unknown and the now considerable body of work in conversational analysis was not yet written. Only the work of Austin and Searle on speech acts, offering the powerful idea that people do things with words, was available then in much the same form as it is now.

In 1970 the only major published attempts to handle the structure of interaction were, fortuitously, all concerned with analysing

classroom interaction – Barnes (1969), Flanders (1970), Bellack
et al. (1966). In evaluating the usefulness and adaptability of these
descriptions for our own aims we used informally the set of minimal
criteria for an adequate <u>linguistic</u> description, later presented
systematically in Sinclair (1973):

(i) the descriptive system should be finite, otherwise one is
saying nothing at all, but merely creating the illusion of
classification.

(ii) the symbols or terms in the descriptive system should be
precisely relatable to their exponents in the data so that the
classification is replicable and clear. There will be problems of interpretation, marginal choices and so on, but that
is a feature of all practical classification.

(iii) the descriptive system should be comprehensive. This is not
in fact an impossible criterion because one can always have a
'ragbag' category, and if one then feels uneasy about putting
certain items together in the ragbag this may well lead to
further insights.

(iv) there must be at least one impossible combination of symbols.

This is the basic notion of linguistic structure.
Barnes described his study as a

preliminary investigation of the interaction between the linguistic
expectations (drawn from home and primary school experience)
brought by pupils to their secondary schools, and the linguistic
demands set up (implicitly and explicitly) by the teachers in the
classrooms (1969, pp. 13-14).

Although preliminary, this is one of the most important studies of
classroom interaction. Besides confirming earlier findings by
Bellack et al. (1966) and Flanders (1965) on amount and quality of
pupil participation, Barnes analyses extracts of lessons in detail to
demonstrate the ways in which teachers interrupt, misunderstand,
confuse, dominate and constrict their pupils. He shows how
apparently 'open' questions are not 'open' at all, as the children
well know:

(1) T: What can you tell me about a bunsen burner, Alan?
P: A luminous and non-luminous flame (ibid., pp. 23-5).

He also shows how some teachers are obsessed with terminology
rather than concepts (pp. 47-51); and how experiences important to
the children and potential openings for a more understandable explanation are often rejected by a teacher anxious to return to his
lesson plan (p. 28).

Unfortunately, the system of analysis used by Barnes is partial –
he focuses in detail on the types of question used by teachers and the
kinds of response these expect, and on the vocabulary items used by
teachers. It is this detailed concentration which provides the educational pay-off, but there is a lot of classroom interaction with
which this system is not designed to cope, and it thus failed to meet
our third criterion – comprehensive description.

A system which does set out to describe all the data is that presented in Flanders (1970). The basic system comprises ten
categories, seven for teacher talk, two for pupil talk and one for

'silence or confusion in which communication cannot be understood by the observer'. The system is intended to be used for coding lessons as they happen, not retrospectively from recordings - the observer notes the appropriate category for the talk every three seconds and builds up a profile of the lesson.

The Flanders system has been widely criticised: for its decision to use time as a basic unit of coding (Forsyth 1971); for its failure to deal adequately with non-verbal aspects (Galloway 1968, Evans 1970); for its inability to deal with informal classroom situations (Walker 1971); for the basic weakness it shares with all other category systems, lack of explicitness, which means that the observer has to 'fill out' the categories as he uses them. It remains, however, the most popular system and with various modifications has been used in literally thousands of studies.

To linguists interested in the ebb and flow of conversation the system appeared to offer a great deal:

> The major feature of this category system lies in the analysis of initiative and response which is characteristic of interaction between two or more individuals. To initiate, in this context, means to make the first move, to lead, to begin, to introduce an idea or concept for the first time, to express one's own will. To respond means to take action after an initiation, to counter, to amplify or react to ideas which have already been expressed, to conform or even comply to the will expressed by others (Flanders, 1970, p. 35).

It was only when we came to examine examples that we realised we had a crucially different concept of the activities of initiating and responding. For us, with our interest in how turns to speak are distributed, any utterance which looks forward and requires another person to speak must be initiating; for Flanders, with a greater interest in how far pupils' contributions are utilised by the teacher, any utterance based on something a pupil has said is regarded as a response.

> S: the rain on the desert would make many plants grow
> T: Mary thinks plants would grow because of the rain
>   WOULD YOU AGREE OR DISAGREE, JERRY (ibid., p. 43)

The difference in aims was a basic one. Flanders's major interest is topical not structural - he focuses on who controls the topic not the talking. This explains why the question above, which we would regard as initiating because it requires a pupil to reply, can be seen as responding because it is part of a pupil-introduced topic. There are other examples of this difference in emphasis. Flanders asks us to imagine a situation where the pupils are contributing eagerly and the teacher's only (sic) role is to decide who talks next, by pointing, nodding or calling out names, and suggests that the teacher's contribution is trivial, 'One of the better ground rules we have used is to ignore the teacher' (ibid., p. 45). However, for us, with a major interest in the way in which the role of speaker or turns at speaking are distributed, this kind of contribution by the teacher is highly significant.

Possibly because of the crude division of all that is said into

instances of initiative or response, possibly because of the
temporal – every three seconds – rather than linguistic unit of
analysis, Flanders discovers no larger structures, except statistical tendencies for categories to cluster into patterns characterised
by a predominance of teacher or pupil initiatives and the system thus
failed to satisfy our fourth criterion, that there should be at least
one impossible combination of symbols.

The system proposed by Bellack et al. (1966) was the most useful
and suggestive for our purposes, although it was only after we had
produced a somewhat similar system that we realised that, while
pursuing educational aims, Bellack had progressed a considerable
way towards the kind of functional and structural analysis of discourse we were seeking. Bellack proposes four major categories,
structuring, soliciting, responding and reacting. The definitions of
these pedagogical moves are as follows:

> Structuring Structuring moves serve the pedagogical function of
> setting the context for subsequent behaviour by either launching or
> halting–excluding interaction between students and teachers.
> For example, teachers frequently launch a class period with a
> structuring move in which they focus attention on the topic or
> problem to be discussed during that session.
> Soliciting Moves in this category are intended to elicit (a) an
> active verbal response on the part of the persons addressed; (b)
> a cognitive response, e.g. encouraging persons addressed to
> attend to something; (c) a physical response. All questions are
> solicitations, as are commands, imperatives and requests.
> Responding These moves bear a reciprocal relationship to solicit-
> ing moves and occur only in relation to them. Their pedagogical
> function is to fulfil the expectation of soliciting moves; thus stu-
> dents' answers to teachers' questions are classified as responding
> moves.
> Reacting These moves are occasioned by a structuring, soliciting,
> responding, or prior reacting move, but are not directly elicited
> by them. Pedagogically, these moves serve to modify (by clarify-
> ing, synthesizing, or expanding) and/or to rate (positively or
> negatively) what has been said previously. Reacting moves differ
> from responding moves: while a responding move is always
> directly elicited by a solicitation, preceding moves serve only as
> the occasion for reactions (ibid., p. 4).

The following is an example of the analysis applied to a piece of
data:

T: STR: lets turn to American investment abroad
   SOL: you suppose we do invest much money outside of the US
P: RES: yes

This system had, for us, three major advantages over that proposed by Flanders. Firstly, the analysis is in terms of linguistic
not temporal units – Flanders's system presents a detailed picture of
the lesson and enables one to discover what was happening at any
point, but it has the disadvantage that one long teacher question
lasting seven or eight seconds will be coded in exactly the same way
as, and therefore be indistinguishable from, three shorter questions.

Secondly, Bellack had to us more acceptable ideas about what constitutes initiating and responding behaviour, sees these as reciprocal, and introduces the category of reacting to cope with teacher
utterances which are related to, but not called for by, pupil utterances. Thirdly, the concept of move is a powerful one. Utterances
typically consist of one or two moves and can never consist of more
than three - a responding or reacting move, followed by structuring
and soliciting moves.
These observations led Bellack to postulate a higher structure.
He observes that

> moves occur in classroom discourse in certain cyclical patterns or
> combinations, which we designated teaching cycles. A [typical]
> teaching cycle begins either with a structuring or a soliciting
> move...continues with a responding move by the student addressed
> and ends with an evaluative reaction by the teacher (ibid., p. 5).

He thus proposes a hierarchical description of classroom discourse
- 'lessons' are said to consist of a series of 'cycles' which in turn
consist of one or more 'moves'.
The major deficiency of Bellack's system from our point of view
was its inability to satisfy Sinclair's second criterion - there was no
attempt to show how the analytic categories related to their exponents
in the data, but we also felt that the categories were not sufficiently
delicate, and that they therefore masked important functional and
structural differences.
When we ourselves first began to analyse transcripts of recordings
we had collected in classrooms we really had no firm assumptions
about what appropriate analytic tools would be like. Working on
short extracts we looked at supra-sentential grammatical relations,
trying to see whether an adaptation of the procedures proposed by
Harris in his article 'Discourse Analysis' would be fruitful; we
looked at grammatical cohesion; we examined topic development as
realised through lexical repetition and substitution; we looked at the
text as a sequence of speech acts. We made very little progress.
Our initial assumption was that a description of the structure of
interaction would include restrictions on the combination of particular kinds of utterance, and our early transcripts embodied the
assumption that at a very simple level much classroom interaction
consisted of a teacher utterance followed by a pupil utterance
followed by a teacher utterance...or T-P-T-P-T...

(4) 1 Can you tell me why you eat
    all that food? Yes.

        2 To keep you strong.

  3 To keep you strong. Yes.
  To keep you strong. Why do
  you want to be strong?

        4 Sir, muscles.

  5 To make muscles. Yes.
  Well what would you want to
  use - what would you want to
  do with your muscles?

        6 Sir, use them

Our first real break-through came when we realised that 'utterance' was not in fact a unit of interaction at all – there are significant breaks in the middle of utterances 3 and 5 in the example above of a kind repeated in many teacher utterances. The first half of the utterance links back to what the pupil has said, the second half links forward to what a pupil will say next. Thus we have a structural unit consisting of three parts, in which the teacher has two turns for every one pupil turn, and a more accurate representation of the structure of the interaction is T-P-T; T-P-T; T-P-T. To the smaller units we gave the label 'move' borrowed from Bellack, to the larger the label 'exchange'.

We labelled the three slots in the exchange 'initiation', 'response' and 'feedback', and defined the moves which occurred there in terms of their function in the discourse: moves in the initiation slot cause others to participate in the exchange; moves in the response slot conform to the constraints and fulfil the predictions of the preceding move and items in the third slot are evaluative of what comes in the second slot. (There is obviously a great deal of similarity with Bellack's soliciting, responding and reacting moves.) Thus:

(5) initiation T: why do you want to be strong
    response P: sir muscles
    feedback T: to make muscles yes

Since Sinclair (1966) we had been very conscious of what was there called 'plane change', points in interaction when speakers focus on aspects of the language or structure of the interaction instead of continuing.

(6) A: isn't the weather awful at the moment
    B: what exactly do you mean by awful

At certain points in lessons teachers in a sense step outside the interaction and comment on it either to summarise what has been done or said, or to prestructure what will occur next:

(7) so what we've just done is given some energy to this pen
(8) well today we're going to do three quizzes

These plane changes appeared to correspond with larger scale boundaries in the lesson and between successive instances there would be a series of exchanges. We had now reached a point where it seemed useful to try to formalise our description. As Labov was later to say 'formalisation is a fruitful procedure even when it is wrong: it sharpens our questions and promotes the search for answers' (1972a, p. 121). As there was no existing linguistic description of interaction, let alone a linguistic theory of inter-action, the only way forward was to analogise from existing gramma-tical theory. The descriptive theory we chose was that outlined in Halliday's paper 'Categories of the theory of grammar' (1961), des-pite the fact that it had already been superseded in its author's opinion by later proposals.

There were two main reasons for this. Firstly, we faced the difficulty that intuitions about permissible sequences in discourse are much weaker than intuitions about grammatical sequences and thus we were forced, despite Chomsky's strong attack on data-based descriptions, to base our analysis very much on data rather than intuition, and Halliday's descriptive principles are well suited to the problem of handling new data - for instance many grammatical descriptions assign particular importance to sentence as a unit of analysis; in a Hallidayan description all units are of equal importance and this was a significant point as we had no idea even of how many units there might be. Secondly, only after many thousands of man-years spent discovering and describing grammatical facts, was it possible to contemplate a deep structure analysis - in beginning the analysis of discourse we were anxious to remain initially on the surface, and 'Categories...' presents principles for designing a powerful but also very simple description of surface structure on the basis of very few a priori assumptions about the data. Now ten years later we are able to contemplate a description based on Halliday's later systemic theory and a first attempt is presented in Chapter 6.

Ranks and levels

A first assumption of a 'categories' description is that the analytic units can be set out on a rank scale which implies that units are related in a 'consists-of' relationship with smaller units combining with other units of the same size to form larger ones. Thus a sentence consists of one or more clauses each of which in turn consists of one or more groups, and so on. In setting out our rank scale we initially suggested four ranks:

> Lesson
> Transaction
> Exchange
> Move

with transactions having their beginnings and/or ends marked by the 'plane-change' items which we now labelled 'focusing' moves, and with lessons seen as consisting of a series of transactions. As is evident there was no place for 'utterance' in this rank scale; although utterances consist of one or more moves there is no larger unit which consists of one or more utterances for, as we discussed above, exchange boundaries typically occur in the middle of teacher utterances.

After proposing this rank scale made up of four analytic units we were faced with the major question of how and where this rank scale made contact with the rank scale morpheme ⟷ sentence devised to handle grammatical structure. Did our rank scale slot on top of the grammatical one, and were moves thus made up of sentences in the same way as sentences were made up of clauses, or was our rank scale not directly related at all? To answer this question we must consider the relationship between ranks and levels.

The lowest unit in a rank scale has, by definition, no structure - otherwise it wouldn't be the lowest, but this doesn't mean that description necessarily stops there. In a very real sense morphemes consist of phonemes or phonic substance and for a long time American structuralism attempted to treat phonetic, phonological and morphological problems as a continuum. Now one of the basic tenets of modern linguistics is that there are two separate kinds of language patterning or 'levels' – the phonological and the grammatical – each with its own rank scale, and the descriptive problem is to show how units at the level of grammar are realised by units at the level of phonology.

The unit at the highest rank in a particular level is one which has a structure that can be expressed in terms of smaller units, but which does not itself form part of the structure of any larger unit. Any attempt to describe structure assumes implicitly that there are certain combinations of units which either do not occur, or if they do occur, are unacceptable – within grammar such structures are classified as ungrammatical. The corollary is that a potential unit upon whose structure one can discover no constraints in terms of combinations of the unit next below has no structure and is therefore not a unit in the rank scale. It is for this reason that sentence must in fact be regarded as the highest unit of grammar, for, despite many attempts to describe paragraph structure and despite the obvious cohesive links between sentences, it is impossible to characterise paragraphs in terms of permissible and non-permissible combinations of classes of sentence. All combinations are possible and thus the actual sequence of sentences within a paragraph depends upon stylistic not grammatical considerations.

In analysis each level and its descriptive units handle part of the linguistic organisation of a stretch of language, but there is no necessary correspondence between either the size or the boundaries of analytic units in different levels. As Halliday stresses, whereas

> all formal distinctions presuppose some distinction in substance ... no relation whatsoever is presupposed between the categories required to state the distinction in form (grammar and lexis) and the categories required to state phonologically the distinction in substance which carries it (1961, pp. 282-3).

A simple example of this principle is the plural morpheme which even in regular cases may be realised at the level of phonology by the unit 'syllable' or the unit 'phoneme' – horse : horses; cat : cats. There are of course, much more complex cases and it is a similar lack of fit between units that provides strong support for postulating the existence of the new level of discourse.

Sinclair and Coulthard (1975) were later to point out not only can the act directive be realised by all four clause structures, imperative, interrogative, declarative and moodless, but also in many cases, as the following examples illustrate, the 'directiveness' appears in some way to derive from the occurrence of the base form of the verb irrespective of whatever other grammatical items precede it – the function of these preceding items seems to be to carry as yet unclassifiable degrees of 'politeness'.

    (9) (i)   shut the door
        (ii)   can you shut the door
        (iii) I wonder if you could shut the door
        (iv)   I want you to shut the door
        (v)   please shut the door
        (vi)   lets shut the door

This set of examples suggests that some discourse categories, whose nature we cannot yet really envisage, cut right across traditional grammatical boundaries with the directive function being realised at times by only part of the verbal group, and a marker of politeness being realised by another set of words which do not comprise a recognisable grammatical unit. One five-year-old appears to be constructing acts on exactly this principle

(10) | fasten my shoe
please may you | open the door
                          | give me a drink

Thus the reasons for postulating discourse as a new level are directly analogous to the ones already accepted for separating phonology and grammar as descriptive levels: that conflation causes added complexity and also weakens the power of the description. It would now appear that grammatical description is suffering problems similar to those earlier encountered by early structuralists because grammarians are unwilling to acknowledge the existence of a further descriptive level. Sinclair and Coulthard suggest that 'a reasonable symptom of the need to establish a further level [is] the clustering of descriptive features in the larger structures of the uppermost level' (1975, p. 121) and observe that the clause or sentence is currently being forced to cope with most of the newly discovered linguistic complexity: 'it now has to manage intricacies of intonation selection, information organisation, semantic structuring, sociolinguistic sensitivity, illocution and presupposition in addition to its traditional concerns' (ibid.).

All this suggests strongly that an artificial ceiling has been reached. However, it is one thing to perceive the problem, quite another to detail the solution and despite the observations above it was still very much as an act of faith rather than as a result of overwhelming evidence that we postulated discourse as a separate level of patterning.

It was as we struggled to show the realisation relationship between moves and sentences that we were forced to recognise the existence of another rank below move which we labelled 'act'. (As we said above, it was this very flexibility of the descriptive system, which in this case allowed us to create a new rank at a comparatively late state in the investigation, which had originally attracted us to Halliday's model.) This new set of units – we eventually recognised twenty-two, which are set out and discussed in detail in Sinclair and Coulthard (1975) – enabled us not only to describe much more successfully and powerfully the structure of classroom interaction but also to see more clearly ways of relating discourse units to the lexical and grammatical items which realise them.

It is obviously not possible to discuss all the acts in detail here and so we will concentrate on three concerned with the teacher's management of turn-taking in the classroom, concentrating on exchanges where the teacher is producing 'elicitations', acts looking for a verbal response, or 'reply'. Obviously there has to be some linguistic etiquette inside the classroom: if thirty pupils shouted out the answer to every elicitation there would be chaos. There are

several ways in which teachers decide who will talk. Sometimes
they 'nominate' a child,

(11) <u>Joan</u> do you know who these people were

sometimes children are required to bid by raising their hand or
shouting 'sir' or 'miss' and the teacher then nominates one of those
who have bid.

(12) T:(elicit)   anyone think they know what it says
     P:(bid)   ⟨raised hand⟩
     T:(nomination) let's see what you think Martin
     P:(reply)   heeroglyphs
     T:(evaluation) yes you're pronouncing it almost right

At times, with a new or difficult class a teacher may find he needs
to insist on this speaker selection process.   The following examples
come from a lesson given by an experienced teacher to a class he
hasn't taught before, when he felt it necessary to provide cues to the
children to raise their hands and bid:

(13) T:(cue)   hands up
     T:(elicit)   what's that
     P:(bid)   ⟨raised hand⟩
     T:(nomination) janet
     P:(reply)   a nail
     T:(evaluation) a nail well done a nail

When he doesn't cue, these children frequently forget to bid and he
has to remind them of the rules.

(14) T:(elicit)   what do we do with a saw
     P:(reply)   cut wood
     T:(evaluation) yes
                 you're shouting out though

Realisation

As we noted above, the major deficiency of the description proposed
by Bellack was that it was not possible to relate the categories precisely to the data; when we came to relate our categories to their
realisations at the level of form we encountered some difficulties.
For some of the acts, like nomination and marker, it was not too difficult to imagine being able to list the realisations exhaustively, but
significantly the easier it was to specify the realisations, the more
marginal a role the acts appeared to play in the development of discourse.   The task was much more difficult for the crucial acts
related to initiating and sustaining the discourse, and particularly
so with the acts elicitation, informative, and directive, which can
informally be regarded as question, statement and command, respectively.

One might expect that the formal grammatical system of mood would
provide a reliable guide to the discourse function of an utterance
such that informatives would be realised by declaratives, elicitations by interrogatives, and directives by imperatives, but in fact
the structural configuration of the subject and predicator of a clause
gives no reliable indication in itself of the function performed and

this is particularly the case with declarative and interrogative structures. It is not difficult, for instance, to construct contexts in which all of the following would be heard as directives although they embody a variety of selections from the mood system.

(15) can you shut the door   (interrogative)
     would you mind shutting the door   (interrogative)
     I wonder if you can shut the door   (declarative)
     the door is still open   (declarative)
     the door   (moodless)
     shut the door   (imperative)

In an attempt to come to grips with this lack of fit between form and function we suggested the need for three sets of labels, with the situational ones mediating between the discourse and grammatical ones (see figure 1.1).

grammatical categories	situational categories	discourse categories
declarative	statement	informative
interrogative	question	elicitation
imperative	command	directive

Figure 1.1 Grammatical, situational and discourse categories

The real descriptive problem was to show how the grammatical and situational categories were related. As we confessed at the time we could 'make only a rudimentary attempt to deal with situation', but what we were trying to do was to use 'at present in an ad hoc and unsystematised way, knowledge about schools, class-rooms, one particular moment in a lesson, to reclassify items already labelled by the grammar' (Sinclair et al., 1972, p. 29). Theoretically the scope and nature of relevant situational informa-tion could have been almost unlimited but it was in fact possible to make a significant delimitation of relevant features of the situation by listing questions, the answers to which significantly determine the interpretation of particular clause types:

   (1) If the clause is interrogative is the addressee also the
       subject?
   (2) What actions or activities are physically impossible at the time
       of utterance?
   (3) What actions or activities are proscribed at the time of
       utterance?
   (4) What actions or activities have been prescribed up to the time
       of utterance?
The answers to these questions enable a given interrogative clause, for example 'what are you laughing at', or 'can you swim a length', to be classified as a question or command. The following systemic presentation attempts to make this clear:

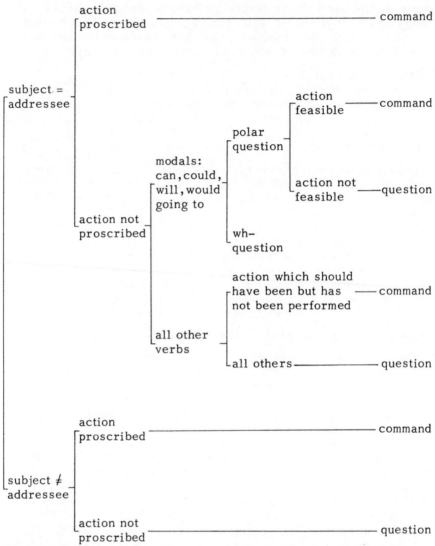

Figure 1.2 The classification of an interrogative by situational information

This interpretive procedure could be reformulated in terms of rules like the following one:

Any declarative or interrogative is to be interpreted as a <u>command to stop</u> if it refers to an action or activity which is proscribed at the time of utterance:

1 I can hear someone laughing   command
2 is someone laughing   command
3 what are you laughing at   command
4 what are you laughing at   question

The declarative command, as in the first example, is very popular with some teachers. It is superficially an observation, but its only relevance at the time of utterance is that it draws the attention of 'someone' to their laughter, so that they will stop. Examples 2 and 3, though interrogative in form, work in exactly the same way. Example 4 is only interpreted as a question when laughter is not regarded as a forbidden or proscribed activity.

The distinction between situational and discourse categories was that between potential and actual function; with this distinction we were trying to cope with the real-time nature of discourse, the way in which items are produced and then 'pushed down' or 'edited' and replaced with a subsequent item to which the next speaker is expected to respond. In the following example we have two questions but only one elicitation to which the pupils are expected to respond, the first question does not realise its potential and become an elicitation because it is replaced by the second. (The category 'starter' includes such 'failed' items.)

    (16) T: Q1 and when you're working what are you using apart from
           your muscles
        Q2 what does the food give you

In the space available it has not been possible to present the proposed analysis in detail, but that in any case would have been to duplicate material available in Sinclair and Coulthard (1975); our aim has rather been to give an insight into why particular decisions were taken and how particular analyses and aspects of the descriptive system emerged.

By the end of this first project we had
(i)   postulated a new level of linguistic organisation, discourse;
(ii) suggested a five-unit rank scale to handle the standard patterns;
(iii) and begun to explore ways of handling the realisation relationship between the smallest units of discourse, acts, and the lexico-grammatical items which realised them at the level of form.

We had, however, only examined one type of discourse, classroom interaction, and had no idea how situation-specific were the units and structures we had proposed.

SECTION 2 DEVELOPING THE DESCRIPTION
SSRC Project 'The structure of verbal interaction in selected situations' 1972-4

The final report of the first project, 'The English Used by Teachers and Pupils', appeared to offer an interesting and in many ways satisfying description of the structure of interaction in one highly formalised situation. It was obvious even at the time, though, that some aspects of the description were less satisfying than others. The criteria for isolating some of the analytic units were not sufficiently explicit and not always consistent. There were, for example, real difficulties at times in deciding where a 'comment' ended and a succeeding 'inform' began and this was related to the general analytic problem of the relationship between discourse units and their lexico-grammatical realisations. Even when long utterances could be unambiguously analysed as a single move, the question remained of

whether it was better to treat a long teacher opening move, for
instance, as consisting of one informing act, or a whole series.
Indeed until the realisation relationship with grammar is solved
there will remain good arguments on both sides.

Nevertheless, despite the obvious shortcomings it was felt that the
basic principles of the description were sound and given that the
ultimate goal was, and still is, a descriptive system that can cope
with all forms of discourse, it seemed that the best heuristic procedure was not to continue tinkering with the system to make it fit
classroom discourse better, but rather to begin work on other kinds
of data. We had argued that there were marked advantages in
beginning an investigation of discourse structure with the classroom,
a situation where the mechanisms were likely to be more apparent,
where 'one participant has acknowledged responsibility for the
direction of the discourse, for deciding who shall speak when, and
for introducing and ending topics' (p. 6), but there was, of course,
the danger that beginning a description of discourse structure with
classroom discourse had been analogous to beginning a grammatical
description of an unknown language by concentrating on newspaper
headlines; work on the structure of other types of interaction would
enable us to test the validity and generality of the descriptive
categories and procedures.

At this stage we had no firm ideas about which factors in a situation might be the most important in determining the structure of the
discourse. We did of course have hypotheses and chose three types
of interaction – doctor/patient interviews, chaired television discussions and industrial committee meetings – which enabled us to vary
the following potentially significant factors: degree of control over
topic invested in one person; degree of control over turn-taking
invested in one person; existence of status difference between
participants either because of acknowledged superior expertise or
situationally assigned role; degree of familiarity between participants; where information lies; purpose of interaction and whether
there is one or more goals achievable within the single interaction.

It is instructive to compare the relationship of teacher, doctor,
media discussion chairman and committee chairman, who all have a
greater or lesser control over turn-taking in their respective situations, to their respective co-participant(s) along the dimensions of
'status difference' and 'where information lies'. They are seen to
be an interestingly contrasting set of interactive roles.

While these factors are quite obviously defined in sociological
terms the investigation remained a linguistic one for, while initially
it was essential to use concepts like 'status', and talk in terms of
social roles like 'chairman', the hope was that eventually it would be
possible to come full circle and define roles like 'chairman' as a set
of linguistic options. Everyone has been in situations when one
participant has 'taken over' a meeting or seminar by acting as, i.e.
selecting linguistic options restricted to, the chairman.

In beginning the description of the new data the research procedure was not to take the description devised for classroom interaction and attempt to impose it on the data, but rather to develop new

descriptions for each situation using the same descriptive principles.
Thus we were engaged in describing what it is that makes TV discussions, for example, different as speech events from doctor/patient
interviews and committee meetings, but of course for a set of such
descriptions to be mutually enlightening they would need to have more
or less common modes of description. Thus we were, as we progressed, moving backwards and forwards from individual situations
to general problems and developing both descriptions of particular
speech events and a theory of discourse to underpin the descriptions.

Macrostructures

The basic theoretical assumption we carried over to our consideration of these new types of interaction was that it would be possible to
describe them in terms of a rank scale, although we were quite prepared for the discovery of new ranks, for some forms of interaction
to be describable in terms of fewer ranks, and for structural complexity to be differentially distributed. We had labelled the largest
rank in our description of classroom interaction 'lesson'; this was
obviously an inappropriate label for a rank in a generalised description of discourse and we therefore substituted the term 'interaction'.
   While being aware from the beginning of the necessity of keeping
distinct not only what Hymes (1972) was later to call 'situation' from
the speech event(s) which occur in a particular situation, but also
our linguistically defined unit 'lesson' from units like 'period' whose
identification depended on other, pedagogical, criteria, we did in
fact assume that the boundaries of lessons were unproblematic and
simply concerned ourselves with describing their internal structure.
This may, of course, have been a product of the basic research procedure of working from tape-recordings in which typically the
beginning of the recording and the beginning of the interaction were
co-terminous. However, even though Turner's (1972) article
addressed this very problem in demonstrating that in therapy sessions the speech event 'therapy' is often preceded by another, 'conversation', and if so the boundary between the two is clearly marked,
we still did not, in this second project, treat the delimitation of
interactions as a problem - this may partly have been because, again
by chance, two of the situations we chose to investigate were ones in
which situation and interaction were co-terminous - doctor/patient
interviews and broadcast discussions. However, we are now able
to offer a very powerful explanation of how the beginnings of interactions are marked but that must wait until we have outlined our
description of intonation (pp. 39-50).
   Uniquely, the doctor/patient interviews had their beginnings and
endings marked by greeting and leave-taking sequences:
   (1) D: come in. hello. good morning
       P: good morning doctor

       D: bye bye
       P: cheerio

However, somewhat to our surprise, one doctor who had been asked
to tape-record his interviews decided that the greetings were not
part of the interview and only turned on the tape-recorder after
these preliminaries, while another turned off the tape-recorder
before he dismissed the patient. In retrospect it appears that the
doctor's intuitions may have been surer than ours, and that the
greeting and leave-taking are not parts of the structure of particular
interactions but markers of the beginning and end of situations during
which interactions can occur. In other words the doctor/patient
interview was perhaps misleading because, including as it did only
one interaction, it also had both greeting and leave-taking which we
assumed to be part of its characteristic structure. If instead we
assume that there is a larger unit than interaction consisting of one
or more interactions typically bounded by the greeting and leave-
taking we get a much more satisfactory picture. The doctor/patient
consultation becomes the limiting case, and lessons and broadcast
discussions are now seen as interactions which are neither initial
nor final in this larger unit of interaction; we can also make sense
of our observation that the hospital consultations tended to have an
opening greeting but no closing, precisely because the patient would
return, after going elsewhere for an X-ray, blood sample, tests,
etc. to the doctor. It is also interesting to recall the ritualised
opening and closing of the school day in many primary schools.

> (2) T: good morning class two
>   P: good morning Miss Rowan
>
>   T: good afternoon class two
>   P: good afternoon Miss Rowan

Within English families beginnings to the day and to a lesser extent
endings tend not to be marked regularly by linguistic items, though
for visitors a morning greeting and a final 'goodnight' seem much
more the rule. To many, once they have encountered it, the French
family habit of marking the beginning and end of the day's interactions
by a handshake or a kiss seems a very sensible one. The whole
question of how far and how often the opening and closing can be
achieved by a non-verbal surrogate is an interesting one, but we are
still trying to cope with the theoretical problems of systematically
incorporating non-verbal items into the description - see Chapter 8.

Transactions

In the description proposed for classroom discourse transactions
were defined as units whose boundaries were typically marked by
frame and focus:

> (3) Frame   well
>   Focus   today I thought we'd do three quizzes

Transactions seemed to be co-terminous with topic boundaries in a
lesson though there were admittedly places in the data where we felt
the teacher changed direction but didn't mark a new transaction
boundary. Frames it will be recalled are realised by a small set of

items, 'good', 'well', 'O.K.', 'now', 'right', spoken with high
falling intonation. We have recently discovered that it is the intonation choice and not the lexical item which is crucial - as we discuss
and justify in detail on pp. 105-6, high pitch can itself, in certain
circumstances, be used to indicate transaction boundaries. However, we did not know this when we began work on the three new sets
of data.

One of the interesting questions to be answered by the new data,
we hoped, was how far the existence of the unit transaction, or
perhaps the realisation of its boundaries by frame and focus, depended on an asymmetrical organisation of speaking roles as in the
classroom and on the particular purpose of the interaction. Intuitively one can appreciate that there is every reason for the teacher
and, as we later discovered, the lecturer and seminar leader both
to divide up the interaction into manageable chunks and also to make
the structure of the interaction as clear as possible by prospectively
structuring and retrospectively summarising.

There were, however, no obvious reasons for a doctor to indulge
in focusing, so perhaps one of the stylistic differences might be the
absence of transactions in doctor/patient interviews. In fact,
transaction boundaries do occur, but realised only by frames; in
other words the doctors contented themselves with marking the
transitions.

(4) D: what sort of things bring that on
    P: when I have a lot of work at the office you know it comes on
    D: again when you're under pressure
    P: yeah
    D: yes
    D: RIGHT
    D: now you said something about some trouble with your neck

To the lay analyst it was not always evident why the doctor had
chosen to begin a new transaction, but there was almost invariably
a frame to mark for the patient the boundary between diagnosing and
prescribing.

(5) D: WELL ALL RIGHT
    D: well I'm going to give you an ointment...

With broadcast discussions we had a situation in which, like the
classroom, focusing items were important and where again it is the
speaker with control over the turn-taking machinery, here the
chairman, who marks the boundaries:

(6) H: I'd like to switch a bit because another theory that I
    developed when I was down in Fleet Street that there are two
    different animals one is called labour and one is tory and they
    are very very different people sort of people a tory is a man
    who is discreet who is sort of believes in the team spirit the
    labour man is garrulous indiscreet argumentative to what
    extent is that generalisation true D-Dick in your view

Items such as these seem to indicate that the topic previously under
discussion is being left in favour of a new one which is set up by the
chairman.

For the committee meetings the facts were similar. It appeared that most transactions could be defined entirely and explicitly in commonsense terms as corresponding to distinct 'items' on the agenda and their boundaries were explicitly marked, usually with a frame and focus, by the chairman:

(7) right thats the financial analyst
    now what do you want us to do next

The remaining transactions were concerned with such matters as discussing procedural problems, e.g. reasons for not discussing an item on the agenda, or negotiating adjournments, but their boundaries were similarly explicitly marked.

It is interesting to note the role of frames and focuses in dividing up the interaction into transactions. In three of the situations one participant, teacher or chairman, sees it as his role prospectively to describe and delimit the topic, in the fourth the doctor intermittently marks the boundaries but, often to the annoyance of the patient, specifically does not overtly gloss the topic of the transaction. Interestingly, in conversation an attempt to produce a focus like, 'we're going to talk about my holidays in France', would be heard as odd, and even frames are unusual, perhaps because, as Sacks observes, in conversations which are going well one has the phenomenon of 'topic drift', in other words marked endings or new beginnings are a thing to be avoided and tend to occur to signal the beginning of a new activity:

(8) Mother: right, coats on boys...

For this reason they are also used, as Schegloff and Sacks (1973) point out (though not of course labelling the items frames), explicitly to mark boundaries to topics in telephone calls, as a way of 'closing down' before the final leave-taking, and it is significant that the other major way of closing is to produce a retrospective focus.

Exchanges

Perhaps the most successful aspect of the description of classroom interaction had been that dealing with exchange structure. Most of the classroom data had been easily analysable into three-move exchanges, each move being relatively short and easily analysable into component acts. Those points where teachers had lapsed into monologue had, however, caused problems which, as we noted above, remained unresolved. In informally characterising our new situations sociologically it had seemed that doctor/patient interviews would be structurally closest to the type of classroom interaction we had already described – one dominant 'expert' speaker with control over topic, relevance and speaking turns and that committee meetings would be most different – a discussion between professional equals with the chairman having only the most general control over topic. Interestingly, this degree of similarity between situations appeared to be reflected in the degtee of similarity between characteristic exchange structures in the different situations.

(a) Doctor/patient exchanges
As we said above, in the classroom typically the teacher asks a
question, the pupil gives a brief answer and the teacher closes the
exchange with an evaluation and then moves on to initiate another
exchange. It is apparently inappropriate for the pupil to make any
response to the evaluation, and since pupils also rarely respond
overtly to any declarative utterances by the teacher following an
answer, it had been possible to treat these as comments and therefore part of the follow-up move, relying simply if not crudely on
length to distinguish comments from informing initiations. In
doctor/patient interviews however, after a patient's answering move
the doctor can do a number of different things. He may simply indicate that he has heard what the patient said:

> (9) D: and **has** this been more lately
>   P: well its been about a fortnight its been like this
>   D: YES

or he may **repeat part** or all of the patient's utterance:

> (10) D: and how long have you had these for
>   P: well I had 'em er a week last Wednesday
>   D: A WEEK LAST WEDNESDAY

or he may 'summarise' or 'paraphrase' or 'draw conclusions from'
the patient's answer:

> (11) D: when did you first start noticing that you er were having
>   attacks of coldness
>   P: erm I've always been very cold feet and hands
>   D: MOST OF YOUR LIFE

After such third utterances from the doctor, the patient may remain
silent and wait for another question or he may himself produce an
utterance similar to the doctor's second. More rarely the doctor
may then produce another utterance from this same set of choices.

For such data then it is not immediately obvious what constitutes
an exchange. Initially we tried to maintain the notion of an exchange
as maximally a three-part structure, as in the classroom analysis,
so that any third utterance which gave the opportunity of a fourth
contribution would be treated as a new initiation. However, in a
number of cases this was obviously unsatisfactory – we found for
instance that the patient could produce a fourth utterance even after
a minimal 'yes' as a third from the doctor and we would therefore
have had to categorise counter-intuitively some instances of 'yes' as
initiations:

> (12) D: but its only the last three months that its been making you
>   feel ill
>   P: ill with it yes
>   D: YES YES
>   P: yes doctor

Therefore we modified the exchange structure proposed for the
classroom to allow, in theory at least, an infinite repetition of the
feedback component. In doctor/patient interviews in fact
I R F F F is the longest structure occurring, and it is hard to
imagine any longer sequence of Fs outside a comedy sketch.

> (13) Initiation D: what's the main trouble

Response P: well about two years ago I started getting
headaches erm and then I was feeling something
heavy on my head like a heaviness you know lift-
ing a heavy weight
Feedback D: like a heavy weight on top of the head
Feedback P: yeah on top of the head
Feedback D: yes yes

However, not only are some doctor/patient exchanges more extended
than classroom ones, some are also briefer. One can by no means
be certain that following a patient's answer the doctor will in fact
begin his utterance with a follow-up move and this creates an
interesting analytic problem, because often items which in the data
function as new initiations are grammatically and lexically indistinguishable from those which function as follow-up moves. In order
to solve this problem we relied on our developing description of
intonation (Brazil, 1973), whose latest revision is sketched out in
Section 4 below, (pp. 39-50), and reported in more detail in Brazil
(1975, 1978a, b) and Brazil, Coulthard and Johns (1980).

By this time we were convinced that pitch-level contrasts between
tone groups were significant and suggested that for each successive
tone group the speaker has to choose high, mid or low key. (At the
time we saw mid key as the speaker's norm; now, while we still use
the concept of key, our definition is different, see below pp. 42-3). We
argued that there was a phonological unit above the tone unit having
the structure

(High, 1...n) Mid (Low 1...n)

It seemed that a high-tone group was to be interpreted as linking
forward carrying the implication 'there's more to follow', and a low-
tone group linking back carrying the implication 'this is said in a
particular situation created by what has gone before'. These
general phonological meanings gave us a way of categorising otherwise identical lexico-grammatical items which followed responses as
belonging either to follow-up or to initiating moves.

Moodless items, that is items without a verb, had caused particular problems in analysis. Now we were able to observe that when
a doctor selected low key for his third utterance in a sequence the
patient appeared to recognise that nothing more needed to be said;
with moodless mid-key summaries or paraphrases of his answer the
patient might feel an invitation to respond but no requirement on him
to do so; whereas high key utterances, unless they were minimal
forms like 'yes', were always interpreted by the patient as elicitations.

We can now give some examples to illustrate our classification of
options following a patient's answer. Lexical repetitions can be
realising either follow-up or elicitation, depending on whether or
not high key is selected as the following pairs of examples illustrate:

(14) Elicit D: and how long have you had these for
Reply P: well I had 'em er a week last Wednesday
Follow-up D: A WEEK LAST WEDNESDAY (low key)
Elicit D: do you bring up sputum
Reply P: only when I get a bit of indigestion and I like
bring the food up as well

Elicit	D: BRING THE FOOD UP AS WELL (high key)
Reply	P: well if I get violent indigestion everything comes up as easy as wink you know got to get rid of it
Follow-up	D: yes

(15) Elicit   D: how long have you had these quick pains on the right side of your head
Reply   P: well again when this trouble started
Follow-up   D: AGAIN FOR ABOUT TWO YEARS (low key)
Elicit   D: when did you first start noticing that you er were having attacks of coldness
Reply   P: I've always been very cold feet and hands
Elicit   D: MOST OF YOUR LIFE (high key)
Reply   P: yes I would say so doctor

Utterances declarative in form are rarer as follow-ups in this data; when they do occur it is the co-occurring low key choice which signals that no response is required:

(16) Elicit   D: he's the only one who's died amongst brothers and sisters
Reply   P: yes
Follow-up   D: SO THERE'S JUST YOUR SISTER AND YOURSELF (low key)
Elicit   D: is your husband well

We can now go on to distinguish at secondary delicacy the sub-classes of act which can occur as head of moves in the three places of exchange structure: initiation, response and feedback. We have already referred to eliciting moves, though strictly we should have referred to them as opening moves in eliciting exchanges. There are two major types having as head, respectively, the acts inquire and propose. Inquiring moves seek a reply which provides informa-tion, rather than simply polarity. We can distinguish three sub-types of act which realise the head of inquiring moves: inquire which is characteristically a wh-question, but sometimes an elliptical form, or a disjunctive question; return, a high-key repetition, seeking further information to clarify a preceding answer; and loop, one of a small set of items, 'pardon', 'sorry', etc., or a questioning-repeat, seeking repetition of the preceding move.

(17)   D: are there any illnesses that run in the family
    P: well my mother suffers with high blood pressure
    D: does she
Inquire   D: YOUR FATHER
    P: he's dead   he died of cancer

(18)   P: I felt a tight pain in the middle of the chest
Return   D: TIGHT PAIN
    P: you know like a sort of ache   tightness as you might say
    D: are you on any tablets for anything
Loop   P: AM I ON WHAT
    D: are you on any tablets for anything

Replies following inquiring moves may be very brief, but cannot be simply 'yes' or 'no'. In some cases they may be preceded by an acknowledging 'yes', and we may be able to distinguish an additional comment as in the following example:

(19) Inquire   D: how long have you had this trouble

    Reply   P: not very long doctor I wouldn't say   p'haps a couple of months   three months I'd say

    Comment   P: THEY'RE THE ONLY THING I WAS COMPLAINING ABOUT

    Follow-up   D: yes

The structure of the answering move in terms of acts was thus seen to be (acknowledge) reply (comment), but, like most pupil answers, most patient answers are brief and consist of only one act, reply.

The other type of eliciting move, proposing, is one seeking information about polarity. It seemed useful to distinguish between marked and neutral forms because each had a different relationship to the answering move which followed. Marked versions are those involving a negative and which therefore indicate the expected polarity of the answer; neutral forms on the other hand have nothing in their grammatical form or lexis to indicate the expected answer. This 'neutrality' needs further comment. Although we do not usually ask questions to which we know the answer, nor do we usually have no preconceptions at all about the possible answer. Thus asking questions can be seen as making hypotheses about what is likely to be the case, and our tendency is to formulate questions so that 'yes' is the more likely answer.

Hence it is often the rule, as Sacks (1972) has observed in his discussion of 'lines of questioning' that if the answer to a question is 'yes' that will suffice, whereas if it is 'no' some further information must be added. Thus it may seem that all apparently and formally neutral questions are in fact marked as expecting a positive polarity answer and certainly in doctor/patient interviews many questions can be seen as hypotheses looking for positive confirmation – for example, on the basis of a number of symptoms the patient has described, the doctor may expect a related symptom. However, on the other hand, the doctor may be asking questions to eliminate possibilities, and the hospital consultant in particular has a stock list of questions on past medical history – asking whether the patient has had pleurisy, tuberculosis or rheumatic fever for example – which are clearly independent of a particular patient's illness – such questions are listed in clinical textbooks and are asked in all case histories.

At secondary delicacy we can distinguish a number of different acts which can occur as head of an answering move following a proposing initiation. These are concur, confirm, qualify, reject and reply. Concur is a mid- or low-key response, and may be a repetition or a paraphrase of items in the question, 'yes' or 'no' or a substitute, e.g. 'I would say so'. 'Yes' may follow a neutral question or one marked for positive polarity, 'no' a neutral question or one marked for negative polarity.

One of the ideas we were playing with at this time was that as soon as the underlying presuppositions changed a new exchange began, and it was this that led us to argue that if opposite polarity occurred following a marked proposal it would be regarded as an informing initiation beginning a new exchange. Thus:

(20) Neutral proposal   D: do you get these attacks at home
      Concur   P: I do doctor yes

      Marked proposal   D: you've not passed any blood in your motions
                          P: no doctor no blood

      Marked proposal   D: don't have to get up out of bed every night to pass water
      Informing   P: YEAH I DO
      Initiation

Instead of concur the patient can choose to confirm, to assert the polarity through the choice of high key:

(21) Neutral proposal   D: do you find that you ever get headaches when you're wearing glasses
      Confirm   P: OH YEAH I DO

Another patient option is qualify, a category that includes parts of responses which make a tentative answer, or detail conditions or exceptions, rather than giving an unconditional polar response:

(22) Propose   D: you never usually get any pain in your chest at all
      Confirm   P: no
      Qualify   P: NOT EXCEPT THE USUAL BIT OF BRONCHITIS STUFF YOU KNOW

The fourth option is for the respondent to reject the underlying presuppositions that he knows the answer or that the question was a relevant and proper one to ask.

(23) Propose   D: was it worse when you took a deep breath
      Reject   P: WELL A WEEK LAST WEDNESDAY I FORGET NOW

(24) Propose   D: is your husband well
      Reject   P: I'VE LOST ME HUSBAND FOUR YEARS LAST APRIL

The final possibility is that the answerer responds not directly to the polar question but to an implicit wh-question, and it is counter-intuitive to treat such responses as new informing moves. There are many conventional polar interrogatives to which a polar response alone would be inappropriate as the answer expected is clearly the information-providing reply:

(25a) have you got the time
       *yes
(25b) have you got the time
       (YES) IT'S TWO O'CLOCK

Sometimes the reply may add more information than the confirm that was apparently asked for, as in the following case

(26) Propose   D: got any children
      Reply   P: TWO

and sometimes it appears to be used by a patient who is unsure of the interpretation of a particular fact to provide the doctor with information so that he can decide whether the answer is 'yes' or 'no'.

(27) Propose   D: is your weight steady at the moment
     Reply   P: WELL ITS SEVEN STONE THREE I
                     THOUGHT I WAS SEVEN STONE FOUR
     Follow-up   D: mm yes it's roughly about the same yes

We have already discussed some of the characteristics of follow-up moves, which distinguish them from new initiations, we now need to distinguish the different acts that can realise follow-up moves.

At primary delicacy we can distinguish three acts: terminate, receive, and react, realised respectively by utterances in low, mid and high key.   All low-key follow-up items close the exchange, indicating that no more needs to be said, though this does not mean that another follow-up move cannot follow.   In the following example all three follow-up moves are low-key terminates.

(28) Propose   D: and its a different sort of pain from the one
                     you had
     Answer   P: yeah quite different burning pain
     Terminate   D: BURNING PAIN YES
     Terminate   P: HEARTBURN I'D CALL IT I THINK
     Terminate   D: YEAH

Receive and react can be further differentiated at secondary delicacy: receive into acknowledge and reformulate, react into confirm and clarify.   Acknowledge includes 'yes', 'oh', 'mm', 'I see', tags like 'have you' and mid key repetitions, reformulate is realised by mid key paraphrases, confirm by high key 'yes' items, and clarify by high key paraphrases.

It will be evident that the definition for clarify is identical to that given above for declarative elicitations and in fact the two are formally identical;   they are distinguished in exactly the same way as starters had been in the earlier classroom description, by their position in sequence.   The declarative elicitations are utterance final, whereas clarifies are always followed by another act which suspends the constraint on the next speaker to begin.   Follow-ups can contain one or several of these five acts:

(29) Inquire   D: and what's been the matter recently
     Answer   P: well I've er pains round the heart
     Reformulate D: PAINS IN YOUR CHEST THEN (mid key)
     Acknowledge P: YEAH (mid key)
     Terminate   P: ROUND THE HEART (low key)

(b) Committee meetings

As we have seen the major complexity in doctor/patient interviews, like classrooms, was seen to be in eliciting exchanges, and the interaction consists in the main of a succession of such exchanges. The committee meeting data was very different in kind, and there was a comparative lack of complexity at the rank of exchange.   An initial commonsense observation about the sequential structure was that speakers made points while others murmured agreement or tried to chip in and interrupt.   This was initially formalised as I Sup^n, where I stands for initiation and Sup stands for a supportive move, selected from acknowledge, accept and endorse and 'n' specifies that Sup can occur an indefinite number of times. Taking Sup to be one kind of feedback item, one basic and certainly the most common exchange pattern was IF^n. This simple structure, however, concealed some complications – the exponents of F could and very frequently did occur in the middle of an I, also I's could be interrupted, either by another I or an attempted I which failed – labelled pre-I. Thus we could instance sequences like

$$I\langle F\rangle; \quad IFFF; \quad I\langle pre\text{-}I\rangle F$$

The three options at F, acknowledge, accept and endorse were all seen as meta-interactional items which accepted an utterance into the discourse by minimally confirming it had been heard, by more explicitly accepting it as relevant, or by more enthusiastically endorsing it. As will be immediately evident here again there is a labelling problem. At the time it was not at all clear that the participants in meetings were doing the same things in the same ways as doctors and patients and the labels and formal realisations of the original study are reproduced here even though they conflict in some ways with those offered for doctor/patient categories.

What is perhaps less evident is that the extremely simple exchange structure contained a feedback move which also had an extremely simple structure, typically a single act, either acknowledge, accept or endorse, and led us to question whether in fact we needed two ranks, act and move, or whether there was only need for one. Certainly the committee data itself would not have led us to set up a separate rank of act.

The three supporting acts appeared semantically to form a cline, though for practical purposes seemed to be distinguishable as follows:

Acknowledge. This is the minimal almost purely meta-interactional category of act which simply indicates that an utterance has been heard and accepted into the stream of talk, and which thus indicates continued auditory presence. Its exponents are 'yeah', 'uhuh', 'mm' with falling tone and low key.
Accept. This is a slightly more committed category of act, which implies at least minimal understanding of the utterance it accepts. Exponents are 'yeah', 'okay', 'yeah I know', 'oh I see', etc.
Endorse. These are items which substantiate and support the 'point' made by the preceding talk. They are acts which back up, add weight to, approve, uphold, chime in with, ratify or recognise as relevant previous talk. Examples are 'yeah that's a point', or 'you're quite right yes'. A possible gloss or translation for such endorsements is: 'I might have said that if I'd thought of it', or 'I wish to be associated with that utterance'. In the example below (b) endorses (a), the endorsement realised by 'yes', repetition, 'because' and the explicit 'I think so too'.
(30) (a) R – I think that a nine
     (b) P – yes I think so too because...
Here, we can see clearly some of the problems of developing a

description. There is a feeling that semantically there is a cline but structurally one must have discrete categories. Then, once one has discrete categories one must provide realisations and whereas it seemed useful to provide intonational criteria for acknowledge it was not possible to do so for accept and endorse. We would now want to propose categories very similar to the three above but to see their realisation as being much more closely linked to the selection of low-, mid- or high-key intonation choices (see p 93)

A second major problem in any developing description is labels – given our decision to develop the descriptions separately, different labels tended to be used for what might seem to be a very similar category and the same label for different categories: it will be evident that accept here is very similar functionally to what was labelled acknowledge in the doctor/patient description; acknowledge is formally identical to the doctor/patient terminate; while endorse is formally very similar to confirm though functionally distinct, but this is probably a result of the sociological difference as to how information is distributed in the two situations, and therefore, arguably, not a difference that should be marked by using a different mnemonic label.

(c) Broadcast discussions
The broadcast discussions we examined were typical BBC productions with 'representatives' of differing viewpoints being asked to present their opinions on particular topics. Unlike in committee meetings, the participants tended not to know each other and also there was no pressure to reach consensus and a decision. Possibly for this reason the exchange structure seemed even simpler. As in committee meetings there was a preponderance of informing exchanges, but many of the exchanges consisted of a single initiating move with no verbalised response or feedback.

To understand the nature of this type of interaction it seemed of major importance to discover whether successive exchanges were supporting or countering previous ones, and we were led to set up a separate class of countering exchanges, which were recognised by the fact that they contained an initial but or though. It may have seemed ill-founded at this stage to base the recognition of an exchange class on the existence of a particular word – given, for instance, the complex correspondence relationships typical of a change of linguistic level, one might argue that basing the identification of a particular type of exchange on the necessary presence of one or two words typically dealt with as clause conjunctions at the level of grammar was to threaten the system. However, that simply raised what was and remains one of the major questions – the way functions are signalled lexico-grammatically.

It is quite striking that whereas we were able to produce a detailed and quite compelling analysis of doctor/patient interaction at exchange rank, broadcast discussions proved pretty intractable, we were left with quite large chunks of speech for which we could produce no analysis at all – yet again we faced the problem of monologue.

Sequences

In our analysis of classroom discourse we concentrated on the ranks
of exchange and below. We saw transactions as unordered series of
teaching exchanges, preceded and optionally followed by a boundary
exchange, though we did have some hazy notion of exchange complex
and labelled some exchanges 'bound' where they were clearly dependent on a preceding exchange, for example, those initiated by loops
or by moves which retriggered an original eliciting move through a
nomination or clue. Evidence from the three new situations made us
growingly more certain that there was additional structure between
exchange and transaction. A crucial question not solved at the time
was how far sequence was a structural unit. In other words, to use
the analogy with grammar, would sequences, like paragraphs, consist of smaller units linked in identifiable ways, have topic relations
and development, but not a structure specifiable in terms of
permissible sequences of classes of exchange? Certainly some of
the linking features were similar to those recognised as stylistic at
the level of grammar. Sometimes we were able to identify sequences
linked by syntactic and intonational parallelism:

(31) | D: bowels are all right

| P: yeah

| D: not passed blood in your motions

| P: no

| D: you haven't passed any black motions like tar

| P: no

| D: no blood in your water no burning when you pass water

| P: no

Sometimes we identified sequences by shared topic which we could
isolate formally by lexical paraphrases between a follow-up and a
subsequent initiation:

(32) | F: you used to.
    D: |
         | I: how long ago

(33) | F: a crawling feeling
    D: |
         | I: it wasn't pain

Sometimes also we identified them through the initiating acts we
labelled return (a repetition of what the previous speaker had said
e.g., 'tight pain' in example 18) or loop. We also felt that key
played a significant part in making exchanges cohere into sequences
and we can now justify this convincingly following subsequent work
on intonation (see below, pp. 155-6).

In the broadcast discussions the situation was less clear; there
was certainly a topic unit consisting of several exchanges and we

could isolate two kinds of criteria for identifying sequence initial
opening moves: firstly the use of a small set of items including
'could I', 'can I', 'if I could', etc.

(34) can I suggest that perhaps there are two categories of
workers we have to take into account not that is er workers...

(35) can I just get back for a moment to the programmes and the
way programmes are er er er are done I'm not for one moment
challenging...

The other basic class of items initiating new sequences seemed to be
chairman specific, the nomination of specific participants.

(36) Brian Pitman would like you to take that up because nobody
knows what they're being charged there's no published...

(37) Alan Alan Hughes let's come to you now because you've got...

However, the most detailed work on sequences was done on the
committee data where two sets of criteria were developed, one for
identifying items that marked sequence boundaries, the other for
items which marked the cohesion between, and therefore sequence
membership of, initiating moves in exchanges. Sequence boundaries
appeared partly to be marked negatively, by breaks in surface cohesion, but there are also several positive boundary markers of which
the most common are three types of preface - 'preface' is a pre-
theoretical term which leaves open the question of how such items
relate to acts:
(i)   misplacement prefaces almost by definition introduce new
      sequences, since they function to indicate a lack of connected-
      ness to immediately preceding talk: 'just one other comment
      Mike...'
(ii) interruption prefaces: 'can I add to that em...'
                            'we've got people in sales if I can just
                                          come in here...'
                            'if I could ask a question again...'
(iii) personal point of view prefaces: 'personally I think we
                                          really...'
Some acts were also seen to be characteristically sequence initial:
(i)   Chairman's frames: (click) well h h...
(ii) Chairman's directs: again could - p'haps eh coffee time
                          Stewart could you again convey...
(iii) Procedural meta-remarks from the chairman;
      well perhaps you'd like to sort of go a little bit more
      because...
(iv) Other items which indicate that a new sequence may be start-
      ing, include chairman nominations and wh-questions (although
      these signals may be over-ridden by strong lexico-referential
      cohesion), and first references to procedural troubles which
      may introduce a side-sequence, in Jefferson's sense,
      'I don't appear to have a job description'
If asked how we had come to discover such items to be sequence
boundary indicators, the answer would have been that intuition told
us that such items introduce a section of talk which is in some sense

'new' or a 'change in topic' and also that such items tend to co-occur.
In addition boundaries, as marked by such items, tend to co-occur
with breaks in discourse cohesion.

As we mentioned above, the committee and TV data had embarras-
singly long stretches for which we could offer no analysis. In an
almost desperate attempt to find links between utterances for which
we had no theoretical perspective, we began to look at cohesive
features which in this data seem to be associated with the unit
sequence. The following items were significant:

(1) Lexico-referential cohesion: i.e. repetition of 'content' words
as opposed to grammatical words. Repetition of phrases or
longer strings of words makes for more obvious cohesion,
because it is one type of syntactic parallelism (see 6 below).

(2) Occurrence of synonyms, antonyms, hyponyms, and words from
the same semantic field (e.g. numerals, or different forms of a
single root word).

(3) Anaphora.

(4) Ellipsis and expansion, i.e. utterances which, by definition, are
non-initial.

(5) Sentence-continuations and completions.

(6) Parallelism of syntax and intonation.

(7) Logical connectors.

It is in fact, even possible to isolate sequences mechanically from
the data using only such surface cues as these. In other words, one
can identify sequences in terms of surface recognition criteria
alone, and to keep this identification problem separate from any
functional or structural analysis of sequences.

The claim is, then, that the surface markers listed tend to
cluster together across strings of utterances, but that fairly sharp
breaks occur in the clustering, and that these breaks are heard as
shifts in 'topic'. What is more interesting is that such breaks
characteristically co-occur with the positive boundary markers
listed above.

H ere is an example of this kind of analysis with sequence
boundaries marked by horizontal lines.

S   the reason I got involved was because (Ron Arthur's-) eh

     Bob Denver came and asked us to get involved they just

     (wanted nothing to do with it)

K   [(right) so   obviously] they've they've said that's   FRAME

     all right as far as they're concerned [anyhow]

Ch ((tongue click, ^{V})) well hh marketing then any   FRAME

comparisons you'd like to draw our attention to stewart   NOMINATION

S there's not really eh many comparisons at all I I (2)

em Donald Hare has (⌐in fact to   )

about possible jobs or they don't really have a a   PARALLEL

marketing co-ordinator they have people that do it and   SYNTAX

their co-ordinator is a is a natural – sort of manager type

Ch mm ((tongue click)) well we'd better look at this against our   FRAME

factors ┌here

K   └we've got people in sales if I can just come in   INTERRUPTION
                                                                    PREFACE + WE

┌here

Ch └yeah sure   ACCEPT

K erm   I don't know what (\ ) exactly what it would go

against but you know we've got people for example like

product and market plans em promotions managers

advertising managers I know it's the job itself is an amalgam

of a whole lot

S that's right it's a a it's a lot of these jobs   ENDORSE

K yeah – but isn't there a – a com comparison with service   ACCEPT +
                                                                    LOGICAL CONNECT

and (k t) ┌on   on the used parts

J   └well I   I would have thought

actually Ken they'd d do very well with a comparison with

fifteen used car conditioning co-ordinator that's a sort

of one off job   in the sales organisation

It must be stressed that this is a very different kind of analysis
from that which has been discussed so far. This is simply a way of
showing how sequences are coherent as units, no suggestions were
made as to what their internal structure, in terms of chained constituent exchanges, might be. We could in fact see no way of
characterising any prospective sequence structure. Our feeling
was, rather, that sequences were characteristically retrospectively
cohesive and coherent.

Thus, at the end of this second project we could claim to have made
some progress in extending our initial description to cope with other
types of interaction, and to have produced a quite detailed description of doctor/patient consultations. However, there were two
major obstacles to further progress, the lack of an adequate description of intonation and the problem of how to analyse long contributions
by single speakers - these we tackled in the next two projects.

SECTION 3 THE STRUCTURE OF MONOLOGUE
British Council Project 'The structure of lectures' 1975-6

As we have seen the earlier work on classroom interaction, broadcast interviews and discussions and committee meetings had highlighted but not solved a major problem - how to analyse long utterances. When a teacher produces a lengthy contribution following a
pupil's response the 'comment' of the follow-up move often shades
into the initiating 'inform' causing evident analytic problems. But,
even when such move boundaries are unambiguous, lengthy informing
moves themselves cause difficulties - should they be treated as consisting of a single long 'inform', or a whole series of shorter ones?
We saw above (pp. 13-14) an initial attempt to cope with the problem,
but in the main we confined ourselves to describing the beginnings
and endings of such moves, the points where they slotted into
exchange structure by responding to or setting up constraints, and
left them otherwise unanalysed internally.

This is not to say that we were unable to perceive some structure
but that we were unable to handle it within the model we were
developing. The difficulty with trying to handle long moves as a
series of informs was that we had no criteria for isolating the
boundaries or for showing their relationship to each other; on the
other hand, if we regarded them as a single inform, should the
structure be handled in terms of a series of smaller units at a new
lower rank in discourse, or should the structure be handled at the
level of grammar as a spoken paragraph?

In order to illustrate some of the most obvious structure in monologue we have chosen the following extracts from a radio interview,
mainly because, for those interested in following things further,
there is a detailed intonation transcript available in Brazil et al.
(1980) and a recording of the extract on the tape accompanying that
book.

(1) Now I think one can see several major areas concerning the
    unions which require to be considered there's first the question
    with which the industrial relations act is mainly concerned and

that is how industrial disputes are handled now I believe myself
the TUC and the CBI and it's interesting that they agree on this
are right in saying that the government by trying to be judge and
jury in its own case has really so tainted the idea of government
interference in industrial negotiation that it's desirable to have
a conciliation service set up as in the United States independent
of government altogether as you know the Labour Party and the
TUC have pretty well reached agreement in details of this and er
I believe the CBI and TUC are very likely to do the same unless
Mr Heath upsets it by insisting on interfering and this is one very
important side er of the act now the <u>second</u> big area of course is
the question of how you handle incomes and I myself very strongly
believe that we have to establish in Britain <u>two</u> fundamental
principles <u>first of all</u> that differentials that's to say the gap
between what one man earns and a slightly more skilled man
earns have got to be rather smaller than they have been in the
past if the people at the bottom of the ladder are to have a chance
of a decent life <u>secondly</u> that increased earnings (earnings above
the average) have got to depend on increased production and the
real trouble is that over the last two years every single thing the
present government has done has been deliberately calculated to
widen differentials rather than reduce them and to reward people
who don't work for their living rather than those who do if you'll
allow me just to give examples...

This is quite obviously a highly structured utterance. For one
thing the speaker himself sets it up in advance as a lengthy contribu-
tion, 'several major areas concerning the unions...require to be
considered'. Then various devices are used to mark the remainder
of the response as fulfilling this initial prediction.
'There's first the question...'
'Now the second big area...'
'Two fundamental principles...'
'First of all...'
'Secondly...'

Several major areas $\left\{\begin{array}{l}\text{first the question} \\ \text{the second big area/two fundamental} \\ \hspace{6em}\text{principles}\end{array}\right.$ $\left\{\begin{array}{l}\text{first of all} \\ \text{secondly}\end{array}\right.$

It is immediately apparent then that the contribution is structured
in terms of the points made and in broad terms this is signalled as
the discourse unfolds by such surface markers as 'first', 'second',
'first of all', 'secondly'. However, it is equally evident that, even
with such a fluent speaker, there are features which would not be
present in a written version of the same information. For example,
setting up the utterance as dealing with 'several major areas concerning unions', not only delimits the broad content of the contribution, but in this context also signals an extended rather than a
minimal reply. It functions not merely as 'topic delimiter' but as a
'floor holder' forestalling an early interruption from the interviewer,
and the word 'several' is usefully vague. Thus a simple topic-

structuring device can be seen to be related also to interactional features because it is also a device for suspending the turn-taking machinery. There are significant pauses at five points within the utterance, but no attempt by the interviewer to fill them – it is only when the speaker has apparently completed the second of the two fundamental principles of the second big area that he needs to fend off an interruption, 'if you'll allow me just to give examples.'

In the hope of casting light on the problems raised by the analysis of longer utterances we decided to investigate the type of extended monologue that occurs in lecture settings. The resulting description – while remaining somewhat pre-theoretical – is none the less of interest and should provide a solid basis for research. We are now planning something which will attempt to combine current work in the description of written texts (Winter 1977, Hoey 1979, 1981), this work on lectures and the description of intonation presented in Section 4, which is a great deal more powerful than the one available to us in 1975.

Lectures, of course, provide a more extreme instance of monologue than those longer utterances which had raised analytic problems. For one thing, such speech events institutionalise the suspension of the turn-taking machinery. None the less, we will seek to show that, even without speaker change and even where both lecturer and student understand the purpose of the lecture in terms of 'information transfer', its discourse is in fact interactively designed; the discourse is 'shaped' or 'structured' with interactive purposes in mind. And if such claims are tenable for the more extreme kind of extended monologue typical of lectures, then we feel confident that the lengthy utterances within multi-party talk will be susceptible to a similar analysis. We should point out in this respect, of course, that we are thinking not of lectures in which the lecturer simply reads a prepared text but of those in which he composes as he talks and reacts to all available non-verbal information from the audience about their state of knowledge and understanding.

Structure

Three units were proposed to analyse the structure of lectures and immediately there arose the problem of labels. As the data was very different from any handled before, it seemed sensible, initially at least, to use a different set of labels, but two of the units on reflection now seem to be sufficiently similar to be given an existing label, for the third we prefer to emphasise its differences. The units we propose are:
Transaction
Sequence
Member

Transaction as a unit is identified by the focusing activity that occurs at its boundaries. As the lecture discourse unfolds, the speaker typically signposts at intervals its prior or subsequent direction:

(2) right so let's turn to mathematics for the next forty-five minutes.
(3) right I'm now going to go right away from this rather abstract

approach and talk about the solution of sets of linear equations. Two kinds of focus can be distinguished; those which open transactions and those which close them.   The former is considered to be a prospective focus and the latter a retrospective focus.   An ideal typical example of a discourse transaction is thus seen as taking the following form, (we ignore for the moment the intervening discourse layer of sequence):
   prospective focus, informing member(s), retrospective focus

Sequences can be informally characterised as smaller-scale topic units and they are isolated on phonological criteria.   It appears that lecturers use one version of the phonological unit pitch sequence, a sequence beginning with high key and ending with low termination, to mark the semantic coherence of a succession of members.

   It will now be obvious why we have characterised this description as so far pre-theoretical.   Although we have identified units larger than member we are not able to provide structures for these units in terms of clauses of the unit next below.   This does not of course mean that the units are not valid nor that the observations we have made are without value, but rather that we are not yet at the stage where they can usefully be formalised.

   If we were proposing a description of multi-party interaction exchange would be the crucial unit of analysis.   It is evident that it does not appear in this proposed rank scale.   It would, however, be naive to imagine that genuine interaction does not occur in lectures and to imagine therefore that it will not at some point be possible to describe exchange-like structures in lectures.   As we said above, lectures are just a more extreme form of long contribution and in both we can informally characterise points where the speaker specifically looks for, if not requests, nods, smiles, even murmurs of agreement or indications of disagreement or puzzlement.   How far these are signalled through intonation and how far through eye contact or even other means, remains an open question.

   In labelling the smallest analytic unit, we wanted and still want to leave open the question of whether it is the same as an act in multiparty discourse - we borrowed the label member from Winter (1977).

Members are isolated on syntactic criteria.   They consist minimally of a free clause or a free clause with its bound clauses.   A member can only consist of more than one free clause when there exists between the clauses a close relationship of the branched type in which the same necessary element of structure is ellipted from the second.

   The major observations we can make are about the ways in which members relate to each other in the unfolding discourse - lecture monologues proceed basically by an interplay between two modes of

discourse. Some discourse members are mainly oriented towards
the subject matter of the discourse, others towards the reception of
this subject matter. Thus, interwoven with the strand of the discourse primarily concerned in lectures of this kind with describing
particular phenomena is another whose concern is with monitoring,
reflecting upon, and commenting on the main thrust of the discourse.
These two strands are seen as constituting discourse activity on
separate planes which are termed 'main' discourse and 'subsidiary'
discourse, and it is interesting to speculate, though we can so far
do no more, that what makes formal read-aloud lectures and papers
difficult to follow is the very lack of subsidiary discourse.

Although members are defined in syntactic terms, our interest is
not in them as syntactic units but rather as functionally related
units. Except where larger-scale discourse boundaries occur,
each member as it occurs is 'played off' against the preceding one
and is heard as doing something in relation to it, such as in the
following examples, reformulation or qualification.

(4) and er these er buds in general have the characteristic of
        indefinite growth
    /once they begin to develop they go on and on

(5) all these equivalent circuits are experimentally determined
    /at least they have a basis in experiment

Each example consists of two separate and crucially different
members: the second depends on the first and acts in the light of
whatever has been accomplished by the first. The first member is
an exponent of main discourse, the second is subsidiary to the first.

This is not to claim that lectures proceed always by an alternation
member by member between main and subsidiary. Indeed a series
of subsidiary members may follow one another uninterruptedly before
the main discourse resumes as in the following example:

MAIN	SUBSIDIARY
(6) (M1) I <u>shall</u> <u>be concentrating</u> mainly on <u>amplifiers</u> for <u>amplifying</u> sinusoidal <u>signals</u> – AC signals, alternating current/	
	/(M2) this is a misnomer/(M3) to say it's an alternating current voltage and AC voltage as so many people do of course is a bit of a nonsense/(M4) erm we all do it/(M5) so I'm afraid that I'm going to have to use this rather loose terminology/(M6) I hope you'll know what I mean/ (M7) I mean a periodically time varying signal which is probab- ly sinusoidal/
/(M8) so we <u>shall</u> be <u>dealing</u> with small <u>signal</u> and large <u>signal</u> <u>AC</u> amplifiers and am- plifiers of steady voltages – DC <u>amplifiers</u>	

After a series of subsidiary members there are various ways in which
the resumption of main discourse is signalled. Typically marks of a
resumption are 'but' and 'so' usually co-occurring with a step up from
low to high key.

   In other words there is usually a sequence boundary at the point
of reversion to main discourse, and the first member of the next
sequence usually reiterates lexical items from the last member of
main discourse – in this example 'signal', 'AC', 'amplifier'.

Main discourse

Between the beginnings and ends of transactions, marked by focusing
members, the main discourse develops through a chain or succession
of informing members.   Although broadly they may be classed as
informatives, they none the less enter into a variety of relationships
with each other. Frequently they are linked together by a limited
range of conjunctive items such as 'and', 'so', 'because', 'but', 'or',
'however', thereby setting up chains of logical relations as the discourse proceeds.   In other words each succeeding member will
adopt one of a restricted set of possible relations with respect to a
prior member.   The wide range of conjunctive items in English is
thus seen as expounding a limited range of relationships connecting
one member with another.   For the purposes of lecture monologue
three relationships in particular are seen as crucial – ADDITIVE,
ADVERSATIVE, CAUSAL – and these correspond with the three
most frequent conjunctive items deployed in the data – 'and', 'but'
and 'so'.   (It is instructive to compare these items and glosses with
Brazil's 'additive', 'contrastive' and 'equative' glosses for the mid-,
high- and low-key choices respectively, p. 50.

   (7) /now the stalk of each stamen, is referred to as the filament
       ADDITIVE /and the head of each stamen is referred to as the
                                                               anther
       CAUSAL /so anther and filament bracket together as stamen

The beginnings of members are typically marked by selection of high
key and they generally end with mid termination; however, if the
preceding member ends with high termination, this appears to signal
that the second is to be heard as an expansion or exemplification of
the first:

   (8) r the WAVE form   PERiodic
       //   //p+may in FACT be
       p the SIMplest one   p is the SINE
       ///   //r+ of COURSE//   WAVE

Subsidiary discourse

There are two main classes of subsidiary members – glosses and
asides, glosses having a closer dependency relationship to main
discourse than asides.   We can identify three main types of gloss,
restate, qualify and comment.   Restates repeat or reformulate the
matter of the immediately prior member and the relationship may be
marked by items such as 'in other words', 'that is', 'for example',
or devices such as lexical repetition and anaphoric reference.

(9) is there a cheaper solution
    /in other words can you use a cheaper device
(10) the output signal will not be quite the same as the input signal
    /it will be a distorted version of the input signal

Qualifys serve to modify the general applicability of an immediately
prior member. Typical surface markers are items such as
'actually', 'in reality', 'at least', etc.

(11) the rank of an array is the number of suffices
    /I should actually be more precise free suffices
(12) all these equivalent circuits are experimentally determined
    /at least they have a basis in experiment

Comments are members which evaluate or comment on stretches of
the discourse. They often include a text reference item such as
'this' or 'that' and an attributive term such as 'important', 'simple',
'difficult', 'trivial', etc.

(13) and that all sounds rather complicated
(14) it may seem very trivial just telling you how to write things down

Comments are particularly significant because they are explicitly
oriented towards the audience's reception of what is being said and
indicate that the speaker is attempting to cope with possible audience
reaction overtly in the discourse itself.
    Glossing members form the core of subsidiary discourse. They
reflect back on the main discourse, expanding it, modifying it and
evaluating it. Members that expound these categories are closely
related to the primary thrust of the discourse and have a close
dependency relationship on main discourse members. They are said
very much in the context of what has gone before.
    The second basic component of subsidiary discourse differs from
glossing activity in so far as it maintains a more tenuous relationship with the main flow of the discourse. Whereas glossing is
typically anaphoric, asides are typically exophoric, functioning to
contextualise the discourse in some way: for example, they may link
abstract description to concrete blackboard illustration or relate
the process of description to some further activity to be undertaken
by the audience or to some previous information supplied to them.
    Almost invariably lectures in science and engineering subjects
are accompanied by some form of visual display. This can take
various forms - from the static diagram to the more dynamic process
of blackboard calculations, but whatever the form, the illustrative
material is referred to in the discourse and, more importantly, both
shapes and is shaped by it. It plays an important role in the discourse almost to the point of operating as a kind of sub-text, and we
have adopted the term 'paradiscourse' to highlight its characteristic
of running parallel to the monologue. One of the major ways in
which paradiscourse is related to the main discourse is by the use of
procedural asides:

(15) MAIN/in the stem er the situation is different because the
            xylem and the phloem are on the same radius
            /now if you have a stem with separate vascular bundles
            like this and so on
ASIDE 1 just show xylem and phloem for simplicity –
            //xylem here phloem towards the oustide
MAIN   /these are on the same radius
ASIDE 2 /er not all incidentally not all stems have this arrange-
            ment of separate vascular bundles
            /these are always taken this type of stem is always taken
            as the type for the herbaceous dicotyledonous stem the
            young herbaceous dicotyledonous stem
            /but er it only really represents about half er of the
            flowering plant kingdom because about an equal number of
            plants have a continuous ring of phloem and a continuous
            ring of xylem on the inside
            /and er why this is never brought out er in er elementary
            courses er I don't know because this is not necessarily
            representative of structure as a whole
MAIN   /but the rule about being on the same radius still holds
            good /if we have a complete ring of phloem and a
            complete ring of xylem then...

Procedurals can also serve to establish the terms within which subsequent communication will take place

(16) /in the stem of protoxylem
     PROCED. /this is the inside of the stem
     /the protoxylem will be found here
(17) /we will look for three properties commutation add
     multiply
     PROCED. /we'll make a little table
     /commutation is the statement under addition that a plus
     b equals b plus a

To complicate matters asides may develop into lengthy digressions,
and then they can assume structural characteristics similar in kind
to stretches of main discourse. The second aside in example (15)
above is of this kind. It is marked at its onset by the item 'incidentally' and the return to main discourse is marked by the utterance
'but the rule about being on the same radius still holds good', where
this first member of the resumed main discourse reiterates items
from those members which preceded the aside: '... the xylem and
phloem are on the same radius', 'these are on the same radius'.
The variable extent of asides may be seen in the same example in
which the first aside is embedded in a member but the second aside
becomes a lengthy digression.
    The other main type of aside is recall, which serves to reinstate
at any juncture in the discourse some information which is treated as
already familiar to the audience. Accordingly recalls typically contain some phrase such as 'you will remember' or 'as I said earlier'.

Some examples are as follows:

(18) /but as soon as you put into a circuit and you do what you have
to to get the thing working
/it's this process I referred to as biassing earlier on
/then currents will flow through it voltages will appear
across it

(19) /in the root the xylem and the phloem occur on different radii
/remember this sort of business the xylem here and the phloem
in the grooves
/so that er thinking of the organ as whole er the xylem main
limbs as it appears in transverse section of the xylem are
on a different radius from the phloem

Concluding remarks

In presenting this description of monologue discourse, we noted its
somewhat pre-theoretical nature: it clearly stands in an uneasy
relationship with the other analyses offered. The notion of rank
scale, for instance, is in this case only weakly developed, primarily
because it proved difficult to specify ordered arrangements of
classes of unit at lower ranks which would combine together in predictable ways to form structures at the rank above. We also noted
the absence of the unit exchange – a unit that had proved crucial in
the consideration of multi-party talk. Despite this, we argued that
even such extended monologues are designed interactively. Of key
importance in this respect is the relationship of main to subsidiary
discourse – a distinction which embodies the claim that the monologue
(even of lectures) is more than an undifferentiated chain of informing
members. Rather the discourse – pre-eminently in its subsidiary
aspect – is seen as constantly reflecting back on its own progression. The functional categorisation of the subsidiary members res-
ponsible for this movement – in terms of repeat, qualify, comment,
etc. – indicates some of interactive work that we can isolate within
the discourse itself. What we are claiming is that through the
operation of such members, the discourse attempts to take account
of, and is oriented towards, possible audience reaction. The relationship of subsidiary to main discourse would seem to reflect the
lecturers moment by moment assessment of the felicity of his utterance with respect to his audience – either in terms of an internalised
projection of the latter's characteristics or in terms of its actual
behaviour.

SECTION 4 INTONATION
SSRC Project 'Discourse intonation' 1975-8

Initially, the need set the limits of the scope of the enquiry. The
intention was to do no more than find a representation of the more
obviously relevant facts of intonation that would conveniently map
onto the categories of the developing description of verbal inter-

action. It soon became apparent, however, that by attending to the status of an utterance as a contribution to the co-operatively produced object we call discourse, it would be possible to characterise the meaning of various intonation features in terms which approached full generality and which related in interesting ways to equally generalisable statements about the meaning of other such features. There seemed to be good reason for postulating a conceptually separable area of meaning potential, wholly realised by intonation, and requiring for its explication reference to interrelated aspects of the here-and-now discourse setting of the utterance concerned.

This is not the place to enlarge upon the factors that seemed to justify engagement with the distinctively discoursal value of intonation nor upon the theoretical consequences of doing so. Neither will any attempt be made to present a case for adopting this approach in preference to one which seeks to incorporate intonation into a grammatical description (see Halliday 1967) or one which attributes to it a range of attitudinal significances (as, for instance, O'Connor and Arnold 1961). The present aim is merely to present a sketch of the descriptive apparatus as it now stands, and as it is referred to in some of the other chapters in this volume. A further contribution, Chapter 7), will confront the question of how the categories of this description are to be related to those needed to describe discourse structure.

The tone unit

Accounts of intonation are in general agreement about the need to identify a stretch of speech with which the meaningful variables they postulate are associated. The category 'tone unit' as it is used here does not exactly match the comparable unit in any other description. It is defined, not by reference to its boundaries, but on the basis of its internal organisation: that is to say, it is characterised as the place of operation of a set of speaker-options. The number of those options and the way they are deployed with respect to each other are, of course, dependent on the view taken of the meaning system. In this important way, the phonological description of the tone unit is set up so as to reflect an already explicit theory of the meaning of intonation.

For reasons to be given later, it has to be recognised that it may not always be possible for the analyst to determine the boundary between two consecutive tone units. It is easiest to proceed by exemplification, and to postpone confronting the segmentation problem by using a fragment of data in which tone unit boundaries are readily identifiable because of a perceived pause:
   (1) // I think on the whole // that these officials // do a remarkably
       good job //
Having thus isolated the entity to be examined, it is easy to see that the three tone units in the sample have these features in common:
(i) Each has two syllables which can be said, on the basis of a number of phonetic criteria, to have a property that will be referred

to as prominence. Upper-case characters are now used in transcripts to represent prominent syllables as follows:
(2)
   // I think on the WHOLE // that THESE ofFICials // do a
   reMARKably good JOB//
(ii) The second prominent syllable, or 'tonic syllable' (underlined in
the transcript) is the place of operation of a speaker choice, most
conveniently referred to as a set of four distinctive pitch movements.
Beginning at this tonic syllable, and continuing to the end of the tone
unit, the pitch of the voice may rise from low to high, fall from high
to low or follow a course which can be described as a fall-rise or a
rise-fall. It is useful to represent the four possibilities

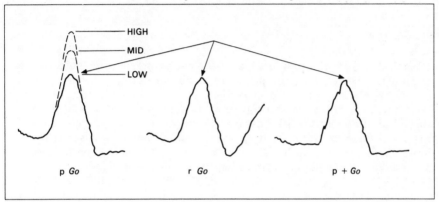

Figure 1.3

diagrammatically as ↗ ↘ ∨ ∧ . These distinctive pitch movements are referred to as tones. (There is a further possibility:
the voice may maintain a level pitch (⟶), but this tone, which
differs in a number of respects from the others, will not be considered here.) There is no comparable choice of pitch movement at
the first prominent syllable.
   In addition to the variable that has been spoken of as pitch movement, there are two further speaker choices in the tone unit, whose
physical correlates can be described in terms of pitch level, one
associated with each of the prominent syllables. Remaining for the
moment with the tonic syllable, Figure 1.3 shows examples of
oscilloscope traces of specimens of each of the tones that have a
falling element in them. In each case it is possible to identify a
turning point, a point of maximum height achieved before the fall
begins. A speaker can vary the level at which this point occurs.
The level is, in fact, continuously variable; nevertheless, a hearer
is able to identify any particular instance as a high, mid or low
choice. The way this is achieved will be described below. Mean-
while, Figure 1.4 shows how the pitch-level criterion can be applied
to the different phonetic shape of the rising tone: here, the significant level is that at which the rise ends and any subsequent fall in
pitch begins. The three-way pitch-level choice located at the tonic
syllable is called 'termination'.

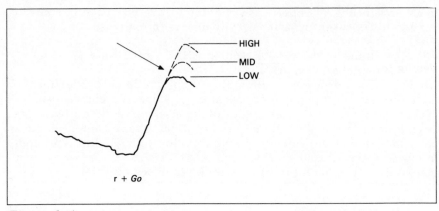

Figure 1.4

Pitch-level is also variable at the first prominent syllable in the tone unit. Here, too, the peculiar pitch pattern which contributes to a hearer's perception of prominence includes a distinctive turning point from rising to falling, and this similarly occurs at a level which has diagnostic significance (see Figure 1.5). Attention to this level enables the hearer to recognise a choice in a separate three-term system, called key. The key and termination options are partly independent, as the simplified traces in Figure 1.5 show.

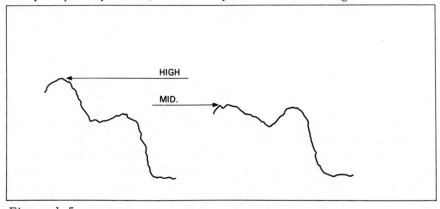

Figure 1.5

It is now easy to see how potentially continuous variation at the tonic syllable can be regarded as realising one of three discrete choices: once key has been identified as, say, mid, a termination choice pitched at the same level is also mid, one above it is high, and one below it low. It follows from this reliance upon relative height that the choices are only partly independent: change within a tone unit can only be to an adjacent level in the three-term system. There are no tone units having high key and low termination or low key and high termination.

The recognition procedure just described assumes that key has already been determined. To see how this is done it is necessary to go back to the immediately preceding tone unit. It is the level of the first prominent syllable there (that is to say the immediately preceding key choice) that provides a reference point with which to compare the present key-determining level. This means that inter-vening termination choices do not affect the issue (see Figure 1.6).

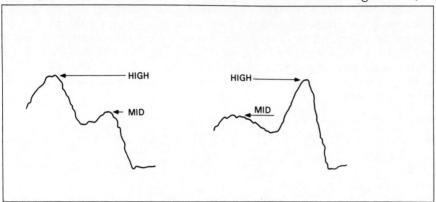

Figure 1.6

It also means that the adjacent level requirement prevents consecu-tive tone units having high key // low key. It is not, however, impossible for a low-key tone unit to be followed by one having high key, a fact which seems to be inconsistent with the application of a relative pitch-level criterion, but which must now be considered in relation to the way a number of consecutive tone units combine to form another, larger, unit, the pitch sequence.

The pitch sequence

Key and termination choices can be shown in transcriptions by placing the relevant syllable at, above or below the mid line:
(3)
    I
// think on the WHOLE // that THESE ofFICials // do a reMARKably good   //
              JOB
(It is important to be clear that this practice is in no sense an attempt to represent the actual phonetic shape of the utterance: the conventions carry no more information than has just been specified for them.)
    The three tone units represented above constitute a pitch sequence, a fact marked by the low termination with which the last one ends. It is assumed either that the first tone unit begins the discourse or that it follows immediately upon one having low termination. Except at the beginning of a discourse, a pitch sequence begins after any occurrence of low termination and extends to the next such occur-rence.
    The example cited provides a useful pattern on which to base

further discussion of key and termination.   It begins with high key
and ends with low termination, all intermediate choices in both
systems being mid.   It would, in fact, be possible to extend the
pitch sequence to indefinite length by introducing further mid-key/
mid-termination tone units.   If, for the present, the opening and
closing choices are regarded as marking the boundaries of the pitch
sequence, and as doing nothing more than this, then there is
evidently scope for two kinds of departure from the simple pattern:
either (i) a key choice or (ii) a termination choice may be other than
mid.   Such deviations will be said to be the result of internal
choices (that is to say internal to the pitch sequences), and poss-
bilities include:

(i) // ^{HIGH KEY} MID TERM. // <u>HIGH KEY</u> MID TERM.// MID KEY ....

// ^{HIGH KEY} MID TERM. // MID KEY   MID TERM.// <u>LOW KEY</u> LOW TERM. //

(ii) // ^{HIGH KEY} <u>HIGH TERM.</u> // MID KEY <u>HIGH TERM.</u> // ...

// <u>LOW KEY</u> MID TERM. //

These examples are not to be taken as implying, however, that all
pitch sequences necessarily begin with high key.   Once a sequence
has been closed with low termination, a speaker has a free choice
of key for the beginning of the next sequence:

(i)   ···_{LOW TERM.} // ^{HIGH KEY} ...

(ii) ···_{LOW TERM.} // MID KEY ...

(iii) ···_{LOW TERM.} // LOW KEY ...

This sequence initial key choice has a different communicative value
from internal choices.   After it has been made, the full range of
options is available in the pitch sequence, subject only to the two
kinds of adjacent-level constraint.   So, for instance, one might
find a mid-key-initial sequence like,

// MID KEY   MID TERM. // <u>HIGH KEY</u> MID TERM. // ....

where the key of the second tone unit has meaning derived from an
internal choice.

The tonic segment

The exposition has so far assumed tone units with two prominent
syllables.   Tone units having more than two are very rare in the
data on which this description is based.   Even when they do occur,
the presence of an additional prominent syllable between those at
which the key and termination choices are made does not disturb the
validity of the following statement: it is the tonic segment, a stretch

which begins with the first prominent syllable and ends with the last, that is tagged with separate increments of meaning derived from each of the three choices. The tonic segment may or may not be preceded by a proclitic segment and/or followed by an enclitic segment, both of which consist entirely of non-prominent syllables. So, in Figure 1.7 it is to the content of the second column that the special value of a particular set of tone, key and termination choices attaches. Sometimes, there is insufficient phonetic evidence in the data to say at what point the enclitic segment of one tone unit ends and the proclitic segment of the next begins. It is because this indeterminacy has no effect upon the domain of any of the choices that the question of boundary recognition is not regarded as crucial.

Proclitic	Tonic segment	Enclitic
	I think on the WHOLE	
that	THESE ofFIC	ials
do a re	MARKably good JOB	

Figure 1.7

Although there are few tonic segments with more than two prominent syllables, there are many with only one:

Proclitic	Tonic segment	Enclitic
	MOST	people do
was going to	ASK	you about it
they did it on	SUN	day

Figure 1.8

In cases like these, minimal tonic segments, all three options are compressed into the same syllable. Key and termination cannot, therefore, be selected independently: high key automatically entails high termination, and so on. It follows that the meaning accruing to both choices will be present in every instance, so that both will have to be appropriate to the situation. It also follows that a minimal tonic segment constitutes a double choice in the configuration of the pitch sequence, as for instance in the second tone unit of:

// HIGH KEY MID TERM. / HIGH KEY and HIGH TERM. // ....

Before attempting to characterise the meaning system, one further point should be clarified. The examples used may have given the impression that the pitch sequence was part of an uninterrupted contribution by a single speaker. In fact, pitch sequences are frequently shared by a number of speakers: the relationship between the phonological unit pitch sequence and the discourse unit exchange is a matter of considerable interest.

The meaning system

Two general observations about the communicative value of intonation as it is here conceived will prepare the way for a brief treatment of each of the options.   The first is that in making any choice
of intonation feature a speaker is invoking some aspect of the conversational setting he shares with his hearer at the moment of
utterance.   The notion of a conversational setting will demand
further explication below; what is here emphasised is the dynamic,
here-and-now, validity of all the decisions that motivate use of any
one intonation feature in preference to others that might have been
used.   The second observation, already implicit in the first, but
easy to overlook, is that it is speakers' decisions and speakers'
choices that have to be reckoned with.   In saying that, say, a
particular tone represents a speaker's assessment of how things
stand conversationally between him and his hearer, there can be no
necessary implication that his assessment is a correct one.
Indeed, the possibility of accidental mismatch between speaker's
and hearer's viewpoints is only part of the problem of setting up a
description.   Intonation features, like all other speaker-options
provided by the language system, are available for exploitation: it
is always possible to represent matters quite differently from what
one assumes they really are for tactical purposes.   Difficulties
associated with speaker-perspective and particularly with exploitation have to be faced in any extended account of the meaning of
intonation.   For present purposes, however , it has seemed better
to avoid blurring the outlines of the system by using straightforward
examples and by referring only to such aspects of the state of
speaker/hearer convergence as seem to be unproblematical.

Prominence

The incidence of prominent syllables has already been said to
delimit the tonic segment.   Additionally, it is possible to ascribe
communicative significance to the simple fact that a speaker does or
does not assign a prominent syllable to a particular word.   The
following fragment of discourse will help to show how:

   (4)

      Speaker A: what card did you play
      Speaker B: // the QUEEN of HEARTS //

It is evident that in B's response hearts represents a selection from
four possible suits and queen a selection from thirteen denomina-
tions.   'Of', by contrast, is the only possible filler of its slot.
Disregarding the slightly more complex case of 'the', the paradigm-
atic options in the response can be represented thus:

  (5)

I	II	III	IV
(the)	king		diamonds
	queen		hearts
	:	of	spades
	ace		clubs

The non-prominence of 'of' can be attributed to the fact that the speaker is not involved in making a selection from a number of available candidates.

Consider now:

(6)
Speaker A: which queen did you play
Speaker B: // the queen of HEARTS //

(7)
Speaker A: which heart did you play
Speaker B: // the QUEEN of hearts //

In these cases, the containing discourse (specifically, the content of A's question) effectively removes the need for any selective process at places II and IV respectively, and we should normally find this fact recognised by the absence of prominence in the word the discourse has made predictable.

There is a difference between example (5) on the one hand and examples (6) and (7) on the other. In the first, it is the operation of the language system that eliminates any alternative to 'of'. In the others it is knowledge of the run of the conversation up to the moment of utterance that is the decisive factor. In each of the following, it is long-standing shared assumptions that speaker and hearer bring with them to the particular conversation that provide the basis for the choice:

(8)
// RED white and BLUE //
// a BOTtle of johnny WALKer //
// in THIS day and AGE //

For anyone participating in the culture that the speaker takes for granted as the background for his utterance, neither white, Johnny nor day will be heard as resulting from a process of selection any more than would of in example (5).

Any verbal interaction can be conceived of as taking place in the context of a certain degree of speaker/hearer convergence. Both participants know about the constraints inherent in the language they use, and both have experience of the present interaction as it has proceeded so far. More variable, and less accessible to a third party such as an analyst, is the extent to which common acquaintance with the subject-matter and mutual understanding of attitudes, expectations and beliefs condition the information value of what is said. It is not possible here to examine the distribution of prominence in a real spoken text and relate it, point by point, to a concept of a constantly changing context of interaction such as this view of interactive discourse provides. It is nevertheless proposed that it is in the light of his apprehension of the context of interaction that the speaker makes his decisions, not only with regard to prominence, but with regard to other intonation choices as well.

Tone: I

The meaning of the four tone choices is best regarded as deriving from two distinct oppositions. Firstly, there is a sense in which the tones that end with a falling movement ($\wedge$ and $\searrow$) are systematically opposed to those that end with a rising movement ($\vee$ and $\diagup$). For reasons that will appear presently, the first pair are designated 'proclaiming' tones (symbol P) and the second 'referring' tones (symbol R). In transcriptions, the symbols are placed at the beginning of the tone unit.

The meaning distinction realised by R tone versus P tone can be illustrated by comparing the following:

(9)

    (i) // R archim<u>ED</u>es // P was a si<u>C</u>ILian //
    (ii) // P archim<u>ED</u>es // R was a si<u>CIL</u>ian //

Version (i) can be paraphrased in some such way as 'Talking of Archimedes, he came from Sicily', version (ii) as 'Talking of Sicily, that's where Archimedes came from'. In both, the tone unit having R tone refers to matter which the speaker assumes is already conversationally in play, while that having P tone proclaims a constituent of the utterance as news. Conceptualisation is made easier in straightforward cases like this by postulating an area of previously negotiated common ground, which can either be invoked retrospectively by choice of R tone or enlarged by the act of proclaiming (or 'telling') something the hearer has not yet been told. In the two versions of (9), the assumption that one or other of the constituents has already been introduced into the conversation amounts to an assumption that its status as common ground can be taken for granted.

To accommodate all speaker-choices between proclaiming and referring, this rudimentary metaphorical apparatus has to be elaborated in two ways. Firstly, matter can become eligible for reference because of its presence in the total context of interaction (the same theoretical postulate as was found necessary to account for the distribution of prominence). Common ground includes, but is not restricted to, shared experience of a particular linguistic interaction up to the moment of utterance; rather it is the product of the interpenetrating biographies of the participants of which common involvement in the interaction constitutes only a part. More radically, perhaps, the most general interpretation of the significance of the P/R choice requires that we make a mental separation between the 'content' of the tone unit and the 'social' implication of the tone choice. Invocation of common ground means, in effect, presenting some segment of the message in the name of the 'WE' of the interaction; proclaiming is tantamount to speaking for the 'I' whose viewpoint is assumed to have not yet been assimilated by the 'YOU' who is the hearer. An explanation in social terms, distinguishing those parts of the utterance that foreground the separative aspect of the conversational relationship from those that foreground the consolidatory aspect, subsumes those partial explanations that make reference to textual recoverability or to shared knowledge.

Tone: II

Attending to the social implications of tone choice is also the best
way of capturing the general significance of the other distinction
realised by tone.   Having said that, for instance $\vee^\nearrow$ and $\nearrow$ are
alternative ways of marking the content of a given tone unit as
matter with which both speaker and hearer can be assumed to be
associated, it remains necessary to discover what motivates the
choice of one rather than the other.   The relevant consideration
here seems to be that the parties to most verbal interactions have
differential rights.   A teacher, for instance, has, by virtue of his
role, a wider range of conversational options available to him than
his pupils have.   The choice of two ways of marking a referring
tone unit is the prerogative of what might be called the dominant
participant; and it follows that, in situations where the allocation
of roles is not predetermined, use of the privileged version, the
rise (symbol r+), indicates the speaker's assumption of dominance
for the time being.   The effect of this version can be compared with
the effect of the fall-rise (symbol r) in:
  (10)
        (i) // r GO if you <u>WANT</u> to //
        (ii) // r+ GO if you <u>WANT</u> to //

The authoritative sound of (ii), which contrasts with something more
like acquiescence in (i), would normally be restricted in its use to
someone to whom social convention had alloted superior status, or
perhaps to someone in an interaction characterised by a generally
symmetrical role relationship who was exploiting the option to assert
temporary dominance.
  Understanding of the r/r+ choice actually contributes comparatively little to present thinking about discourse structure.   So, too,
does the little that can be said about a similar difference between
two versions of the proclaiming tone, the fall (p) and the rise-fall
(p+), where the symbol + again stands for the component that has
been characterised as dominance.   Usually, it is enough to do as
was done in the previous section and identify tone as R (that is, as
r or r+ without distinction) or as P (p or p+).

Key

Only choices of key internal to the pitch sequence will be considered
here.
Compare:
  (11)
        (i) // p they LIVE on the es<u>TATE</u> // p in a <u>SEMi</u> //
        (ii) // p they LIVE on the es<u>TATE</u> // p in a <u>SEMi</u> //

  The second tone unit of (i) proclaims information about where they
live additional to that presented in the first tone unit; also, the
prominent syllable in 'semi' marks it as a selection from a range of
possibilities (villa, bungalow, maisonette, terraced house, etc.).

In (ii), the second tone unit is still proclaiming, but because of the high key, semi does not now result from the same simple process of selection. Probably, its significance is most readily interpreted as indicating surprise; but surprise turns out to be only one of a large number of implications that the same key choice can carry, depending upon the lexis and other aspects of the context. This instance permits paraphrases like: 'They don't <u>not</u> live in a semi as one might have supposed they. did' or 'They don't <u>live</u> in the kind of house you seem to think they do'. Superimposed upon the paradigm of possibilities that can be listed, as they were listed above, it is necessary to think of a binary opposition between 'semi' and some alternative which the speaker regards as being present in the context of interaction. If a mid-key tone unit means 'A selected from the set A,B,C,D, etc.' then an otherwise identical high-key version means 'A not Y', where the value of Y is assumed to be known to the hearer. The term 'contrastive' is frequently used in linguistics with the significance attributed here to 'selective'. In its present use, it is to be regarded as being reserved for instances of the existentially valid 'A not Y' kind. Tone units having high key are thus <u>contrastive</u> and those having mid key are <u>additive</u> when looked at from the point of view of their contribution towards speaker/ hearer convergence.

Consider now:

(11)

    (iii) // p they LIVE on the esTATE // p in a SEMi //

Here, the low-key version of 'semi' has selective force: a villa or a bungalow would be among the other possibilities. But what the key choice adds is the information that 'living on the estate' necessarily entails 'living in a semi'; another selection might mean it necessarily entails, say, living in a bungalow. The content of the two tone units is presented as being, in the context of inter- action, equivalent to each other. Low key, whose value is <u>equative</u>, can be represented as 'A, which equals Y', where Y is the content of the immediately preceding tone unit.

Examples (11) (i), (ii), (iii) all have minimal tonic segments. A further variant will serve as a reminder of the possibility of separate key and termination choices:

(11)

    (iv) // p they LIVE on the es<u>TATE</u> // p in a PRE-war <u>SEMi</u> //

In such a case, it is the relative pitch level of <u>pre-</u> that decides whether the value of 'pre-war semi' is contrastive, additive or equative. The pitch level of 'semi', now the last prominent syllable in the tonic segment, realises termination. If this happens to be low, it can already be said on the basis of what has gone before that this will bring about pitch sequence closure. A systematic account of the communicative value of termination needs, however, to take note, in a very direct way, of the relationship between one speaker's utterance and the succeeding one. For this reason, it is better dealt with in the chapter that attempts to relate intonation categories to discourse structure.

Chapter 2

Sentences in discourse

Kay Richardson

This chapter presents, schematically, an argument about descriptive units which is at odds with the general view of discourse structure presented in this book. As other chapters demonstrate, the prevailing view is that units of discourse analysis, in the context of the rank scale to which they belong, are realised by sentences and other grammatical items – and also, on occasion, by non-linguistic items. According to this view, it is a mistake to take syntactically defined units as the basis of the discourse description, since discourse is not a kind of higher-order syntax, but a completely independent level of patterning. The relation between the two levels is thus analogous to the relation between syntax and phonology. I shall be arguing that it is possible, appropriate and revealing to make the opposite assumption – that syntactically defined units can be seen as entering directly into the structure of discourse, rather than via a 'realisational' relationship.

Importantly, it is the description of the structure of discourse which is affected by this reconceptualisation of syntax–discourse relations. The Birmingham discourse analysis model, with its rank scale of units, is predominantly designed with structural description as its goal. Nevertheless, a distinction which I feel to be crucial is largely missing from this tradition – the distinction between structuration and synchronisation as principles of linguistic organisation at the supra–sentential level. The importance of this distinction is that certain features of interactive discourse are then removed from the domain of structural description, into the domain of synchronisation, with a distinctive and independently motivated set of guiding principles. These principles, and the principles of structuration, I shall now briefly explain.

Synchronisation

From the point of view of discourse synchronisation, the basic unit is discourse turn. 'Turn' is a theoretical concept borrowed from the ethnomethodologists (see, for example, Sacks et al. 1974). I have tried to simplify this concept, to make it workable as a descrip-

tive tool.   In the ethnomethodological writings, there is no systematic conceptual distinction between synchronisation and structuration.   Consequently, 'turn' can refer to both an uninterrupted
stretch of language produced by one speaker, which is how I shall
be using it, and an item of a particular kind constituted by the discourse for which I shall be using the term 'contribution'.

The model of two-party spoken discourse which underlies my
notion of 'synchronisation' is one in which both speakers are equally
involved from the moment of the conversation's commencement to the
moment of its termination.   This is obviously an idealisation.
Diagrammatically, it can be represented as two parallel strands,
one for each speaker, with asterisks standing for 'positive phases'
(see below) and dotted lines for 'negative phases':

```
           2                  4                 7
A: _____*****?****_____*****?****_____***?****
    1                  3       5        6
B: *****?****_____*****?****__**?____*****?****_____
```

In this particular 'conversation', there are no discontinuities such
as might occur if one speaker went out of earshot whilst the other
continued talking on the assumption he or she could still be heard.
A positive phase is equivalent to a discourse turn, and the turns of
this 'discourse' have been numbered for convenience; a negative
phase corresponds to a listening period.   In other words a discourse turn occurs when a speaker is exercising the option 'talk'
from the paradigm 'talk/no talk' whilst a listening period occurs when
the option 'no talk' is being exercised.   A description of this imag-
inary conversation would show that turns 1, 2, 3, 4, 6 are all
neatly sequenced, one after another, that the transition from 6 to 7
involves some overlap, and would contrast these sequenced turns
with the parallel organisation represented by 4/5.   In a sense, 5 is
not a turn at all; for its place in the sequence of turns is not as
significant as its place parallel to, and 'underneath', turn 4.   I have
labelled such occurrences as 'parallel subordinate turns'.   The
following example illustrates the occurrence of parallel organisation
in a real conversation:

(1) A: oh this is for the NUT⌈party tonight ⌈yes
    B: ⌊yeah   ⌊this evening

(This, and all other numbered examples in the corpus, forms part of
the data used in my MA thesis (Richardson 1978), and the letters
used to indicate speakers, e.g. 'A' and 'B', follow the usage in that
study.)   'oh this is for the NUT party tonight yes' constitutes the
whole of A's turn.   As the bracketing shows, B's 'yeah' starts in
the pause between 'NUT' and 'party', and his 'this evening' follows
A's 'tonight'.   The relationship between A's turn and B's 'yeah' is
of superordinate to a subordinate turn, whereas the relationship
between A's turn and B's 'this evening' is one of overlap.

Structuration

'Structuration' encompasses a concern with the nature of, and relationships between, units of linguistic structure larger than the sentence. In the Birmingham discourse analysis tradition, I see units of description related to one another hierarchically on a rank scale, although there is a crucial difference between the approach to discourse structure outlined in Sinclair and Coulthard (1975) and the present approach, which concerns units at the lowest rank of the discourse hierarchy. However, this difference in approach does not follow through into the higher ranks: consequently I am happy to adopt their terms 'move', 'exchange' and 'transaction' as names for the units at higher ranks. Of these three, only 'moves' will, briefly, be dealt with; more details about moves, and exposition concerning exchanges and transactions, is given in Richardson (1978).

A first step is to distinguish structuration from synchronisation and to explain why turn will not do as the basic unit of discourse structure. The main reason why it is inappropriate to use the turn as the basic unit of discourse description, and why the 'strand' model of discourse outlined in the previous section is of little use for an analysis of discourse structure, is that this presupposes an essentially arbitrary view of who speaks, how much he or she says, and how these linguistic productions are put together.

There is no a priori reason for a turn to be of any particular length, and no constraints at all governing its internal structure. While there is room, in a comprehensive view of the nature of discourse, to acknowledge this kind of arbitrariness, it is important that the acknowledgment should not interfere with the apparatus for describing discourse structure, for here we shall always want to talk of units which can be 'complete' in themselves, or recognisably and accountably incomplete: we shall need principles for deciding where to recognise boundaries between units of the same rank in a continuous piece of text, and we shall need to recognise that certain ways of initiating units at all ranks actively predict the nature of the unit even before it comes to be complete.

At the lowest rank, the sentence is the perfect candidate to carry this kind of responsibility. (Although I have used the term sentence to refer to the syntactically defined bottom-rank unit of the rank scale, I really prefer to use syntactic contribution, for reasons which will become clear as the argument progresses.) The obvious objection to regarding the sentence as a starting point is that discourse does not consist only of sentences, and that even when stretches of discourse do, the sentences are not always well formed according to idealised grammatical rules. I shall show, below, how a syntactically based discourse description copes with this apparently anomalous situation. In Sinclair and Coulthard (1975) it is claimed that the basic units of discourse need to be defined in functional terms, and realisation rules invoked to specify how these discourse acts are encoded in syntactic forms. But this approach leads to problems, not least of which is the problem of deciding what

constitutes a functionally defined discourse act. Unless very carefully handled, the list of acts may become arbitrary: whereas, in
any piece of discourse the recognition of sentences is relatively
straightforward, the recognition of elicitations and the like is not.
The formalisation of sentence recognition in discourse seems a
possible goal, whereas the formalisation of 'act' recognition is very
difficult to imagine. This seems sufficient motivation to shift attention to sentences, and to investigate the consequences of this shift.

One reason for being unhappy with the insistence of function as
the defining criterion for units at the lowest rank, is the ambiguity
surrounding the notion of function itself, which in Sinclair and Coulthard (1975) is used partly to mean 'position', partly to mean 'use',
as in the following quotation:

> Statements, questions and commands are only informative, elicita-
> tions and directives when they are initiating; an elicitation is an
> initiating question of which the function is to gain a verbal res-
> ponse from another speaker – questions occur at many other places
> in the discourse but then their function is different and this must
> be stressed (p. 34).

From 'an elicitation is an initiating question of which the function is
to gain a verbal response', we get the impression that function is
equal to 'use': 'to gain a verbal response'. But then they state that
to change the use of an item you change its position, and this suggests a structural view of 'function'. It seems that structural position is one of the things which helps to determine an item's function,
rather than defining function, thus giving priority to the function–use
equation. If this is a correct interpretation, then the set of 'uses'
ought to be defined by criteria which are independent of discourse
structure, and the relevance of the one to the other ought to be
argued for more centrally.

It is not over-optimistic to suggest that sentences in discourse are
easy to recognise. There are certainly problems, but the problems
mostly consist in deciding what does and what does not count as a
sentence, and in trying to describe the function of the things which
do not count as sentences. These problems actually pinpoint some
of the most interesting things about spontaneous discourse. The
next stage in this argument is to illustrate how the process of classification can proceed, once one accepts the crucial first stage of
giving sentences a privileged status in discourse description.

A first step is to recognise that, in fact, items other than sentences can function at the lowest rank of analysis:

(2) C: now we didn't know which would come out best either
        with it altered like that ** or whether ** with a
        piece of paper stuck over it like that
    A: mm, well the only thing is um ** you'll probably get
        a * you know, there'll be a little mark (?)

(* indicates a pause, longer pauses are indicated by adding more
asterisks; (?) indicates talk which cannot be deciphered.)

From this section of a spontaneous conversation, once the grammatical sentences have been identified, the analyst is left with
unanalysed items like 'now', 'mm', 'well', 'um' and (arguably) 'you

know'. From the present perspective these items are considered
not to be sentences or parts of sentences, but to have separate
status as non-syntactic contributions, a label chosen to mark the
contrast with sentences, or syntactic contributions. The terminology adopted is also intended to stress that, at the lowest rank of
description, the two kinds of contribution have equivalent status.
As well as having distinctive internal structuration, the two types of
contribution crucially have different jobs to perform in terms of the
structure of the discourse.

A syntactic contribution is an item structured around a finite verb.
This definition is of course at odds with some versions of English
syntax, such as that of Sinclair (1972) which employs a category of
'moodless' sentence (pp. 19-20) which subsumes many of the things
here classified as non-syntactic contributions, i.e. contributions
not structured around a finite verb, as well as some elliptical forms
which would be regarded as syntactic contributions under the present
scheme.

It is worth noting that Sinclair and Coulthard (1975) also allow
both syntactic and non-syntactic contributions to function as discourse 'acts',

directive	d	Realised by command. Its function is to request a non-linguistic response.
bid	b	Realised by a closed class of verbal and non-verbal items - 'Sir', 'Miss', teacher's name, raised hand, heavy breathing, finger clicking. Its function is to signal a desire to contribute to the discourse.
		(p. 41)

The present article can thus be seen as presenting a different way
of coping, analytically, with the same 'fact', but instead of implicitly treating this fact as part of the case for not giving sentences a
privileged status in discourse description, the strategy has been to
make it the basis of a primary classification into two types, and to
see whether any independent evidence, other than internal principles of structuration, can be brought to bear to sustain the distinction. I believe that it is possible to discover such structural
evidence, as I shall now try to illustrate.

The structure of moves

Non-syntactic and syntactic contributions can be seen as combining
with one another in structural patterns to form moves. There are
two types of move, syntactic and non-syntactic: a well-formed non-
syntactic move consists of at least one non-syntactic contribution:
a well-formed syntactic move consists of one and only one syntactic
plus (optionally) non-syntactic contributions before and/or after.
Thus the form of a syntactic move can be notationally represented as
(f^n) h (f^n), where f refers to the element of structure frame, which

must be realised by non-syntactic contributions if present, and h
refers to the element of structure head which is obligatory and must
be realised by a syntactic contribution (sentence).

In example (2) presented above, both kinds of move occur. I will
now concentrate on the part provided by speaker A, which can be
analysed as follows:

(2a) A: mm. well/the only thing is (um) ** you'll probably get
     a * (you know) there'll be a little mark.

(Full stops indicate the end of moves; slashes (/) indicate a boundary
between a frame and a head in a syntactic move; and brackets indicate that the enclosed item is an inappropriately placed (disruptive)
non-syntactic contribution, a phenomenon which will be discussed
below.)

According to this analysis, speaker A first utters a non-syntactic
move consisting of one non-syntactic contribution. She then utters
a syntactic move, consisting of an initial non-syntactic frame (the
optional element) followed by a syntactic head (the obligatory element). A framing element may be realised by more than one non-
syntactic contribution:

(3) A: mm, yes/that would probably be better

(Commas are used to separate the independent contributions which
together constitute the move's frame.)

As examples (2a) and (3) show, there is no automatic way of
deciding whether a sequence of non-syntactic contributions constitute separate moves, or discrete parts of a single move. In
example (2a) I have shown a move boundary between 'mm' and 'well',
both non-syntactic contributions, whereas the boundary between
'mm' and 'yes' in example (3) is treated as a boundary between contributions, within the frame element. When analytical problems of
this kind arise, it becomes necessary to look to dimensions of
patterning other than the structural, for evidence which would support one analysis over another. Another dimension of patterning,
not hitherto acknowledged in this chapter, is the dimension of intonation. Although treated here as a conceptually distinct dimension of
patterning, it can provide evidence to help decide an analytical
problem in the description of structure. Intonation does in fact
distinguish example (2a) from example (3). In the former 'mm' has
an intonation contour of its own, and is further separated from 'well'
by a pause. In the latter, one intonation contour covers the whole
of the turn, from 'mm' to 'better'. This is not to be taken as an
argument that units of intonation are always coterminous with units
of structure (or it would be pointless to conceive of intonation and
structure as distinctive dimensions of patterning): simply that if
there is an ambiguity along the structural dimension, it is justifiable
to assume that the mapping between different dimensions takes the
unmarked form.

Before moving on to discuss the relationship between turns, contributions and moves, there are two further points about syntactic
and non-syntactic contributions which ought to be raised. The first
point concerns those 'non-syntactic contributions' which seem to
occur in mid-sentence, for instance 'um' and 'you know' in example (2a)

The second point concerns circumstances under which certain apparently syntactic forms, such as 'you know', are better seen as 'honorary' non-syntactic utterances.

To take the first point. From a commonsense point of view it makes sense that 'hesitation phenomena' should occur when a speaker is constrained to produce a sentence 'on the spot'. Another example:

    (4) C: I'm sorry about want always wanting things in a rush
            but its (uh) * really not our fault not in the office anyway.

The hierarchical model specifies that non-syntactic contributions can only frame syntactic ones, that is, stand on either side of them. This need not be a contradiction if we assume that non-syntactic contributions like 'uh' here which disrupt a flow of syntax are not entering into a structural relationship with that syntactic structure. The speaker can, and frequently does, carry on from where he or she left off in the sentence before the disruption took place. This also illustrates that understanding syntax is a process of continuous classification. A hearer who is aware of listening to a syntactic contribution, will be able to classify everything before a possible termination point for that contribution as either structurally belonging to that contribution or not. He or she is also able to monitor for possible completion points in the ongoing sentence. I suggest, therefore, that in this sentence 'uh' will be heard as not adding anything to the syntactic structure of this sentence, but that neither will it be heard as preventing that sentence from being completed. The same is true of short pauses, which are less disruptive than non-syntactic contributions of this kind.

It was suggested above that 'you know' is appropriately classified as a non-syntactic contribution, in spite of the syntactic structure which it appears to possess. The reason why this particular form is awarded the status of an 'honorary' non-syntactic contribution is that it participates in the discourse in the positions character-istic of these, in framing contributions and as disruptions, and not in the positions that syntactic contributions occupy - in example (2a) above 'you know' interrupts the ongoing syntactic structure. It is significant that when the speaker returns to her syntactic contribu-tion, she links back to 'the only thing is', thus eliminating or ignor-ing not only 'you know' but also everything else that occurred between 'is' and 'there'll', which includes another interrupting non-syntactic contribution and two pauses, as well as the syntactically coherent though incomplete series 'you'll probably get a'.

Another exponent of the class 'honorary' non-syntactic contribu-tions is 'I see', illustrated here as part of a framing element:

    (5) A: oh, I see, mm/this the headed paper.

I would like to concentrate for a moment on the question: how could syntactic expressions have become functionally equivalent to non-syntactic ones? Only a longitudinal study could answer this ques-tion, for it is a historical process, although it is possible to invent plausible scenarios. For example, perhaps at one time the syntax of 'I see' was important, say, in a response move within an exchange. If so, why would that lexicogrammatical pattern be

chosen rather than any other? Common sense suggests that it would
have been metaphorical for 'yes, I understand/ accept what you say',
or something like that, because that is often what a hearer is supposed to do when given information by a speaker. In other words it
was never, in this context, literally about 'seeing'. Now it happens
that any utterance from the co-participating speaker, after a piece
of information from the first speaker, will seem to have that 'I accept
what you say' meaning. Even a statement like 'I don't understand
you' accepts the preceding information, since to accept is simply to
acknowledge that you have heard it. But an utterance like 'yes'
carries that meaning more transparently than others because in that
context it carries no other meaning. By using, regularly, items
more substantive than 'yes' in this slot, any additional meaning comes
to be 'eroded', in the same way that metaphors in general gradually
cease to evoke their original meaning.

Turns, moves and contributions

This chapter began with the concepts of turn and synchronisation as
a dimension of patterning in spontaneous discourse involving more
than one speaker. It is appropriate now to return to the concept of
turn in order to clarify the relationship between turns, contributions
and moves, bearing in mind that this discussion hinges upon how best
to conceive of the integration of two distinct dimensions of patterning, synchronisation and structuration.
    The structural environment within which a contribution is located
is the move, as discussed above. However, as a matter of pragmatic necessity, the opportunity to initiate a move occurs within a
discourse turn. It has been shown (Sacks et al. 1974) that conversations are organised on the basis of the principle that speakers
take turns, and turns are allocated according to a rule that says
only one speaker at a time has the right to talk. Although the turn-
taking principle is appropriate for the description of the synchronisation of the talk, it is not a useful principle with which to describe its structuration, for not only can we point to many turns which
accommodate more than one contribution, many contributions in fact
occupy more than one turn.
    Consider the following examples. In (6) the whole series occurs
within the space of one turn:

(6) C: well/that's what I thought.   I think that's better.

There is a combination of one complex syntactic move, structure fh,
with one simple syntactic move. The converse of this is the extension of a contribution to occupy more than one turn of the discourse.
In the following example, one contribution has parts of its realisation in three separate turns of the discourse. Not only does the
co-participant have intervening turns featuring independent contributions, but so does speaker E himself:

(7) T   E: yeah/I'll (er)

    T   A: (?)

```
        E:  be bringing the cheese and wine (er) the (er) not
            the cheese and wine, the wine

T    A:  oh/this is for the NUT┌party tonight/┌yes
TT   E:                        └yeah         └this evening

T    A:  mm

T    E:  and (er) what I'll have to do is to drop it off and
         go to hospital to see my ma-in-law who's in hospital/
         you see

T    A:  oh yes, mm

T    E:  and then my wife and I, and then we'll, after
         we've visited then we'll come back
```

(The letter T in the margin indicates the start of a new turn.)
Allowing for self correction pausing and disruptive non-syntactic
contributions, and also for the 'side sequence' (Jefferson 1972), F
can be seen as providing a syntactic move which reads as follows:

(7a) yeah/I'll be bringing the wine and what I'll have to do is
     to drop it off and go to hospital to see my ma-in-law who's
     in hospital and then my wife and I after we've visited then
     we'll come back

There are other possible analyses, such as treating 'and then my
wife and I...come back' as a separate move, following the termination of the preceding one with the non-syntactic final frame 'you see'.
Unfortunately, it is beyond the scope of the present chapter to discuss the complex issues involved when making decisions of this kind.

If interaction of this kind is the norm in the relations between
elements of structure and turns, how can it be legitimate to speak of
the discourse turn as being the relevant environment within which
structural options are exercised? The considerations here are
pragmatic ones. It is easy to adhere to the principle that, when one
speaker stops talking, another can/must take over. It is
especially easy when there are only two speakers, for the problem of
which person is to take over talking when the current speaker stops
does not arise. This turn-taking system is the system which is used
to minimise the occurrence of overlap and of silence – and it provides the basis for the more complex dimension of structural organisation. It is only possible to organise communication structurally
if there is an accepted procedure for distributing turns to the
speakers, and a speaker needs to be allocated a turn in order to
start any contribution which he or she might have to supply to the
discourse. It is also crucial to describe this mapping of structuration on to synchronisation in terms of the continuous classification
of discourse, since obviously the option to start a new contribution
does not operate at the start of every new turn. This option will be
low on the list of priorities if the speaker's previous turn was
occupied by an incomplete syntactic contribution.

In the following example speaker C uses a syntactic structure
employing the binder 'either', which is standardly paired with 'or',
in order to introduce two syntactic structures of equal rank. By

the end of C's first turn, this structure is still incomplete, in the sense that there has been no use of 'or'. So when her next turn begins with 'or' it can be seen that she is not starting a new move, but completing the contribution and thereby the move which was initiated in the previous turn:

> (8) C: now/we didn't know which would come out the best,
>   either with it altered like that
>   A: mm
>   C: or whether ** with a piece of paper stuck over it like that

Related to this point, it is also worth noticing the way in which speakers tend to use turns to produce what come to be seen as move-continuations even where the move, in its previous turn, had appeared to reach its completion. This strategy involves the use of linking words:

> (9) B: er we (er) *** you'll get one from both Lyndhurst and
>   the Beckett
>   A: oh yes
>   B: but we are in some dis well not disarray but
>   A: mm
>   B: we have (er) * time problems there

In this example, the move which B initiates in his first turn could be terminated at 'Beckett': this would be a syntactically complete contribution, and it may be that A responds believing B's move to be finished. However, in his next turn, he produces a string which can be seen as syntactically dependent upon the string in his previous turn, and thus as continuing that contribution/move, rather than initiating a new one.

In this chapter I hope to have shown some of the positive advantages, as well as the practical possibility, of recognising that sentences do have a part to play in the structural organisation of discourse. In the thesis from which these arguments are taken (Richardson 1978) yet more of these gains are outlined. The frame of reference which is developed allows us to ask 'why choose a syntactic move rather than a non–syntactic move?' for example. All choices are context–dependent, and I think it can be shown that the motivation for a choice sometimes concerns the giving or withholding of information (where one speaker knows something that the other does not); the manifesting of closeness or distance in the interpersonal relationship; the current set of constraints imposed by the discourse, and the stylistic effects produced by choosing the option which is not the one that the discourse constraints would have predicted.

Chapter 3

Analysing spoken discourse

Deirdre Burton

1 Introduction

There can be little doubt that the seminal ideas presented in
Sinclair et al. (1972) and Sinclair and Coulthard (1975) are the most
significant contribution to the rigorous socio-linguistic analysis of
naturally spoken discourse at present available to linguists. The
strict adherence to both the Hallidayan model and the four criteria
discussed on page 2 offer an approach to the analysis of spoken text
that satisfies formalists and structuralists alike.

However, the one obvious drawback to the descriptive apparatus
is the difficulty of applying it to data collected in, for example, non-
formal, non-authoritarian, non-collaborative contexts. Sinclair
and Coulthard do, of course acknowledge this (p. 6):

> the system ... is now able to cope with most teacher/pupil inter-
> action inside the classroom. What it cannot handle, and was not
> designed to handle is pupil/pupil interaction in project-work,
> discussion groups, or the playground (my emphasis).

Similarly, they stress that their descriptive apparatus is specifically intended as a base model, to be modified in subsequent research
to greater generality (pp. 112-15). The recent literature suggests,
though, that researchers who have collected data from other 'situations' (see below, for comments on this concept) have encountered
considerable problems in trying to use and adapt the Sinclair-
Coulthard model (see, for example, McKnight, 1976; McTear, 1977
and various working papers from Birmingham ELR). Below, I offer
a set of modifications to that model which allows a comparably
rigorous analysis of any naturally occurring talk, but two crucial
points need to be stressed here.

Firstly, I am convinced that, wise as it was to begin the original
work in discourse analysis by focusing on the formal, recognisably
and markedly orderly interaction of the chalk-and-talk classroom,
later attempts to extend the generality of the application of the
descriptive apparatus were severely hampered by having this data,
and its structural patterns, as a central conceptual base. Clearly,
since classroom talk was intuitively singled out for analysis because
it was generally acknowledged as 'odd', then a comprehensive

61

method for analysing all styles of talk must be expected to demonstrate the oddities of classroom talk and its linguistic structural
choices in contrast with a different set of stylistic choices evident
in other kinds of talk.   One would expect features that are prominent in classroom talk to be less prominent, or even not apparent at
all, in other types of talk and vice versa.   Researchers examining
other 'situations' have seemed surprised that their data could not be
forced into, say, a pattern of neatly recurring three-part IRF
exchanges, whereas, in fact, exactly the opposite should be the
case.

That is, a researcher should be extremely surprised if other data
does exhibit such patterns, since it is precisely those types of pre-
dominant structural choices that call out for commonsense recognition and glossing of the talk as, say, 'an authoritarian conversational situation', whose archetypal member category is formal
teacher-pupil talk.   Clearly, there are other talk-situations which
do exhibit such choices: middle-class mother-child talk, some
doctor-patient talk, some native-speaker to non-native-speaker
talk, for example, and accounts, explanation and discussions of
such similarities are important and far-reaching in terms of
language, education and society.   However, the fact that speakers
recognise the stylistic-sociological significance of such patterns is
precisely why such choices are not tolerated in many other situations, and are not realised in, say, casual conversation.   The
junior lecturer who offers his or her head of department recurrent
accepting and evaluating acts as feedback in casual coffee-table talk
does so at the risk of losing tenure!

The second, related, point concerns the spate of research work
inspired by the Sinclair-Coulthard model, where individuals have
gone out to collect recordings of talk they have already tagged by a
commonsense notion of 'situation' or 'type' dependent on pre-
theoretical, loosely sociological features.

Thus we have attempts to analyse, for example, mother-child talk,
child-child talk, doctor-patient interviews, psychiatric therapy
sessions, alternative classroom interactions, committee negotiations, seminar discussions, etc.   Many of these studies certainly
do contribute to our overall understanding of the structure of talk,
but, in their stated goals of hoping to compare these 'situations'
with the original classroom 'situation', several researchers miss an
important central linguistic issue.   If there are such things as 'talk
situations' (and I think there are, but would prefer to taxonomise
them as styles of talk), then all the data collected must eventually be
charted against a general model designed to show the potential
structure of discourse, and which demonstrates linguistically why it
is that actual instances of talk are perceived as similar or dissimi-
lar by both analysts and conversationalists.   That is, talk situations should not be tagged a priori according to quasi-sociological
features like 'setting', 'participants', 'the job being done', etc.
Though obviously this is an unavoidable aspect of our member's
knowledge, it is the beginning of interesting analytical questions,
and not in any way a convenient answer.   Rather, data should be

analysed according to a model sufficiently general and powerful to handle all types of talk. And it is the analyses which should be compared to see whether or not they display similar stylistic choices from the underlying linguistic structural options available for all talk.

It is a model of this type that I describe below. It is never easy to describe a hierarchy in a linear text, so I will firstly present an informal and discursive description (Section 2), and then the formal rank scale (Section 3). The coded data which then follows (Section 4) includes short extracts from(i) casual conversation, (ii) teacher-pupil talk, (iii) mother–child talk. This is partly to clarify the practical aspects of actually coding data according to the model offered, and partly to enable further discussion of the points made in the preceding paragraph here.

2 An informal description of the proposed rank scale

There seem to be two sets of problems that recur when analysts of data, other than classroom data, try to apply the Sinclair-Coulthard coding scheme. The simple problems concern the topmost and bottommost ranks – interaction, transaction, act – where the analyst needs only to see what recognition criteria are descriptively adequate, to account for these structures and items. Apart from questions of economy, precision and delicacy, this activity is not unduly difficult, and alterations are not necessarily radical. The really interesting interactive ranks are those of exchange and move. And since the description of exchange structure hinges on what moves are used in what orders and relationships, and since move is also the minimal interactive unit, it seems that most analytical problems centre on this rank first and foremost.

Outside the classroom there are several specific problems with the notion and description of moves as set out in Sinclair and Coulthard. Firstly, feedback or follow–up hardly ever occurs. Only in minimal ritual encounters (see Goffman, 1971, chapter 3), or in extended formal talk can this be seen as a recurrent feature that needs a central place in a structural description of conversations. I think it may be used in informal talk as a device for conveying sarcasm. I will not dwell on that suggestion here, except to say that, if it is the case that casual conversationalists can use feedback items per se as a sarcasm device, regardless of the realisations of that item, then it must also be the case that feedback does not occur as an unmarked norm in the structure of those casual conversations.

This repeated lack of feedback or follow–up being the case, any coder using the layout of three major columns, opening, answering, follow–up, that works so neatly for the classroom data, merely finds himself with an empty third column. Surely an adequate reason for deleting that third column.

This leaves opening and answering moves. Inside the classroom all parties are agreed that time will be spent in the transfer of

information from teacher to pupils, with a ritualised structure of
informatives, elicitations and directives, etc. to be employed by the
teacher to that end, and a set of appropriate reciprocal acts and
moves to be employed by the pupils to assist in the attainment of the
teacher's end. In a formal classroom the teacher is in control of
structural choices right through the hierarchy, in that when the
pupils, or selected pupils, are given a place to interact, the type of
act they can appropriately use is selected and predetermined by the
preceding teacher-act. The teacher is also in control of 'content'
right through the hierarchy, in that he or she selects the topic for
the lesson, the topic for transactions, the topic for exchanges, the
topic for appropriate moves and acts. Outside the classroom, it is
not news to anyone that the situation is nothing like as simple, particularly since interactants, far from having a job to be done via the
talk, may simply talk for the sake of talking.

Certainly, structural and topical control are rarely in the hands
of one participant only, indeed the commonsense interpretation of a
conversationalist finding himself in such a position would be that his
co-conversationalist was 'difficult to talk to'. Whilst openings
which coincide with transaction boundaries are easy to find, in that
of course the recognition criteria also coincide, following moves
are often difficult to categorise, in that they can seem simultaneously to answer a preceding move and open up the way for a new move.
An extreme analytical view would be to see multiple openings, where
anything that was not a simple, appropriate response to a preceding
act (say a reply to an elicitation, or an acknowledge to an ongoing
inform) would be seen as another opening. This would not, however,
be of much structural or descriptive interest, since there clearly
are relationships between successive utterances in casual conversations, even though they do not fit the classroom format. The big-
gest difference between classroom data and everyday talk is, of
course, the wide range of verbal activities available to anyone
answering an opening. The polite consensus-collaborative model
just has no room for the number of possibilities, where, for
example, the 'answerer' can refuse to answer, can demand a reason
for the question being asked, can provide an answer that simultaneously answers a preceding move, but seems to open the next
exchange, etc. This last possibility appears in many people's
data, and analysts feel that they need to 'double code' – a theoretically unsound solution. It certainly appears in my data, such that
to remain within two simple columns representing opening (including
framing and focusing) and answering would only be possible by forcing the data into categories that it does not really fit, and by ignor-
ing other interesting structural complexities that should be represented.

My solution to these problems has been to reconceptualise conversational moves in this fairly commonsense way. It seemed to me to
be true that, given an opening move by speaker A, B has the choice
of politely agreeing, complying, supporting the discourse presuppositions in that move, and behaving in a tidy, appropriate way in his
choice of move and acts, or he has the choice of not agreeing, not

supporting, not complying with those presuppositions, possibly counter-proposing, ignoring, telling A that his opening was mis-guided, badly designed, etc. This range of possibilities open to B (and of course subsequently to A, then to B and even to C, D and E) seemed to cluster under two types of conversational behaviour, which for mnemonic convenience I labelled supporting and challeng-ing moves. I am trying here to keep within the 'game' analogy sug-gested loosely by the notion move. Whilst it would be misguided to press this analogy too far, it is nevertheless helpful to see moves as items which define the positions of the participants' utterances in relation to each other in the course of say, a 'round' of talk, leav-ing a different set of information to be conveyed by the choice of constituent acts for these moves, and other information still to be conveyed by varying combinations of act and move choices.

The problem then was to find explicit criteria for recognising these moves (as well as other more familiar types of move). The problem can be solved quite neatly by importing three concepts: (i) a notion of 'discourse framework' based on a concept of recipro-cal acts and cohesion; (ii) Keenan and Schieffelin's idea (1976) of 'Discourse Steps' necessary for the establishment of a discourse topic; and (iii) an extension of Labov's (1970) preconditions for the interpretation of any utterance as a request for action. I think the clearest way to explain the rank scale is from the bottommost rank upwards, so I will do that, and explain these three concepts more fully under my description of moves.

Acts

Wherever it was possible, I tried to restrict my coding at act rank to the 22 acts listed in Sinclair and Coulthard, 1975, pp. 40-4. Obviously, though, where this would have meant forcing the data into inappropriate categories, I revised and reconsidered that list. For the most part the 22 acts were adequate, but I made some alter-ations and some additions.

1 Markers
In the classroom this item is realised by a closed class including 'well', 'right', 'ok', 'good', 'all right'. Its function is to mark boundaries in the discourse, and it occurs either as the pre-head signal in an opening move, or as the head of a framing move, in which case it is used with a falling intonation and followed by a silent stress. Maintaining this functional criterion, and given that I also recognise both framing and opening moves in my data (the latter somewhat amended – see below), I also find this set of markers, but need to extend the realisation list to include items which, following Schegloff in Keenan and Schieffelin (1976), I call expressive particles, for example:
　(1) A: hey　　　　　　　　　　Marker and Silent Stress
　　　　what are you doing out there

2   Summonses

A similar attention-getting item recurs, when one participant uses
the name of another in order to establish contact before introducing
a discourse topic.   Again, this marks boundaries in the discourse,
and can occur either as the head of a framing move or as the signal
in an opening move.   I have again borrowed the term itself from
Schegloff (1968) in that this verbal items seems structurally and
functionally analogous to non-verbal summonses like telephone or
door bells.

    (2)   A: deidre   Summons
          B: what
          C: look at this

3   Requests for speaker's rights – Metastatements

Like summonses, these requests for speaker's rights (cf. Sacks,
1972) occur as pre-topic items, being variations on the classic
'you know what' formula of small children with restricted speaker's
rights, or questions, or statements containing 'tell', or 'ask', for
example:

    (3)   A: you know what I told her
          or
    (4)   A: can I ask you a question

They occur as the heads of focusing moves, like metastatements or
conclusions.   So I have decided to list them as a sub-category of
metastatements, in that they do contain explicit reference to doing
talking, and since, outside the classroom, there seems only a very
fine line between these items and items that are more clearly metastatements, in that they indicate what the next piece of talk is going
to be about, for example:

    (5)   A: let me give you your instructions

The important structural distinction between the use of metastatements inside the classroom and outside it, is that in the latter situation other participants may choose not to allow the speaker using the
metastatement to go ahead with his designated talk.   Thus since both
ordinary metastatements and requests for speaker's rights require
the approval of the other speaker, and occur in the same structural
place, it would seem economic to see them both as metastatements.

4   Permission to go ahead with a topic – Accept

Outside the classroom summonses, metastatements and requests for
speaker's rights do not always go unchallenged, and, as a consequence of this possibility, in fact usually require some sort of 'go-
ahead' signal from a co-participant.   This may be realised by a
non-hostile silence, appropriate attention-giving gestures, formu-
laic responses like A: do you know what, B: what or A: can I tell
you a story?, B: yes, etc.   I label these accept, bearing in mind
part of the functional definition of that act in Sinclair and Coulthard
'to indicate that the teacher has heard or seen and that the preceding act was appropriate'.

    Of course in the classroom, accept is a follow-up act, whereas in
my coding, it is the head of a supporting move.

5 Greetings – Summonses/Accepts

Greetings do not of course occur in the classroom, although they
frequently do so outside the classroom.   In that they are inevitably
markers of boundaries in the talk, I see them as similar to summonses, for an opening greeting, and accepts for a reply greeting.
The first-pair part is coded as summons, the second-pair part as
accept, thus as the head of a framing move, followed by the head of
a supporting move.

6 Accuse-Excuse

A particular feature that again does not seem to be relevant in the
classroom, but recurs often in other data, occurs when speaker A
uses a statement, question or command that is heard as requiring
either an apology or an excuse/explanation, or justification (cf.
Austin, 1962).   This statement, question or command varies in
intensity from mild criticism to serious attack.   Wherever the responses to this type of act can be coded as an apology, or excuse, I
label the first-pair part accuse, the second-pair part excuse.   The
rather nice ambiguity between the meaning of the noun 'excuse' and
the verb 'excuse' covers the related but different types of response
rather well.

7 Inform-Comment

Where there are long passages of informatives offered in the text it
seems inadequate to give one label of informative to the whole
passage, or even to label the first clause inform and all subsequent
units comment – using the definition of comment in Sinclair and
Coulthard as 'to exemplify, expand, justify, provide additional
information'.

I have here followed some of the ideas suggested by Montgomery
(1976) in his analysis of the discourse structure of information-
transfer lectures.   His very neat and interesting work is outlined
on pp. 31-9 and described in detail in Burton (1978a).   In coding
my data, I have found the following categories useful: additive,
adversative and causal items;   repeat, restate and qualifying items;
where, it seems to me, the first three are sub-categories of informative, and the second three are sub-categories of comment.   So given,
say, an initial informative as the head of an opening move, later
informing acts can easily be classified under these six headings.

Montgomery adapts the first three from Halliday and Hasan's more
complex suggestions (Halliday and Hasan, 1976) on clause relationships.   Additive items are typically, but not necessarily, introduced
by 'and', adversative items are typically but not necessarily introduced by 'but', and causal items are typically but not necessarily
introduced by 'so'.   They represent, of course, the three primary
relationships to which, according to natural logic, all propositions
can be reduced.

All these types of informative can be 'expanded' by the use of the
other three comment items.   Repeats are acts which, more or less,
repeat the exact words, or some of the words of an earlier informative.   Restate items rephrase an earlier informative, and qualify-

ing items modify the general applicability of a preceding informative
All comment items may also be used to expand preceding comment
items as well, of course. Coding with these seven labels is no
longer coding at primary delicacy, but in that the data does not conform to the rather simple informing patterns required by the informa-
tion-transfer of the classroom, it seems uninteresting to do less.
In my formal representation of the rank scale, I have restricted
items to the two primaries, inform, and comment, but these should
be understood as superordinates. See also the notes below on
coding conventions.

8 Prefaces

Following work on committee data discussed briefly on pp. 24-6, 28-31
and in detail in Stubbs (1974), I have labelled acts which introduce
re-opening moves as prefaces. Stubbs recognises three types of
prefaces: misplacement prefaces, interruption prefaces, and
personal-point-of-view prefaces, which, for my purposes, I find it
adequate to collapse into one general act.

Misplacement prefaces point out that the utterance following them
will, in some way, be out of sequence. The term is borrowed from
Schegloff and Sacks (1973) where they consider the notion of misplacement markers. They are typically, in committee data, rather
elaborate:

(6) just one other comment Mike - you asked me just now what ...
or
(7) John - y'know this other information ...

Stubbs gives the full possible form of a misplacement preface as
follows:

1	2	3	4	5	6
terms of address	mitigation	account	placement marker	self-referential metaterm	metareference to other speakers' talk

and produces a hypothetical example of how the full form of a misplacement preface might be realised:

(8) 1   2   3   4

  John - erm I think perhaps it would be useful before we go
       5   6

  any further if I sum up some of the things Harry was saying
Interruption prefaces are described as a particular type of misplacement preface, exhibiting surface markers which typically
preface items designed to break into a flow of talk, for example:

(9) look - look let me let me let me let me make it patently clear ...
The markers include: repetition of the first syllable or two; addressing someone by name; standard adversative words and formulae;
'but', 'no but'; items such as 'can I', 'could I', 'I must', 'let me',
plus a self-referential statement. The suggestion for the full form
of an interruption preface looks like this:

1	2	3
terms of address	can I could I I must let me	self-referential metastatement

Personal-point-of-view prefaces overlap to a certain extent with interruption prefaces in terms of their exponents. If, however, there is a clear indication that the speaker is expressing his own point of view, then the item is categorised specifically as a personal-point-of-view preface, for example:

> personally I think we really ...
> my real opinion is ...
> I certainly don't ...

This list, though useful for committee data, is in fact rather over-built for the general model. Thus I have collapsed the three types of preface into one category of preface.

Coding conventions
A word or two here about my conventions in coding acts on the analysis sheets (see Section 4 of this paper). I have loosely followed a suggestion in Halliday and Hasan, 1976, where they analyse texts for cohesion, in that I have given each act, usually a single clause (given the inclusion of Montgomery's categories), a number, indicating its sequential position within the transaction. In this way the coded sheets can show relationships between acts, these relationships being rather more complex than the often simple sequences exhibited in classroom data. Again this is arguably not coding at primary delicacy, but, again, it seemed interesting to add this rather simple feature in the coding, for the extra information that it gives.

Moves

In the data I recognise seven types of move: framing, focusing, opening, challenging, bound-opening, re-opening. A discursive description follows:

1 and 2 Framing and focusing moves
Frames and focuses are explicit markers of transaction boundaries, and involve acts that are essentially attention-getting, pre-topic items.   Thus frames are made up of a head which is either a marker or a summons, and silent stress as qualifier. Focuses comprise an optional signal (marker or summons), followed by an optional pre-head (starter), a compulsory head (metastatement or conclusion), and an optional post-head (comment - including Montgomery's additions to this).

3 Opening moves
Opening moves may also be transaction-initial, in which case the recognition criteria are the same as those for transaction boundaries where frames and focuses are not employed; that is, they are informatives, elicitations or directives which have no anaphoric reference to the immediately preceding utterance.   This preceding utterance can then be seen to be the concluding utterance of a transaction. Opening moves, then, are essentially topic-carrying items which are

recognisably 'new' in terms of the immediately preceding talk.
Where they are not transaction-initial, they follow directly after
frame and/or focus, where these have been used to attract the
attention of the co-participant(s) to announce that a new topic will be
coming.

4 Supporting moves

Supporting moves occur after all the other types of move: frames,
focuses, openings, challenges, bound-openings, and re-openings.
The data has chains of supporting moves, but essentially the notion
of a supporting move involves items that concur with the initiatory
moves they are supporting.   This means that in these chains, each
supporting move can be related back to one of the other six types of
move.   This being the case, whilst a supporting move may follow
another supporting move, functionally it serves to support a preceding initiatory move.   Recognition of supporting moves depends upon
a concept of discourse-framework, which I will outline briefly here.

Discourse framework concerns the presuppositions set up in the
initiating move of an exchange (that is, in any move other than a
supporting move), and the interactional expectations dependent on
that move.   I want to argue that, for casual conversation, exchanges can be seen to last as long as this framework holds.   The discourse framework set up by an initiating move has two aspects,
which, loosely following Halliday (1971) I shall label: (i) ideational
+ textual: (ii) interpersonal.

The first of these, the ideational and textual, is defined lexico-
semantically and can be retrieved from the lexical items used in the
topic-component of any initiating move.   The potential discourse
framework dependent on that move then includes all items that can be
categorised as cohesive with that move, using the notions covered in
Halliday and Hasan (1976): substitution, ellipsis, conjunction, and
lexical cohesion.

The second aspect, the interpersonal, concerns interdependent
or reciprocal acts, where certain initiating acts set up the expectations for certain responding acts.   Here the discourse framework
can be retrieved differently from the acts used pre-topically (in the
optional initial moves of a transaction – frames and focuses) and
from acts used in topic-carrying moves (in the compulsory opening
move of a transaction, and subsequent re-openings, bound-openings
and challenges).   Pre-topic acts include the following: markers,
summonses, metastatements.   Topic-carrying acts include the
following: informatives, elicitations, directives, accusations.

If the appropriate and expected second-pair parts are added to
these initiatory acts the outline for the interpersonal aspect of the
discourse framework is as follows:

Marker.........Acknowledge (including giving attention/
                                       non-hostile silence)
Summons.......Accept
Metastatement....Accept
Informative......Acknowledge
Elicitation.......Reply

Directive.......React
Accuse.........Excuse

Given this concept of discourse framework, a supporting move is any move that maintains the framework set up by a preceding initiatory move. If speaker A sets up the framework, then, once speaker B has supported it, he may support it too. The idea in general is, that in casual conversation, speakers can support a previous piece of text rather than a previous speaker.

5 Challenging moves

As supporting moves function to facilitate the topic presented in a previous utterance, or to facilitate the contribution of a topic implied in a previous utterance, challenging moves function to hold up the progress of that topic or topic-introduction in some way. Challenging moves can occur after any other move, with the exception, in two-party talk, of following a supporting move. There are different types of challenging move whose recognition depends on three different concepts - the idea of discourse framework outlined just above, the idea of discourse-topic steps, presented in Keenan and Schieffelin (1976), and an expansion of the necessary pre-conditions for interpreting any utterance as a request for action, as suggested by Labov (1970). I shall take each of these separately.

(i) Challenging moves and discourse framework. A simple kind of challenging move is made by withholding an expected or appropriate reciprocal act, where the expectation for this act was set up in a preceding initiatory move. Thus, absence of, say, a reply after an elicitation, or an accept to a request-for-speaker's-rights meta-statement is seen as a challenge (cf. Sacks, 1972; Turner, 1970 and Schegloff, 1968, on the notion of justifiable absences).

Similarly a challenging move can be made by supplying an unexpected and inappropriate act where the expectation of another has been set up, for example, by producing a marker where a react has been indicated as appropriate. At its most extreme of course, this type of challenge filters upwards through the system and effects the opening of a new transaction. Notice that although I have chosen the mnemonic 'challenge', I do not intend it necessarily to indicate hostility. A challenging move may divert the ongoing talk in quite an amicable way.

(ii) Challenging moves and discourse-topic steps. Keenan and Schieffelin's very interesting paper on topic as a discourse notion suggests that the following four steps are required in order for the speaker to make his topic known to his hearer:

1 The speaker must secure the attention of the hearer.
2 The speaker must articulate clearly.
3 The speaker must provide sufficient information for the listener to identify objects, persons, ideas included in the discourse topic.
4 The speaker must provide sufficient information for the listener to reconstruct the semantic relations obtaining between the referents in the discourse topic.

To reformulate this in terms of challenging moves, the listener in

this above-described situation may do one of four types of challenge
- again, either hostilely, or because of poor recipient design in the
first place:

1. He may refuse to give his attention.
2. He may ask for a repetition of the utterance.
3. He may ask for clarification of information about the identification of objects, persons, ideas in the discourse topic.
4. He may ask for more information concerning the semantic relations that obtain between the referents in the discourse topic.

(iii) Challenging moves and Labov's rules of interpretation.   Labov,
amongst his other extremely useful rules of interpretation linking
'what is said' with 'what is done', offers a general rule for interpre-
ing any utterance as a request for action - a directive.

If A requests B to perform an action X at a time T, A's utterance
will be heard as a valid command only if the following conditions
hold: B believes that A believes that (it is an AB-event that)

1. X should be done for a purpose Y.
2. B has the ability to do X.
3. B has the obligation to do X.
4. A has the right to tell B to do X.

His own data is interesting in that it shows a speaker challenging
various of these pre-conditions.

I want to add to these four pre-conditions, more pre-conditions
for hearing any utterance as either a valid informative or a valid
elicitation:

If A informs B of an item of information P, A's utterance will be
heard as a valid informative only if the following pre-conditions
hold: B believes that A believes that (it is an AB-event that)

5. A is in a position to inform B of P.
6. P is a reasonable piece of information.
7. B does not already know P.
8. B is interested in P.
9. B is not offended/insulted by P.

If A asks B for a linguistic response from B concerning a question
M, it will be heard as a valid elicitation only if the following pre-
conditions hold: A believes that B believes that (it is an AB-event
that)

10. B hears M as a sensible question.
11. A does not know M.
12. It is the case that B might know M.
13. It is the case that A can be told M.
14. It is the case that B has no objection to telling M to A.

Again, each of these preconditions has its corresponding challenging
move, as Labov himself makes clear in his own data.   In my coding
of the data, I index each challenge, where it is not a simple breach
of the discourse framework, with reference either to Keenan and
Schieffeling (KS1, 2, 3, 4) or to Labov (L1-14), in order to indicate
what sort of challenge I understand the data to represent.

6 Bound-opening moves

Bound-opening moves occur after a preceding opening, bound-opening or re-opening move has been supported.   They enlarge the discourse framework by extending the ideational-textual aspect of the original opening move, employing the various types of informative and comment acts presented in the discussion of Montgomery (1976) above.

7 Re-opening moves

Re-opening moves occur after a preceding opening, bound-opening or re-opening has been challenged.   They re-instate the topic that the challenge either diverted or delayed.   They are made up of optional prefaces, as pre-heads, compulsory informs/comments as heads.

Exchanges

I recognise two types of exchanges: explicit boundary exchanges, and conversational exchanges.

1 Explicit boundary exchanges

These are optional exchanges at the openings of transactions.   They are made up of a frame, or a focus, or a frame and focus together, and must be supported by another speaker.   This support may be negatively realised - as it is in the classroom - and it is then a matter of interpretation for both the analyst and the co-participants to determine whether support has in fact been given.

2 Conversational exchanges

These exchanges begin with an initiation which may be either an opening, or a re-opening or a challenging move.   They may be followed by one of several supporting moves, and may then be followed by a bound-opening, which may itself be supported one or several times, after which bound-openings may recur together with recursive supports.

Transactions

Since transactions either begin with frame, focus, or an opening move, the recognition criteria for transaction boundaries are the same as those for the beginnings of these moves.   It might be useful, however, to repeat them here.
  1 Frames: the presence of a marker or a summons, together with
           silent stress.
  2 Focuses: the presence of metastatement (which may be a request
           for speaker's rights) or a conclusion.   The optional
           use of marker or summons preceding this, and the
           optional use of a starter immediately before the meta-
           statement or conclusion.
  3 Opening moves: the presence of an informative, elicitation,
           directive or accusation with no anaphoric referent in
           the preceding utterance.   This may be preceded by
           marker or summons, and/or starter, and may of
           course ⌐e followed by comment or prompt.

Transactions themselves are made up of an optional explicit boundary exchange, a compulsory conversational exchange with an opening move as initiator, and an unordered sequence of conversational exchanges with bound-openings, re-openings and challenges as their initiators.

3 A formal description of the rank scale

I here follow the layout used in Sinclair and Coulthard, 1975, page 24 onwards.

Rank I: Interaction

Elements of structure	Structures	Classes of transaction
	an unordered string of transactions	

Rank II: Transaction

Elements of structure	Structures	Classes of exchange
Preliminary (P)	$(P)O(C(R)^n)^n$	P: Explicit Boundary
Opening (O)		O: Conversational with Opening as Initiator
Challenging (C)		C: Conversational wtih Challenge as Initiator
Re-opening (R)		R: Conversational with Re-Opening as Initiator

Rank III: Exchange (Explicit Boundary)

Elements of structure	Structures	Classes of move
Frame (Fr)	$(Fr)(Fo)S$	Fr: Framing
Focus (Fo)		Fo: Focusing
Supporting (S)		S: Supporting

Rank III: Exchange (Conversational) – Opening, Challenging, Re-Opening

Elements of structure	Structure	Classes of move
Initiation (I)	$I(R(I^r(R)^n)^n)^n)$	I: Opening or Challenging or Re-Opening
Responses (R)		R: Supporting
Re-initiation (I^r)		I^r: Bound-opening

Rank IV: Move (Framing)

Elements of structure	Structures	Classes of act
head (h)	hq	h: Marker or Summons
qualifier (q)		q: Silent stress

Rank IV: <u>Move</u> (Focusing)

Elements of structure	Structures	Classes of act
signal (s)	(s) (pre-h)h(post-h)	s: Marker or Summons
pre-head (pre-h)		pre-h: Starter
head (h)		h: Metastatement
		or Conclusion

Rank IV: <u>Move</u> (Opening)

Elements of structure	Structures	Classes of act
signal (s)	(s) (pre-h)h(post-h)	s: Marker or Summons
pre-head (pre-h)		pre-h: Starter
head (h)		h: Informative
		or Elicitation
		or Directive
		or Accusation
post-head (post-h)		post-h: Comment
		or Prompt
		or Clue

Rank IV: <u>Move</u> (Supporting)

Elements of structure	Structures	Classes of act
pre-head (pre-h)	(pre-h)h(post-h)	pre-h: Accept
head (h)		h: Acknowledge
		or Reply
		or React
		or Excuse
post-head (post-h)		post-h: Comment

Rank IV: <u>Move</u> (Challenging)

Elements of structure	Structures	Classes of act
pre-head (pre-h)	(pre-h)h(post-h)	pre-h: Starter
		or Preface
head (h)		h: Informative
		or Elicitation
		or Directive
		or Accusation
post-head (post-h)		post-h: Comment
		or Prompt

Rank IV: <u>Move</u> (Bound-Opening)

Elements of structure	Structures	Classes of act
pre-head (pre-h)	(pre-h)h(post-h)	pre-h: Starter
		or Preface
head (h)		h: Informative
		or Elicitation
		or Directive
		or Accusation
post-head (post-h)		post-h: Comment
		or Prompt

Rank IV: Move (Re-Opening)

Elements of structure	Structures	Classes of act
pre-head (pre-h)	(pre-h)h(post-h)	pre-h: Starter or Preface

head (h)		h: Informative
		    or Elicitation
		    or Directive
		    or Accusation

post-head (post-h)		post-h: Comment or Prompt

Summary of the acts

Label	Symbol	Realisation and definition
marker	m	Realised by a closed class of items – 'well', 'OK', 'now', 'good', 'all right' and expressive particles, e.g. 'kaw', 'blimey'. Its function is to mark boundaries in the discourse and to indicate that the speaker has a topic to introduce.
summons	sum	Realised by a closed class of verbal and non-verbal items – the use of the name of another participant, or mechanical devices like door bells, telephone bells, etc. Its function is to mark a boundary in the discourse, and to indicate that the producer of the item has a topic to introduce once he has gained the attention of the hearer.
silent stress	∧	Realised by a pause, indicated in the text by an exclamation mark, or following a marker. It functions to highlight a marker or summons when they act as the head of a boundary exchange.
starter	s	Realised by a statement, question, command or moodless item. Its function is to provide information about, direct attention to, or thought towards an area, in order to make a correct response to the coming initiation more likely.
metastatements	ms	Realised by a statement, question or command which refers to a future event in the ongoing talk, or a request for speaker's rights. Its function is to make clear the structure of the immediately following discourse, and to indicate the speaker's wish for an extended turn.

Label	Symbol	Realisation and definition
conclusion	con	Realised by an anaphoric statement, which can be seen as the complement to meta statements, in that its function is to make clear the structure of the immediately preceding discourse.
informative	i	Realised by a statement whose sole function is to provide information. The appropriate response is the giving of attention and indication of understanding.
elicitation	el	Realised by a question. Its function is to request a linguistic response. Occasionally it may be realised by a command requesting a linguistic response.
directive	d	Realised by a command, and functions to request a non-linguistic response.
accusation	accn	Realised by a statement, question, command or moodless item. Its function is to request an apology or a surrogate excuse.
comment	com	Realised by a statement, question or command, or moodless item, and functions to expand, justify, provide additional information to a preceding informative or comment.
accept	acct	Realised by a closed class of items; 'yes', 'OK', 'uhuh', 'I will', 'no' (where the preceding utterance was negative). Its function is to indicate that the speaker has heard and understood the previous utterance and is compliant.
reply	rep	Realised by statement, question, moodless items and non-verbal surrogates such as nods. Its function is to provide a linguistic response appropriate to a preceding elicitation.
react	rea	Realised by a non-linguistic action. Its function is to provide an appropriate non-linguistic response to a preceding directive
acknowledge	ack	Realised by 'yes', 'OK', 'uhuh', and expressive particles. Its function is to show that an informative has been understood, and its significance appreciated.

Label	Symbol	Realisation and definition
excuse	ex	Realised by a formulaic apology, or a statement or moodless item which substitutes for an apology, and is thus heard as an excuse. Its function is to provide an appropriate response to a preceding accusation.
preface	pr	Realised by combinations of placement markers, self-referential metaterms and metareference to preceding talk. Its function is to show that a diverted topic is being reintroduced.
prompt	p	Realised by a closed class of items – 'go on', 'what are you waiting for', 'hurry up'. Its function is to reinforce a preceding directive or elicitation.

4 Examples of coded data

The following coded sheets take extracts from three conversations. Whilst it is not possible to find reasonably sized selections that would demonstrate all the coding categories, they show a representative sample of problems, and should serve to clarify the approach to data in general.

(i) casual conversation

	CHALLENGING MOVE	ACT	OPENING MOVE	ACT	SUPPORTING MOVE	ACT
			1 A: I'm going to do some weeding	inf	2 B: yes please	ack
	3 A: what (KS 4)					
RE-OPENING			4 B: yes please			
B-OPENING			5 A: you don't listen to anything I say	inf		
	6 B: I thought you said you were going to pour some drinks (L6)	inf				
	7 A: no I said I'm going to to do some weeding (L6)	inf				

(ii) teacher-pupil talk

BOUNDARY	CHALLENGING MOVE	ACT	OPENING MOVE / FOCUS	ACT	SUPPORTING MOVE	ACT
BOUNDARY		1	T: right ∧	m		
		2	read us what you've written Joan	d		
					3 P: the cat sat on the rug	rea
					4 T: yes, that's right	acct
B-OPENING		5	T: I changed the last word	s		
		6	now what are the letters that are missing	el		
					7 P: e	rep
					8 T: yes	acct
					9 P: a	rep 6
					10 T: a	acct
					11 P: o	
B-OPENING		12	T: and	el		
					13 P: e	rep
B-OPENING		14	T: and	el		
					15 P: u	rep
					16 T: u yes	acct
B-OPENING		17	those letters have special names	s		
		18	do you know what it is	el		
	19 P: θ (DF)					
RE-OPENING		20	what is one name we give to these letters	el		
		21	Paul	nom		
					22 P: er, vowels	rep
					23 T: they're vowels aren't	

(iii) mother–child talk

	CHALLENGING MOVE	ACT		OPENING MOVE	ACT		SUPPORTING MOVE	ACT
			1	A: oh look Tommy, what are these	el	2	B: cakes	rep
						3	A: cakes, yes	acct
B-OPENING			4	A: they're lovely cakes aren't they	el	5	B: yeah	rep
B-OPENING			6	A: now what do we need	s	8	B: butter	rep
			7	(pointing to picture) there's some –		9	A: butter, yes	acct
			10	A: and some –	el	11	B: eggs	rep
						12	A: eggs	acct
			13	A: and –		14	B: sugar	rep
	15 A: no, this one's the sugar (L 6)	inf						
RE-OPENING			16	A: what's this one do you think	el	17	B: don't know	rep
B-OPENING			18	A: it's flour isn't it	inf			

Chapter 4

Exchange structure

Malcolm Coulthard and David Brazil

SECTION 1 THEORETICAL PRELIMINARIES

1.1 Descriptive problems

Following any piece of scientific research the investigator is faced
with the problem of demonstrating the validity and generality of his
discoveries, of showing that an explanation, based of necessity on a
fairly small sample of data, is applicable to similar data collected by
other investigators. During the past twenty years this problem has
been elegantly solved within linguistics by the development of generative grammars. A linguist can now present and exemplify his findings quite briefly and then encapsulate them in a few abstract rules
which will generate all and only acceptable instances of the phenomena. The reader can then insert his own lexical items and check
the outcomes against his own data or more usually his own intuitions
and thereby evaluate the description for himself

By contrast, most of the descriptive problems in the analysis of
spoken discourse remain to be solved. There has so far been no
detailed theoretical discussion of the peculiar nature of verbal interaction or of the components and categories appropriate to describing
it – there is no 'Discourse Structures' or 'Aspects of the Theory of
Discourse'. Indeed it is by no means certain that the kind of generative description grammarians have used so successfully is an
appropriate tool for handling the structure of interaction. As a
result there are virtually no commonly agreed descriptive categories
– it is still not even clear what is the largest structural unit in discourse – and descriptions tend to concentrate on fragments.

One notable obstacle in the way of developing a description of
interaction is that speakers seem to have weaker intuitions about
permissible sequences of interactive units than they do about permissible sequences of grammatical units. It may be that this only
appears to be the case because relatively little work has been done
on the structure of interaction, but nevertheless we have found the
safest working assumption to be that, in the co-operatively produced
object we call discourse, there is no direct equivalent to the concept
of grammaticality. Indeed, the concept of competence, as it has

been understood since Chomsky set it in sharp contrast to performance, may ultimately be unhelpful in our field.

Since 1957, competence has been related conceptually to the
ability to discriminate between well-formed and deviant sentences.
The application of the criterion of well-formedness has never been
unproblematical, and developments in transformational/generative
theory have tended to make its application more difficult rather than
less so, but if we consider it in relation to each of our three levels
in turn, we can throw some light on the problem.

Beginning with the phonological level, we note that any deviance
there can be recognised fairly easily, perhaps unequivocally. Word
initial /ŋ/, for instance, excludes any sequence of phonemes from
the set of well-formed English words, as does final /h/, and other
sequences having certain specifiable combinations of phonemes
medially are similarly excluded. Linguists have had recourse to
various ways of characterising the segments that enter into the
phonological structures of a given dialect of English, employing the
theoretical postulates of phoneme, distinctive feature and prosody.
On whatever basis the classification is made, the membership of the
resulting classes does not vary.

We may, perhaps, relate this to the fact that there are physiological and physical aspects to the classification and thus the distinction
between allowable and proscribed sequences is not 'arbitrary' in the
sense that it is at the formal level. Sorting into classes is not
merely a matter of observing distributional privileges, which is why
/h/ and /ŋ/, although in complementary distribution in the syllable
are never seen as allophones.

When we move to the formal level, the situation is not so simple.
Admittedly, structure enables us to reject certain sequences as ungrammatical: 'cat the ...' contravenes the rule that words of the
word-class 'determiner' always precede the head of the nominal
group. However, in the pair of groups 'the cuddly black cat' and
'the black cuddly cat' the situation is somewhat different. 'Cuddly'
is one of a large group of adjectives which belong to two separate
sub-classes of adjectives and it is the sequential position, before or
after the colour adjective 'black', which determines the differential
classification of 'cuddly' as a qualitative or a classifying adjective.
So here, it is his knowledge of nominal group structure that provides
the hearer/reader with information about how to interpret a particular item. The way this predictive power of the structural frame can
be exploited to allocate words to classes quite different from those to
which they are normally interpreted as belonging is a commonplace
of literary commentary. A particularly vivid example is 'Thank me
no thanking, nor proud me no prouds' (Romeo and Juliet, III, v) but
the phenomenon itself is very common. The point we are trying to
make is that although the semantics of such a sentence may present
difficulties, there is no real problem in providing a grammatical
analysis. To recall the comparison with phonology, we may note
that such exploitation is possible because items like 'cuddly', 'thank'
and 'proud', as they are used conversationally, do not have a necessarily stable relationship with anything that can be objectively

specified on an extra-linguistic basis. Exploitability would seem to
be in inverse proportion to the stability of the relationship that is
commonly assumed to hold for the word in question, a fact we can
relate to the improbability of a closed-class item like 'the' being
reclassified.

The intermediate position given to the formal level in our description accords with the observation that structure there sometimes
separates the possible from the impossible (or perhaps more
accurately, the probable from the highly improbable), but sometimes
provides the basis for interpreting whatever elements actually do
occur. Crossing the watershed between form and function to the
level of discourse we find a situation that contrasts with that at the
phonological level in an interesting way. Here we are concerned
with an object created by the combined efforts of at least two
speakers, and under these circumstances it is difficult to see how
anything can be ruled out as 'not discourse'. Indeed, to set out
with the expectation that it might be possible to make such a ruling
seems counter-intuitive. There is no way in which one speaker can
place absolute constraints upon another speaker which are in any
sense comparable to the grammatical rules which block the production of certain sequences of elements within his own utterance.
When 'mistakes' occur, and are remarked upon, they are usually of
the type

(1) A: so the meeting's on Friday
     B: thanks
     A: no I'm asking you

where B wrongly classifies A's contribution, and rectification
requires help of a metalinguistic kind from the latter. There is no
way in which B can come to recognise the wrongness of his response
simply by reflecting upon it in the way he might become aware of –
and spontaneously correct – a grammatical mistake. The most promising theoretical assumption seems to be that a speaker can do anything he likes at any time, but that what he does will be classified as
a contribution to the discourse in the light of whatever structural
predictions the previous contribution (his own or another's) may
have set up. To take an·obvious and over-simplified example, an
elicitation may get the response it predicts, or it may be followed by
a totally irrelevant new initiation.

Reflection upon the latter possibility forces us to focus upon two
important facts. The first is that, because of the predictive power
of the structural frame, a first speaker is likely to treat a next
utterance as a non-response only after he had failed to discern a
possible relevance. Utterance pairs like

(2) A: so the meeting's on Friday
     B: Tom will be back in town

where A hears B as meaning unambiguously either 'yes' or 'no' are
common enough in most kinds of conversation. The absence of a
deterministic relationship between form and function makes it possible for virtually any imaginable rejoinder to have coherence given
the shared background of understanding of the participants – in
example (2) B's classification of A's utterance as an elicitation

could itself have been made only on the basis of assumptions arrived at intersubjectively. In our earlier discussion of intonation (pp. 39 ff) we have already shown how certain important aspects of the here-and-now state of play between participants are systematically invoked in spoken discourse. It is partly because a quality of relevance, accessible only to participants, and valid only at the time and place of utterance, can attach to any utterance regardless of its form, that no generalised judgments about well-formedness in discourse can be made.

A problem that sometimes confronts conversationalists and sometimes analysts is that of interpreting an apparent non-sequitur like (2). The satisfactory progress of interactive discourse depends upon participants seeing eye to eye about the classifying power of each successive contribution. In the case of (1) we can reasonably say that things go wrong because A's initiation is ambiguous, and because of this the misapprehension is easily rectified. Example (2) is not so simple. B's contribution may, as we have said, fully meet the expectations of the initiation and so be seen from both participants' viewpoints as a response. There are other possibilities, however. B may have misunderstood the implications of A's initiation and so said something which, according to his own view of the state of convergence could be a response but which A is unable to interpret as such because his view is different. Or B may have interpreted A's comment in the way A intended but responded on the basis of some assumed understanding which, in fact, was not accessible to A. A further possibility is that B has exercised his option not to reply to the initiation. In a situation where both participants were fully aware of the structural implications of their own and each other's actions, B could simply have decided that before pursuing the matter of Friday's meeting there were other matters to consider. His reinitiation which ignores A's initiation might under some circumstances be considered rude, but this would depend upon their relationship.

This brings us to the second point: that if a speaker's behaviour is heard as deviant, the deviance can be most satisfactorily characterised as deviance from a social norm as is popularly recognised in the use of labels such as 'rude', 'evasive', and 'eccentric'. It is worth noting that, when speaker A fails to recover any coherent relationship between the two components of a pair like

(3) A: will you come for a drink
    B: my brother's just left for the States

his precise choice of label will reflect his knowledge of B's manners, his drinking habits, or perhaps his state of mental health. As a linguistic event the latter's contribution simply represents one of the set of options open to him at this point in the discourse, and what a competence/performance dichotomy might separate out as an 'error' is much better regarded as an event which has its own meaning, characterised not in terms of whatever social judgments A may be induced to make of B but rather in terms of the prospective constraints that now apply to any rejoinder A might make. Thus we are not arguing that interaction has no structure but rather that the

structural framework operates by classifying each successive discourse event in the light of the immediately preceding one.

A consequence of this view is that the virtual impossibility of
arguing simply by appeal to intuition is a fact that has to be lived
with and thus research in this area will for a long time be data-
based out of necessity.

1.2 Linguistic description

Obviously one danger inherent in a purely data-based investigation
is that the resulting description handles only the corpus from which
it is derived, but this is not a necessary consequence. The British
linguistic tradition has always seen theory construction and corpus
description as inherently linked, not main and subordinate activities,
and in Halliday (1961) we have a theory of linguistic description
which explicitly confronts the problem of setting up a description of
new and unfamiliar data. Despite its title – Categories of the theory
of grammar – and although it is founded on experience in describing
phonological and grammatical structure, the paper is in fact an
explicit, abstract discussion of the nature of linguistic description
and thus, for anyone seeking, as we are, to describe a new kind of
data, but at the same time to follow well-tried linguistic principles,
it is a perfect starting point.

The first questions one asks of a linguistic description are what
are the descriptive units and how do they relate to each other?
Within a Hallidayan framework such information about the interrela-
tionships between units can be presented very simply in terms of a
rank scale, whose basic assumption is that a unit at a given rank –
to take an example from grammar, word – is made up of one or more
units at the rank below, morpheme, and combines with other units at
the same rank, i.e. other words, to make up one unit at the rank
above, group or phrase.

Even such an an apparently simple operation as organising descriptive units into a rank scale can be part of the heuristic process.
Sinclair et al. (1972) report that it was their attempt to fit utterance
into their rank scale which made them realise that it was not in fact
a structural unit, while if we try to create a rank scale from the
ethnomethodologists' descriptive units, 'sequence', 'adjacency pair'
and 'turn' as used in a series of papers by Sacks, Schegloff and
Jefferson, we get similarly enlightening results. One criterion for
placing units at a particular point on a rank scale is relative size
and thus we would expect the following

sequence

pair

turn

However, in a rank scale larger units are related to smaller ones,
by definition, in a 'consists of' relationship, and we can in no way
pretend that, as the label is used by the ethnomethodologists, a
sequence consists of one or more pairs; rather both consists of two
or more turns and thus we realise that, structurally, sequence and

pair are varieties of the same unit, with pair being a label for one
type of sequence just as transitive is a label for one type of clause.
The unit at the highest rank in a particular level is one which has
a structure that can be expressed in terms of smaller units, but
which does not itself form part of the structure of any larger unit.
Any attempt to describe structure assumes implicitly that there are
certain combinations of units which either do not occur, or if they do
occur, are unacceptable – within grammar such structures are classified as ungrammatical. The corollary is that a potential unit upon
whose structure one can discover no constraints in terms of combinations of the unit below has no structure and is therefore not a unit
in the rank scale. It is for this reason that sentence must be regarded as the highest unit of grammar, for, despite many attempts to
describe paragraph structure and despite the obvious cohesive links
between sentences, it is impossible to characterise paragraphs in
terms of permissible and non–permissible combinations of classes of
sentence. All combinations are possible and thus the actual
sequence of sentences within a paragraph depends upon stylistic not
grammatical considerations.
    In making a first attempt at a rank–scale description of discourse
Sinclair et al. emphasised that they had been 'constantly aware of
the danger of creating a rank for which there was only pedagogical
evidence', and in fact postulating the largest unit, lesson, was an
act of faith as it was impossible to describe its structure in terms of
combinations of classes of transaction. After broadening the data
base to include doctor/patient interviews, committee meetings, media
discussions, ordinary conversations, and broadening the rank label
to interaction, it begins to look as if this postulated largest unit of
discourse structure has a great deal in common with paragraph as a
postulated largest unit in the grammatical rank scale.
    Sacks (ms) confronts the same problem when he asks whether one
can use conversation as an analytic unit. He proceeds by asking
whether there are some universal features which all conversations
share and suggests that opening greetings are close to universal,
while endings of conversations are also marked and recognisable –
speakers don't just stop speaking. Similarly, Turner (1972) discusses how, in group therapy situations and by analogy in many other
situations like classrooms and meetings, there is a clear boundary
between pre-therapy, pre-lesson, pre-meeting talk and the intended
interaction.
    However, such observations, while they do demonstrate that con-
versations, interactions, lessons, have clearly delimited boundaries,
do not demonstrate that they are structural units – there are apparently no structural constraints on what occurs between the opening
and closing markers and thus these items are in fact directly analogous to the indentations at the beginnings of paragraphs. There is,
of course, in any rank–scale description the problem of where to
take account of any particular distinction and thus one could,
trivially, suggest that lessons, interactions or conversations begin
with a particular kind of transaction which is distinguished from all
subsequent transactions by beginning with a particular kind of

exchange distinguished from all other exchanges by beginning with a particular kind of move distinguished from all other moves by beginning with a particular kind of act. However, that way madness lies.

This is not, of course, to say that there may not be other types of organisation which give coherence and structure to a whole interaction - Sacks (passim) has some interesting observations on topic organisation - nor that there may not be another, as yet unimagined, level of organisation beyond discourse, but simply to demonstrate that, in terms of the rank scale we are using to describe discourse, there is no structure above the rank of transaction. Just as we must accept that paragraphs, while being composed of sentences, do not have a structure which can be specified in terms of combinations of classes of sentence, so we must accept that interactions too do not have a specifiable structure.

In discussing the structure of transactions, the units at the rank below interaction, Sinclair and Coulthard observe that 'transactions normally begin with a Preliminary exchange and end with a Final exchange. Within these boundaries a series of Medial exchanges occur' (1975, p. 56).

Here there was an attempt to specify a structure for transactions, though not a very detailed specification - it was impossible to describe constraints on occurrences of types of medial exchange, while initial and final exchanges could be disconcertingly absent, and when they were present might be realised simply by frames - moves realised by a closed set of items 'right', 'well', 'OK', 'good', 'now', uttered with high-falling intonation. Thus, while there were no real doubts about the existence of transaction as some kind of topic unit, nor about the fact that its boundaries were typically marked by frames, it was beginning to look as if this might also be a unit like paragraph whose structure could not be specified and as if the largest discourse unit might be exchange. Now, however, work on the function of intonation in discourse and particularly the isolation of the pitch sequence (see below, p. 156), gives us evidence that transaction is indeed a structural unit. Thus we are now seeing transaction as the largest structural unit of discourse, and the rank scale consisting of four or perhaps five units

> transaction
> (sequence)
> exchange
> move
> act

1.3 Relations between ranks

Isolating descriptive units and setting them out on a rank scale is only the first step in a description. For each unit it is necessary to provide two kinds of structural information - how many classes of unit there are, that is, sub-varieties classified in terms of their differing occurrence at particular places in the structure of the unit above, and how many types of unit, that is sub-varieties classified

in terms of their own differing structure. We can exemplify the
difference with the unit group from the grammatical rank scale.

Clause structure can be described in terms of four elements of
structure – subject, predicator, complement and adjunct – and there
are four classes of the unit group, one for each slot. The class
for the slot adjunct includes three types of group with markedly
different internal structures – nominal, adverbial and prepositional
– which are 'classed' together at clause rank because they have the
same privilege of occurrence, but differently 'typed' at group rank
because their internal structure expressed in terms of classes of
work is markedly different:

	Subject	Predicator	Adjunct	Group types
			last night	nominal
(4)	John	came	very quietly	adverbial
			to the house	prepositional

This distinction between class and type of unit can be overlooked
because there are instances when the members of the two sets are
coincidentally identical – the set of groups identified as type nominal
in terms of their internal structure appears almost entirely to overlap the class of groups which can occur as intensive complements.
However, it is crucial to maintain the distinction and, as we discuss
below, a failure to do so led to descriptive complications in our
earlier work.

SECTION 2 MORE ON ELICITING EXCHANGES

In the classroom data the most interesting exchanges were the
eliciting ones whose typical structure was not initiation–response,
but rather initiation–response–feedback where the third part functions to evaluate and/or comment upon the second. It is not difficult to explain the occurrence of this structure – most teacher questions are in some sense bizarre in that the questioner usually knows
the answer already, while the answerer himself is often unsure and
thus genuinely needs to be told whether the answer he has offered is
the answer required. In many classrooms this structure is so
powerful that if there is no evaluative third part it is 'noticeably
absent', and its absence a clue that the answer is wrong:

(6) T: can you think why I changed 'mat' to 'rug'
     P: mat's got two vowels in it
     T: ∅

     T: which are they   what are they
     P: 'a' and 't'
     T: ∅

     T: is 't' a vowel
     P: no
     T: no

While such three-part exchanges with evaluatory feedback are a
marked feature of classroom discourse, they do occur in other situations as well:

(7)   mother: have you brushed your teeth yet
      child: yes
      mother: no you haven't

though, as here, they normally presuppose an asymmetrical status relationship. For this reason occurrences in adult-adult inter-action tend to be heard as aggressive:

(8)   A: what time did you come in last night
      B: about midnight
      A: no you didn't

Those who have investigated other kinds of data have in the main come up with structures which would be, in our terms, two-move eliciting exchanges - though Jefferson's (1972) 'misapprehension sequence' is an obvious exception.   Sacks (passim) discusses two-part question-answer sequences, and Labov (1972b, p. 124) illus-trates the category 'request for information' with the following sequence of obviously two-part exchanges:

(9)   Therapist: oh so she told you
      Patient: yes
      Therapist: she didn't say for you
      Patient: no
      Therapist: and it never occurred to her to prepare dinner
      Patient: no
      Therapist: but she does go to the store
      Patient: yes

Nevertheless we want to argue that eliciting exchanges are always potentially three-part structures, while accepting that a two-part realisation may, and in the case of requests for polar information often does, occur.   As we can see in the following extract three-part exchanges are in fact by no means uncommon, though obviously the third move is very different in function from a third move in classroom discourse:

(10)   Doctor: and what's been the matter recently
      Patient: well I've had pains around the heart

      Doctor: pains   in your chest then
      Patient: yes

      Doctor: whereabouts in your chest
      Patient: on the   heart side here
      Doctor: yes

      Doctor: and how long have you had these for
      Patient: well I had 'em a   week last Wednesday
      Doctor: a week last Wednesday

      Doctor: how many attacks have you had
      Patient: that's the first one
      Doctor: you've only had one in all
      Patient: well as far as I know   there's only been one this
                     severe like
      Doctor: yes

The description of intonation outlined on pp.39-50 now gives us a principled way of categorising all the options open to a speaker

following a response and of explaining their significance and therefore the likelihood of their occurring in a given situation.   The first
intonation option we need to invoke is key.   For every tone unit the
speaker must select high, mid or low key and these choices attach an
additional meaning to the matter of the tone unit that can be glossed,
at the most general level as:

> High key   contrastive
> Mid key   additive
> Low key   equative

The way in which these intonational meanings combine with lexico-
grammatical ones is discussed in detail in Brazil (1979a) but can be
simply illustrated in the following invented examples where only key
is varied.*

(11)

p he GAMbled //ᵖ and LOST//   CONTRASTIVE (contrary to
expectations, i.e. there is an
interaction-bound opposition
between the two)

p he GAMbled //p and LOST//   ADDITIVE (he did both)

p he GAMbled //ₚ and LOST//   EQUATIVE (as you would expect, i.e. there is an inter-
action bound equivalence
between them)

In example (11) we see key being used to indicate particular relationships between successive tone units in a single utterance, but
the same relationships can occur between successive moves.   If we
begin with the polar options 'yes' and 'no' we quickly realise that
only when they co-occur with high key are they in opposition.   In
other words if he wishes to convey 'yes, not no' or 'no, not yes' a
speaker must select high key:

(12) A: p well you WON'T be HOME//p before SEVen//

   B: (i) p YES//p i WILL//

      (ii) p NO//p i WON'T//

In (i) the speaker chooses contrastive high key for 'yes' to mark the
choice of opposite polarity in his response; in (ii) he chooses to
highlight an agreed polarity and this apparently unnecessary action
is usually interpreted as emphatic and then in a particular context as
perhaps 'surprised', 'delighted', 'annoyed', and so on.   Much more
usual than (ii) is (iii) where the speaker indicated that he agrees with
the previous speaker's assertion:

(12a) B: (iii) p NO//p i WON'T//
      *(iv) p YES//p i WILL//

while (iv) sounds odd because the speaker is heard as simultaneously
agreeing and contradicting or rather agreeing with something that
wasn't in fact said, and the normal interpretation would be that he

---

* The transcription conventions are the ones introduced on pp. 40-50
  and summarised on p. ix.

had misheard. The contradiction is in fact only made explicit by
the repeated auxiliary, which carries the polarity, because interestingly 'yes' is the unmarked term of the pair and thus as a result,
if the speaker does not repeat the auxiliary he can select either
'yes' or 'no', to mark his agreement with the previous speaker, a
choice which at times causes confusion even for native speakers:

(12b) A: p well you WON'T be HOME//p before SEVen//

       B: (v) p NO//(I agree I won't)
          (vi) p YES//(I agree with your assessment)

When the polarity is positive, however, there is only one choice:

(12c) A: p well you'll be HOME//p before SEVen//
       B: (vii) p YES//(I agree I will/I agree with your
                                 assessment)
        *(viii) p NO/(I agree I won't)

One of the teacher's major functions in reacting to pupil replies is
distinguishing right from wrong and, as we would expect, occurrences of high key 'yes', i.e. 'yes, not no' are frequent:

(13) T: would you say then that P: yes sir T: p YES//
     your pen was doing some
     work

(14) T: would you say then P: energy sir T: p YES//
     you're using something

A teacher, of course, has more problems with answers which are
incorrect or only partially correct. He has the high–key option but
seems only to use it when an answer is unequivocally wrong.

(15) T: what are three twos P: eight sir T: p NO//

or at times of annoyance or exasperation; more normally he will say
'yes' selecting mid key which carries the meaning of agreement, but
also selecting referring tone to indicate incompleteness. Thus the
move can be glossed as 'OK so far but ...'

(16) T: can you tell me why do P: to keep you strong T: r YES//
     you eat all that food

(17) T: and why would you want P: to make muscles T: r YES//
     to be strong

It is noticeable how rarely teachers use 'no', a phenomenon we can
readily explain in social terms, and it is instructive to look at the
following occasion when it does occur:

(18) T: can you think what P: does it mean there's T: r NO//
     it means   been an accident
                            further along the
                            road
                   P: does it mean double T: r NO//
                            bend ahead
     T: look at the car P: slippery roads T: p YES//

Both teacher and pupils work hard to create a situation in which
'no' is a non–threatening, socially acceptable follow–up move.
Firstly the teacher implies that the question is a difficult one by

changing from her earlier 'what is X' formulation to 'can you think what X means'. Then the children respond with interrogatives marking the tentativeness of their answers and simultaneously overtly requesting a 'yes/no' follow-up. Finally the teacher does not select evaluative high key, but mid key and referring tone which together indicate that she is agreeing with their implied expectation that their answer is not correct.

We have so far discussed 'yes' and 'no' co-occurring with high and mid key as options for the third move in an exchange; much more frequent in fact, is a repetition or reformulation of the response. Teachers very often highlight part or the whole of a pupil's response by repeating it in high key and thus marking it as important by contrast with whatever else might have been said, before going on to produce a mid-key, agreeing item:

(19) T: how do you use   P: by working   T: $^{p \; by}$ $\underline{\text{WORking}}//_p$ $\underline{\text{YES}}//$
          your muscles

We will discuss further the function of high-key repetitions and reformulations in other forms of discourse below; now we turn to mid-key items. Reformulations in mid key, where the key choice marks the item as additional information, or a suggested contextually meaningful paraphrase, are quite common:

(20) A: what time is it   B: ten o'clock   A: $//p$ TIME to $_{\underline{\text{GO}}}//$

and we can see the teacher in the following example exploiting the option after a high-key evaluative repetition:

(21) T: why do you put petrol in
       P: to keep it going
       T: $//p^{\text{to KEEP it}}$ $\underline{\text{GOING}}//$ p so that it will GO on the $\underline{\text{ROAD}}//$

A common option in non-classroom discourse is low key which, when co-selected with 'yes' or a pure repetition, indicates that the move is doing little more than acknowledge receipt of information.

(22) D: whereabouts in your chest   P: on the heart side   D: p $\underline{\text{YES}}//$

(23) A: what's the time
       B: ten o'clock
       A: $//_p$ ten o'$\underline{\text{CLOCK}}//$ or $//_p$ i $\underline{\text{SEE}}//$

If the speaker reformulates in low key he is indicating that he doesn't feel he is adding any new information but simply verbalising an agreement that the two versions are situationally equivalent in meaning.

(24) A: what's the time   B: ten o'clock   A: $//_p$ $\underline{\text{BED}}$ time$//$

2.2 Pitch concord

It has long been accepted that some polar questions predict or expect a particular answer like 25 (i), while others like (ii) appear to allow for either:

(25) (i)   you'll come won't you
        (ii) will you come

We want to suggest that in fact all moves set up expectations at a
very general level about what will follow but that some set up quite
specific expectations because of pitch concord. In order to demonstrate this we need to discuss termination, the pitch choice made at
the tonic syllable. When we look at transcribed texts we discover a
remarkable tendency for concord between the termination choice of
the final tone unit of one move and the initial key choice of the next;
in other words it appears that with his termination choice a speaker
predicts or asks for a particular key choice, and therefore by implication a particular meaning, from the next speaker. This is easiest
to exemplify with elicitations. In the first example above the
speaker is apparently looking for agreement, i.e. a mid key agreeing
'yes', and his move is likely therefore to end with mid termination,
to constrain the required response:

(25ia) A: p you'll $\underline{COME}$//p $\underline{WON'T}$ you// B: p $\underline{YES}$//(I agree I will
(remember that key and termination can be realised in the same
syllable). Choice of high termination for 'won't you' needs some
ingenuity to contextualise; the conflict between the lexico-grammatical markers of a search for agreement and the intonational indication that there is a 'yes/no' choice makes it sound like a threat or a
plea:

(25ib) //p you'll $\underline{COME}$//p $\underline{WON'T}$ you//

By contrast the second alternative (25ii) naturally ends with high
termination looking for a 'yes/no' contrastive answer:

(25iia) A: p WILL you $\underline{COME}$// B: p $\underline{YES}$// or p $\underline{NO}$//

although the persuasiveness of

(25iib) A: p WILL you COME// B: p $\underline{YES}$//

can be explained by seeing the intonational choice of mid termination
being used to convert an apparently open request into one looking for
agreement. These are, of course, constructed examples, but we
can see pitch concord clearly working in the two examples below,
both from the same doctor/patient interview:

(26) D: p its $\underline{DRY}$ skin//p $\underline{ISn't}$ it// P: p $\underline{MM}$//

(27) D: p VERy $\underline{IRritating}$ you say// P: p VERy $\underline{irritating}$//

The initial key choices in these answering moves have the meanings
we have discussed above and in both examples we can see the first
speaker asking for or constraining a response of a particular kind
by his final termination choice. Thus in (26) the doctor ends with
mid-termination because he wants the patient to agree with his
observation while in (27) he wants the patient to exploit the contrastive 'yes not no' meaning of high key to confirm what he has said.
Had the doctor stopped at 'skin' in example (26), his move would have
had a very different force, and he would again have been heard as
asking for confirmation of a fact in doubt, but both the key and the
lexical realisation of the rest of the move show that what is required
is agreement with a presumed shared opinion.

The pressure towards pitch concord can, of course, be

disregarded: the patient could have responded to the doctor's mid key 'isn't it' with a high key 'yes' or 'mm', but telling the doctor he was right would, in these circumstances, sould like non-compliant behaviour, suggesting perhaps annoyance at an unnecessary question. In the following example the patient solves his dilemma by selecting the predicted agreeing mid key after first lexicalising the correctness just to be sure:

(28) D: p FIVE tiller ROAD//p ISn't it//
    P: r THATS corRECT//p YES//

While high and mid termination place concord constraints on what follows, low termination does not: it marks, in fact, the point at which prospective constraints stop and thus occurs frequently at exchange boundaries:

(29) D: where abouts in your chest
    P: on the heart side here
    D: p YES//

(30) D: and how long have you had those for
    P: well I had them a week last Wednesday
    D: p a WEEK last WEDnesday//

It is, however, not unusual in certain types of interaction for a response to end with low termination. The following is unremarkable:

(31) A: p have you GOT the TIME// B: p its THREE o'CLOCK//

The second speaker doesn't preclude the first from making a follow-up move, but he doesn't constrain him to do so as he could have done by choice of high termination:

(31a) B: p its THREE o'CLOCK//

If the first speaker chooses to produce a follow-up move after (31) one option would be a low key //p THANKS//, which one might expect if the exchange occurred between strangers in the street, and in that case the follow-up would serve to simultaneously acknowledge receipt of the information and terminate the encounter. If the exchange occurred during a longish interaction the acknowledging function could equally well be realised by //p MM//, a repetition //p THREE o'CLOCK// or an equative reformulation //p TIME to GO//.

2.3 Form and function

We can now use these observations on the significance of pitch concord to explain one of the major problems in discourse analysis – why some items which are declarative or moodless in form are taken to be eliciting or questioning in function. Following example (31) above we discussed the possibilities for the follow-up move. Options we did not discuss were those in which the first speaker

ends his second move with mid or high termination, rather than low.
The exchange could have ended as follows:

(31b) A: have you got the time

B: its three o'clock

A: $//_p$ TIME to $\underline{GO}//$

and the message would have been I take 'three o'clock' as equivalent
in meaning in this context to 'time to go' (indicated by choice of low
key), and 'I assume you will agree' (mid termination predicting mid
key 'yes I agree').   Another alternative would be:

(31c) $//p$ TIME to $\overset{GO}{\underline{\quad}}//$

and this time the speaker will be heard as adding the information that
he considers 'three o'clock' to be 'time to go' and asking for positive
confirmation in the form of a high-key 'yes/no' response.

We can see the difference that termination choice makes in the
following two extracts from a doctor/patient interview;   in the first,
(32), the repetition with low termination is heard as exchange final,
in the second, (33), the repeated item with high termination is heard
as eliciting:

(32) D: how long have you had these for

P: well I had them a week last Wednesday

D: $//p$ a WEEK last $_{WEDnesday}//$

D: $//p$ HOW many at$\overline{TACK}$S have you $\underline{HAD}//$

(33) D: what were you doing at the time

P: coming home in the car I felt a tight pain the
middle of the chest

D: $//^p \underline{TIGHT}$ pain$_{//}$

P: $//^{r\ YOU}$ $\underline{KNOW}$ $//$ like a – $//$ r DULL $_{\underline{ACHE}}$ $//$

There are two significant points about these observations: firstly,
although the move final items with mid or high termination are initiating and in some sense questioning, the pitch movement on the
tonic is falling not rising as is often claimed in the intonation
manuals – in other words, it is definitely termination and not tone
choice which carries the eliciting function of the move;   secondly, we
are now able to identify the function of these moves through the
phonological criteria which realise them and do not need to invoke
assumptions about speakers and hearer's knowledge or A–events and
B–events as suggested by Labov (1972).

SECTION 3 A REVISED DESCRIPTION OF EXCHANGE
STRUCTURE

3.1

Now that we have reconsidered eliciting exchanges in the light of
findings from examining other kinds of data and have incorporated our
description of intonation, we have reached a position where we can
look again at the structure of exchanges.

In the original description initiation and response were conceived of as complementary elements of structure; a given realisation of initiation was seen as prospectively constraining the next
move, while a given realisation of response was thought of as retrospective in focus and an attempt to be 'appropriate ... in the terms
laid down' (Sinclair and Coulthard, 1975, p. 45). The third
element of structure, labelled feedback, was seen as an additional
element in the exchange, not structurally required or predicted by
the preceding move, but nevertheless related to it.

The label 'feedback' turns out to have been an unfortunate choice.
Not only does it seem to imply that this element, unlike initiation and
response, is defined semantically, it also leads to conceptualisation, and even at times definition, in highly specific semantic terms,
as an item whose function it is 'to let the pupil know how well he had
performed' (ibid., p. 48). It was this very confusion that led to the
problems with pupil-informing exchanges. The informing move
filling the initiation slot should, by definition, require a complementary move in the response slot, but as the item which occurred
tended to be one which 'let the pupil know how well he/she had performed', it was categorised semantically, rather than structurally,
and thus labelled as a feedback item. It was therefore suggested
that the two types of informing exchange differed structurally,
teacher-informing exchanges having a structure IR and pupil-
informing moves a structure IF. In fact the pupil-informing
exchanges should have been distinguished in terms of the different
range of items which could occur in the responding slot. In re-
considering the three elements of structure and their definitions we
will now use the structural label 'follow-up' for the third element to
avoid any semantic implications.

We need only two criteria to define the elements of exchange
structure: (i) does the element generate constraints which amount to
a prediction that a particular element will follow; and (ii) has a preceding element predicted its occurrence? An initiation is then seen
to be an item which begins anew and sets up an expectation of a response; a response is predicted but itself sets up no expectations;
a follow-up is neither predicted nor predicting in this particular
sense. Thus:

		Predicting	Predicted
1	Initiation	Yes	No
2	Response	No	Yes
3	Follow-up	No	No
4	?	Yes	Yes

When we set out the criteria in the form of a matrix like this, we
discover a gap, and this prompts us to ask whether there is not also
a fourth element of exchange structure which is both predicted and
predicting. It is not in fact difficult to find pupil responses which
appear actually to be looking for an evaluatory follow-up from the
teacher:

(34) Teacher: can anyone tell me what this means
     Pupil: does it mean danger men at work
     Teacher: yes ...

We have here in the pupil's contribution an element which partakes of the predictive characteristics of both response and initiation: to put it another way, we may say that it functions as a response with respect to the preceding element and as an initiation with respect to the following element.

We are now in fact able to explain a paradox in the original description of classroom discourse. On the one hand the follow-up move is, as defined optional, on the other it is so important that 'if it does not occur we feel confident in saying that the teacher has deliberately withheld it for some strategic purpose' (Sinclair and Coulthard, 1975, p. 51). One explanation of the paradox may lie in the peculiar nature of much classroom questioning – the teacher is not seeking information in the accepted sense, as he already knows the answer, but it is essential for the pupils to know whether their answer is the one the teacher was looking for, and hence there is a situational necessity for the follow-up move. There is, however, a more satisfactory explanation. When we look at examples like (35),

(35) T: $//^p$ WHY would you want to be STRONG//

P: //p to MAKE MUSCLES//

T: $//^p$ to MAKE MUSCLES//r+ YES//

we discover that very often pupils, by using the predictive concord implications of high termination are in a very real sense requesting a high key evaluative 'yes not no' response from the teacher. Thus we have in (35) an example of a move which looks both ways, or which is, in the terms used above, both predicted like a response and also predicting like an initiation.

We can here point to an interesting analogy in grammar where phased predicators (Sinclair, 1972) are frequently separated by an element of clause structure that 'faces both ways', standing as object to the first predicator and as subject to the second:

(36) Let him go

For much the same reason that 'him' in example (36) above is labelled O/S, object/subject, we shall use the label R/I, response/initiation, to capture a similar dual function. We are thus suggesting that many classroom eliciting exchanges have the structure I R/I F with the R/I move being distinguished from the R by high termination and/or interrogative syntax. This doesn't mean that there will be no IRF exchanges, there obviously will

(37) I: p FINished miri//

R: p YES//

F: p GOOD//

and there will also be occasions when a pupil selects low termination with a discourse implication that no further move is needed, and a social interpretation of truculence or insolence:

(38) I: p what's the CAPital of FRANCE//

R: p PAris//

We are now proposing an exchange structure

I (R/I) R (F) (F)

to convey the information that an exchange is minimally a two-part
structure but that it can consist of up to five moves, though such long
exchanges are comparatively rare. It may seem strange to have the
move R/I both optional and 'predicted', but with this move we are
coping with the ongoing interpretive process. In example (31), re-
cited below, A can assume that B is fulfilling his predictions and
producing a responding move but does not know whether or not it is
an R/I to which he is expected in turn to respond until he hears the
termination choice:

(31) A: p have you GOT the TIME// B: p its THREE o'$\left[\dfrac{\text{CLOCK}}{\text{CLOCK}}\right.$ //

R/I is apparently theoretically recursive, but we haven't suggested
in our formulation that it is actually recursive; we will explain why
below.

3.2 Move classes

In the original formulation there were three major classes of move –
opening, answering and follow-up – proposed, one for each of the
places in structure, IRF. However, as we mentioned above there
was a difficulty in analysing classroom exchanges caused by the fact
that both pupil informs (opening moves with an informative as head)
and pupil replies (answering moves with a reply as head) tended to
be followed by the same kind of item, a move with evaluation as head,
which we had labelled as feedback. As we have seen, the definition
of initiation in fact excluded a possible structure IF but we were
still misled by the fact that the items occurring in second place in
two-part exchanges and third part in three-part exchanges were
identical. However, when we look at grammar we see that the
group sub-class nominal can occur as part of the class of items
which realises both subject and complement and adjunct and thus we
should not be surprised if one or more of the move sub-classes can
occur as a member of more than one move class.

When we come to look at non-classroom exchanges we discover a
very similar situation – the set of items following opening moves with
an inform as head is very similar to that following answering moves
with replies as head and the reason is not too difficult to discover:
from a lexico-grammatical point of view the items realising informs
and replies are very similar.

It is this observation which leads us to argue that exchanges are
basically concerned with the transmission of information, in its most
general sense, and thus must contain one informing move, which can
occur in either the initiating or the responding slot. In some case
one participant initiates by offering a piece of information and then
wants to know, minimally, that it has been understood and hopefully
accepted and agreed with – in such cases, as the IR structure makes
clear, the acknowledging move is socially required. In other cases
the information is elicited and then the reason for its occurrence and
its interpretation should not be problematic, so an acknowledging
move is not essential though it often occurs – a fact captured by the
observation that in such cases it occupies the follow-up slot.

As soon as we conceptualise the exchange in these terms, with
the initiating slot being used either to elicit or to provide information and the responding slot to provide an appropriate next contribution, we achieve the following differential relationship between
slots and fillers:

eliciting move

I

informing move

R

acknowledging move

F

It will be evident, even though this description has so far been
only partially presented, that there will be more move classes than
the three in the original description, but this increase in complexity
at move rank will be more than compensated for by a marked reduction in the number of acts. For instance, inform and reply, accept
and acknowledge can now be recognised as pairs of identical acts
which were distinguished in the original description because they
occurred in the structure of what were conceived of as different
move classes, but that are now seen as the same sub-classes,
informing and acknowledging respectively which can each occur as
members of two move classes.

3.3 Prospective classification

The powerful structural relationship between I and R means that any
move occurring in the I slot will be heard as setting up a prediction
that there will be an appropriate move in the R slot. The result is
that a speaker will make every effort to hear what follows his initiation as an appropriate response, and only in the last resort will he
admit that it may be an unrelated new initiation. Thus, to take the
simple case of an eliciting move in the I slot looking for information
about polarity, it will classify whatever comes next as conveying
polar information, if this is at all possible:

(39) can you come round tonight
$\begin{cases} \text{no...} \\ \text{I've got an essay to finish} \\ \text{thanks} \end{cases}$

The joke in the following example from Labov (1972b) derives from
the fact that Linus either fails to interpret Violet's informing move as
an adequate response, or deliberately rejects the underlying assumption that age is important:

(40) Linus: do you want to play with me Violet
      Violet: you're younger than me (shuts door)
      Linus: she didn't answer my question.

The same interpretive strategy is used with wh-elicitations:

(41) where's the typewriter
$\begin{cases} \text{its in the cupboard} \\ \text{try the cupboard} \\ \text{isn't it in the cupboard} \\ \text{in the cupboard} \end{cases}$

Again all the items in the response slot are interpreted as attempts

to provide the required information.   However, these items are not
necessarily informing moves; the third and fourth alternatives in
(41) above, assuming a high termination, are in fact polar eliciting
moves, an option available to a speaker to enable him to both comply
with the constraints of the initiating move and to mark the potential
unreliability of his information.   The following is a perfectly normal
exchange:

(42)   I: elicit: p WHERE's the $\frac{\text{TYPE}}{}$writer$//$

      R/I: elicit: p IS it in the $\frac{\text{CUP}}{}$board$//$

      R: inform: p $\frac{\text{NO}}{}//$

3.4 The limits of the exchange

In the earlier, Sinclair and Coulthard, version of exchange structure, each move class could only occur once; however, it has now
been claimed that two eliciting moves can occur in the same exchange
and it will soon be suggested that two informing moves can also co-
occur.   How, then, can one recognise an exchange boundary?

We have argued earlier that the exchange is the unit concerned
with negotiating the transmission of information and that it will contain an informing move at I or R.   We now want to argue that the
exchange only carries one (potentially complex) piece of information
and its polarity, and that the information and the polarity can only be
asserted once.   As just described it looks as if we are using semantic and not structural criteria, but in fact we can support and exemplify our claims structurally, for the power of the exchange is that as
one progresses the available options decrease rapidly.

Before we go any further we need to subdivide both the eliciting
and informing moves into two sub-classes:

e_1 eliciting moves which seek major information and polarity

e_2 eliciting moves which seek polarity information

i_1 informing moves which assert major information and polarity

i_2 informing moves which assert polarity information

We now argue that each of these moves can only occur once in an
exchange in the sequence e_1 i_1 e_2 i_2 and that a second occurrence of
any move marks a new exchange.   This gives us a strong structural
criterion to account for our intuitions about exchange boundaries,
which we recognise for instance between the following pairs of utterances, even though in each case the first exchange is structurally
incomplete.

(43) e_1 A: where are you going
      e_2 B: why do you ask

(44) i_1 A: well I've applied to fairly selective big biggish
             civil engineering contractors
      i_2 B: most of the people I'm applying to aren't pre-selective

(45) e_2 A: would you like to come round for coffee tonight

       e_2 B: are you being serious

We must of course always be careful not to misinterpret a particular linguistic realisation: in (45a) below each of the alternatives offered for B could in other contexts be realising respectively e_1, i_1 and e_2 moves, but here they are all interpretable as paraphrases of the basic i_2 realisation 'yes'.

(45a) e_2 A: would you like to come round for coffee tonight

       i_2 B: $\begin{cases} \text{who wouldn't} \\ \text{I'll be there by nine} \\ \text{are you kidding} \end{cases}$

Although the most frequent exchanges are the ones with the sequence $e_1 i_1$ or $e_2 i_2$, it is as we mentioned above, possible to have the (incomplete) sequence $e_1 e_2$, as in example (42) above, and also $i_1 i_2$ as:

(46) i_1 A: I think its raining

       i_2 B: //p $\xrightarrow{\text{YES}}$ //p it $\underline{\text{IS}}$ //

where, in a structure typical of classrooms, B proclaims the polarity of A's utterance without A suggesting it was in doubt.   More typical, of course, is a move indicating acceptance or understanding of the information:

(46a) i_1 A: I think its raining

       ack B: //p $\underline{\text{YES}}$ //p it $\underline{\text{IS}}$ //

       ack A: //p $\overline{\underline{\text{YES}}}$ //

Whereas all the other moves can only occur once in a particular exchange, acknowledge can, though it rarely does, occur twice, but in such cases it is almost invariably lexicalised the second time as mid-key'yes' and is used by a speaker to 'pass' when it is his turn to speak and allow the other speaker to select the next topic.

Two further restrictions need to be noted: firstly, if e_2 is selected following e_1 as in:

(42) e_1: where's the typewriter

       e_2: is it in the cupbaord

there are obviously massive content restrictions on the available realisations for the e_2 if it is to be regarded as within the same exchange; secondly i_1 and e_2 cannot occur within the same exchange. As we said above information and polarity can only be asserted once within an exchange and thus to follow an i_1 with an e_2 is in Burton's terms, to challenge and thereby to begin a new exchange - though one must never forget that acknowledging moves can have interrogative syntax

(47) i_1: its raining again

       ack: is it really

while on the other hand e_2 moves predict i_2 moves and will prospectively classify potential i_1 items if at all possible as i_2 thus:

(45a) e_2: would you like to come round for coffee tonight

       i_2: I'll be there by nine

The restrictions on co-occurrence - that each eliciting and informing move can occur only once and that e_2 and i_1 cannot both occur in the same exchange now enable us to account both for the fact that the largest exchange consists of five moves:

(48)   I: e_1 where's the typewriter
       R/I: e_2 is it in the cupboard
         R: l_2 no
         F: ack   oh dear
         F: ack   yeh
and for the fact that R/I is not recursive.   R/I can only be realised
by e_2 and it would be pointless for a second speaker to seek information about polarity from one who has just indicated he hasn't got that
information:
  (48a)   I: e_1 where's the typewriter
         R/I e_2 is it in the cupboard
        *R/I e_2 is it <u>OR</u> isn't it

3.5 Residual problems

This new analysis of exchange structure while being intuitively more
acceptable obviously leaves several problems unresolved and creates
others that apparently didn't exist before:

3.5.1 <u>Informing moves</u>
In what has gone before we have assumed and indeed implied that the
distinction between class 1 informing moves and class 2 eliciting
moves is unproblematic.   We certainly pointed out that while a class
1 eliciting move predicts a class 1 informing move and indeed gets
one in example (49i), it may be followed by a class 2 eliciting move as
in (49ii)
     (49) where's the typewriter   (i) it's in the cupboard
                                    (ii) is it in the cupboard
However, there are times when it is difficult to decide which category
an item belongs to because it is difficult to describe/delimit the
boundary.   A high-termination choice at the end of a move certainly
constrains the other speaker to make a contribution as in (50) and
(51):

  (50) r and so <u>THEN</u> //p i went to the $\overline{\text{MARket}}$ // $\left\{ \begin{array}{l} \text{p } \underline{\text{REally}} \text{ //} \\ \text{p } \underline{\text{GOSH}} \text{ //} \end{array} \right.$

  (51) p its ALready $\overline{\text{FREEzing}}$ //
and it is instructive to compare (43) and (44) with (43a) and (44a)

  (50a) r and so <u>THEN</u> //p you went to the $\overline{\text{MARket}}$ // $\left. \begin{array}{l} \\ \text{p } \underline{\text{YEH}} \text{ //} \end{array} \right\}$

  (51a) p you're ALready $\overline{\text{FREEzing}}$ //
which are unproblematically heard as elicitations.   We are obviously
on the borderline here – is it better to see utterances like (50) and
(51), which appear to constrain the next speaker to verbalise his
reaction to the information, as the most extreme type of inform, or
the mildest of elicit?   As the class of items which follows high-
termination items like (50) and (51) can also follow unproblematic
informs but cannot follow class 2 elicits it does appear more sensible to categorise (50) and (51) as informs but there are still doubts.

3.5.2 Directing moves
We have so far not mentioned directing moves.   Sinclair and
Coulthard (1975) proposed a basic two-move structure for directing
exchanges in the classroom, the initiating move realised minimally
by a directive, the responding move minimally by a react defined as
the performing of the required non-verbal action.   The structure
allowed for the occurrence, additionally, of an <u>acknowledgment</u> of
the directive, like 'yes sir' though actual instances are rare and
confined to exchanges between a teacher and a single pupil.   Indeed
the following hypothetical example could only occur in a class taunt-
ing its teacher:

(52)   Teacher: open your books at page 39
       Class together: p <u>CER</u>Tainly sir //

In other forms of interaction, between more equal participants,
acknowledgment is much more common if not absolutely compulsory,
and one of the ways a child can irreproachably indicate his annoyance at being asked/told to do something, is by performing the
action in silence with no acknowledgment.   Indeed, the required
verbal acknowledgment is overtly constrained in the most frequently
occurring grammatical realisations of directives – the interrogative
ones:

(53)   could you open the window
       open the window will you

Here the interrogative simultaneously fulfils a double role: it provides for the verbal acknowledgment and also realises 'politeness'
by allowing the directive to masquerade as an elicitation – an exploit-
able masquerade as children know only too well:

(54)   could you just ...   ⎡yes but I'm a bit busy just now
                            ⎣no I'm a bit busy just now

As philosophers have frequently pointed out the two major assumptions underlying directives are that the speaker has the right to ask
the listener to do X and that the listener is, in the most general
sense, willing or agreeable to doing X.   From what has been said
above about termination, the key concord it predicts and the meanings of the choices in the key system, one would expect directives to
end with a mid-termination choice, looking for a mid-key agreeing
//p <u>YES</u> //, //p <u>SURE</u>ly //, //p <u>CER</u>tainly //.   It is thus quite
fascinating to discover that most classroom directives, even those in
a series and to the whole class, when no verbal acknowledgment is
possible or expected, also end with mid termination, symbolically
predicting the absent agreement:

(55)   FOLD your <u>ARMS</u> // ^{LOOK at the} <u>WIN</u>dow // ^{LOOK at the}
       <u>CEI</u>Ling// ^{LOOK at the} <u>FLOOR</u> // ^{LOOK at the} <u>DOOR</u> //

It is also instructive, if not worrying, to realise that, when parents
and teachers get cross because their directives are not being succes
successful, they typically switch to high termination, which para-
doxically allows for the high-key contrastive refusal:

(56)   Parent: p PUT it <u>DOWN</u>//   Child: p <u>NO</u>//

Despite these interesting observations it is not clear whether it is better to regard directive moves as a separate primary class of moves, or whether to regard them as a sub-class of informing moves concerned with what the speaker wants B to do – certainly the linguistic options following a directive move are remarkably similar to those following an informing move; and it therefore becomes a question of the significance to be attached to the non-verbal action.

3.5.3 Act classes

While we have argued that this new description will enable a marked reduction in the number of primary act classes, we have not yet fully worked out these new act classes, nor the way in which the primary classes will, or perhaps will not, at secondary or tertiary delicacy make contact with categories proposed by other analysts. For example the category inform includes what in many descriptions would be distinguished as promise, prediction and statement to name but three. However, in order to demonstrate that these are in fact structurally distinct units which would then be distinguished in this description at secondary delicacy, and not semantic labels for members of the same class, it would be necessary to demonstrate that as well as sharing many possible realisations for next move as is evident in (57) below, they also have a set of possibilities which follow them alone; it is this crucial criterion that no one has yet been able to meet.

(57) I'll be there by eight   ⎫ ⎡ great
he'll be there by eight   ⎬ ⎨ are you sure
I know he'll be there by eight ⎭ ⎣ just in time to eat

3.6 One problem solved

We mentioned earlier the special significance of termination choices at move boundaries, arguing that they predicted the initial key choice and therefore the significance of the next move. The particular significance of low termination is that it does not place any constraints on a succeeding move, and we find it useful to regard all the tone units occurring between two successive low terminations as a phonological unit which we call the pitch sequence. Pitch sequences are often closely associated with topic – speakers appear to to use a drop to low termination to signal their apprehension that a particular mini-topic is ended. Next pitch sequences may begin in mid key, with the key choice indicating that what follows is additively related, or topically linked, with what has just ended:

(58) D: p its DRY skin //p ISN'T it//

P: p MM //

D: p SCALY // p LETS have a LOOK /// r OPen your mouth WIDE//

On other occasions a next pitch sequence may begin in high key and the contrastive meaning serves to mark the beginning of a completely new topic unit which is usually very similar in scope to that of the transaction – indeed when we return to classroom discourse with the concept of the pitch sequence we discover that what Sinclair and

Coulthard isolated as frames are in fact high key proclaiming tone items which occur immediately following a low termination ending a preceding pitch sequence.

(59) T: so we get energy from petrol and we get – energy from food

$$//p \text{ TWO kinds of } _{ENergy}///p \underline{NOW} \text{ then } // ..$$

Indeed, once one has the concept of pitch sequence boundaries it is possible to discover transaction boundaries at points where one had previously wanted to make them, but where there were, unfortunately, no frames:

(60) T: good girl, energy, yes, you can have a team point; thats a very good word

$$//^r \text{ we } \underline{USE} //^r \text{ we're } \underline{USing} //p \underline{ENergy} //p \text{ we're } \underline{USing} //$$

$$//_p \underline{ENergy}///^r \text{ when a } \underline{CAR}//r \text{ GOES into the } _{GARage}//..$$

In other words the low termination/high key pitch sequence boundary appears to be the transaction boundary signal which may incidentally also be lexicalised.

Acknowledgments

In writing the final version of this chapter we have benefited greatly from detailed comments on an earlier draft from Margaret Berry and Mike Stubbs.

Chapter 5

Motivating analyses of exchange structure

Michael Stubbs

'We must follow the argument wherever it leads.' (Socrates)

A concentrated amount of work on discourse analysis over the past
ten years has demonstrated that spoken discourse is highly organised and amenable to analysis using traditional linguistic concepts
such as sequential and hierarchic organisation, system and structure, and so on. However, the demonstration has so far been
largely informal: insights have been gained, features of conversational organisation have been noticed, but few attempts have been
made to develop such insights in a rigorous fashion. Two main
problems are as follows.

Many structural analyses of spoken discourse have now been published, but little attempt has been made to motivate different rival
analyses of the same data, and to decide which analysis is the best.
This is a powerful procedure and is standard in phonology and
syntax, where much of the literature consists of analyses followed by
counter-examples and rival analyses. A prerequisite of such a
procedure is, of course, the statement of analyses in a form which
allows counter-examples to be searched for and found, that is, a
degree of formalisation.

Second, there is the problem that intuitions about discourse
sequences are notoriously untrustworthy. Some control over the
analyst's intuitions is required, as well as the development of techniques for collecting other types of data. Methodology therefore
requires more attention than it has often had so far.

Well-formedness in discourse

Linguistics has traditionally been concerned with characterising
well-formed versus deviant strings, that is, with stating the constraints on the distribution of units such as phonemes and morphemes.
The basic aim is to predict the correct surface distribution of forms,
and the basic assumption is that any given string is recognisably
well- or ill-formed, with only a few doubtful cases, if any. This
assumption seems satisfactory for phonotactics, although even here

a few marginal cases could be cited. The concept of grammaticality is more difficult, and certainly the optimism of early work in transformational grammar has faded: the confidence in clear-cut grammaticality judgments has declined as more and more marginal cases have come to light which are crucial for the theory. However, grammaticality still seems a meaningful concept, and some strings are clearly ungrammatical.

On the face of it, the concept of well-formedness also applies to discourse. Speakers can distinguish coherent from incoherent discourse. Thus in the following genuine interchange between a husband A and wife B, utterances (3) and (5) indicate that (1-2) has been heard as an ill-formed sequence by one of the participants.

A: I'm going to do some weeding	(1)
B: yes please	(2)
A: what	(3)
B: yes please	(4)
A: you don't listen to anything I say	(5)
B: I thought you said you were going to pour some drinks	(6)
A: no I said I'm going to do some weeding	(7)

There are however various problems in applying the concept of well-formedness to discourse. First, in the normal course of events, deviant phoneme strings, say */mbuvb/, and grossly ungrammatical strings, say

*table-mats over up hockey swims

simply do not occur. Yet it is quite common to find conversational interchanges, such as that cited above, which are ill-formed but do occur, and to find also that speakers then have routine ways of recognising and repairing the ill-formed discourse.

Second, although utterance (2) above does appear to be inappropriate, and due to a performance error, there is no real difficulty in thinking of a way to interpret (2) so that it makes a perfectly coherent response to (1). It could be interpreted, for example, as 'yes, please, that's a good idea, it's about time you did tidy up the garden a bit'. Given any two utterances in discourse, it is usually possible to relate them, even if they were not intended to be related. Hence the unintended humour of this introduction to a magazine programme on Scottish radio, also genuine: 'Today we have a discussion of vasectomy, and the announcement of the winner of the do-it-yourself competition.' The literature contains various examples of one scholar proposing two items which form an ill-formed sequence, only to have someone propose a context in which the sequence would be coherent. For example, Van Dijk (1972, p. 40) cites: 'We will have guests for lunch. Calderon was a great Spanish writer.' He argues that the sequence is nonsense, 'definitely ungrammatical', and that it is impossible to assign a semantic interpretation to it. But Widdowson (1977) proposes a situation in which the sentences could occur and make good sense.

We require therefore a more careful statement of the concept of well-formedness in discourse, to take account of the fact that anything can follow anything in conversation, or that 'irrelevance is always one of the speaker options' (Coulthard and Brazil, 1979.

See this volume, p. 84). Deviant strings occur, and may be due to performance factors, but deviance may be used to convey rudeness, irony and so on. Deviance has no such analogous uses in phonotactics at all; and no such analogous uses in syntax, although it may there have stylistic functions, particularly, although not exclusively, in literary varieties.

A further obvious difference between discourse on the one hand and phonology and syntax on the other, is that discourse structure is characteristically the joint product of two or more speakers. It is difficult to see how speaker A could place absolute constraints on speaker B's contribution. We might therefore expect discourse structure to be less predictable in principle than phonotactic or syntactic structure. But if we allow that discourse structure is less predictable, this appears to mean that conversational behaviour is simply not predicted, at any given point, by what has gone before.

One way out of the problem is to switch from thinking about what might occur at any point in discourse, to thinking about the interpretation of what does occur. Speaker B may, as we have noted, say anything. However, whatever speaker B does say, will be interpreted in the light of what A has said. A's utterance will set up expectations and predictions. B's utterance may not fulfil them, but it will be interpreted as having failed to fulfil them. In other words, a structure can provide a basis for interpreting what does occur. Labov and Fanshel (1977) formulate this point by arguing that there are invariant rules of discourse. Discourse itself is not invariant, but the operation of the rules is. Therefore, whatever occurs is invariably interpreted in the light of our knowledge of the rules. Formulated in this way, we can maintain a useful distinction between competence (what speakers know about what can be expected to occur) and performance (what actually occurs).

This view of discourse derives from the concept of discourse function proposed by Sinclair and Coulthard (1975, p. 120): 'the meaning of an utterance is its predictive assessment of what follows'. That is, each utterance is classified in the light of the preceding one. (See also Coulthard and Brazil, in this volume, p. 84.)

Exchange structure

The rest of this paper will discuss some of these ideas with reference to the concept of exchange, which is the unit of discourse which seems most amenable to linguistic-structural analysis.
   I will use the following notational conventions:
[ ] Square brackets indicate exchange boundaries
( ) Round brackets indicate optional items.
n   Indicates recursion, e.g. F^n: any number of Fs.
$\longrightarrow$ Predicts a following utterance, and is therefore non-terminal in an exchange.
$\longleftarrow$ Is predicted by a preceding item, and is therefore non-initial in an exchange.
$\longleftrightarrow$ Is predicted and predicts, and is therefore medial in an exchange.

An exchange is a minimal interactive unit, in which an initiation I
by A is followed obligatorily by a response R from B, and optionally
by further utterances.   The minimal structure is therefore
[I R].
Several researchers have proposed concepts which are broadly
comparable to exchange.   For example, Sacks (1967-72) uses the
concept of 'adjacency pair', which includes two-place structures
such as question-answer and greeting-greeting.   If the second-
pair-part is missing, it is 'noticeably absent', giving, in the terminology I am using here, an ill-formed string *[I].   Such a string
could occur, for reasons discussed above: but if it does, it will be
recognised as deviant and interpreted accordingly.   Goffman (1971)
uses the term 'interchange' to refer to various structures, of up to
four places.   And Sinclair and Coulthard (1975) propose the term
'exchange' for structures of up to three places, structures which
they label, for example, [IRF], for initiation-response-feedback,
and which are particularly applicable to teacher-pupil interaction of
the type:

    T: can you tell me why you eat all that food – yes   I
    P: to keep you strong   R
    T: to keep you strong – yes – to keep you strong   F

I will discuss in more detail below how the structure of such three-
part exchanges might best be represented.
    My own use of the term exchange in this paper derives most closely
from Sinclair and Coulthard (1975) and from more recent work by
Coulthard and Brazil (1979 and in this volume, cf. Stubbs, 1979).
Also adapting Sinclair and Coulthard (1975), I am assuming exchange
to be a rank in a rank scale:
    speech event   e.g. conversation, committee meeting
    ...
    exchange   i.e. minimal interactive unit
    move
    act
The relationship between units at different ranks is one of constit-
uency: exchanges consist of moves which in turn consist of acts.
No detailed proposals have been made about structural constraints
above the rank of exchange, hence the dotted lines between exchange
and speech event.
    Concepts such as exchange and adjacency pair are useful and
intuitively appealing.   It does give insight into the organisation of
some conversations to regard them as comprising question-answer,
statement-acknowledgment pairs, or initiation-response-feedback
triplets, which in turn form larger units.   But there are many un-
solved problems, such as the following.   Is it possible to give
formal recognition criteria for exchanges?   Are exchanges always
well-defined units, with clear-cut openings and closings?   Or do
they have well-defined openings, but ill-defined ends?   As Labov
and Fanshel (1977, p. 62) suggest: 'ending is a more complex act
than beginning'.   Or are some utterances simply Janus-faced,
closing one exchange and opening the next?   Is all conversational
data analysable into exchanges, or is the concept applicable only to

a narrow range of discourse (e.g. teacher-pupil dialogue) whilst
other discourse (e.g. casual conversation) drifts along in a less
structured way?   Can one exchange be embedded within another,
giving discontinuous exchanges?   And so on.   Any work which makes
structural claims about the organisation of spoken discourse must
provide answers to such questions.

This paper will not answer all these questions, but it will at least
propose three ways of beginning to tackle them: first, the use of a
restricted set of intuitive judgments by the researcher about well-
formed discourse;   second, the use of informants' judgments elicited
by manipulating naturally occurring conversational data;   and third,
the use of further naturally occurring data to provide corroboration
or refutation of structural claims.

Basic discourse categories

First, I will discuss a way of defining basic discourse categories,
and then see what implications follow about exchange structure.   We
have seen above that a starting point for discourse analysis is to use
the concept of continuous classification (Sinclair and Coulthard,
1975, p. 120): that is to say, each utterance is classified or interpreted in the light of the structural predictions, if any, set up by the
preceding utterance.   That is, given any utterance we ask whether
it predicts a following item, whether it is itself a response to preceding items, whether it marks an initial boundary of a relatively
large unit of discourse and thus predicts such a unit, and so on (cf.
ibid., p. 14).   Such an approach proposes a small number of minimal
interactional categories, at primary delicacy, which might include
moves such as initiate (I), respond (R), respond-initiate (R/I), and
feedback (F).

Coulthard and Brazil (in this volume, p. 97) define elements of
exchange structure in terms of two features, + predicting and
+ predicted.   This gives four logically possible combinations of
features.

	predicting	predicted
I	+	−
R	−	+
F	−	−
R/I	+	+

Let us follow through what such definitions imply for exchange
structure.

First, these features entail other features.   The feature +pre-
dicting entails −terminal: if an utterance predicts a following utterance, it cannot be terminal.   Similarly, the feature +predicted
entails −initial: another utterance must have preceded it.   But the
features −predicting and −predicted do not entail anything about the
position of utterances within an exchange.   We can therefore
immediately expand   the matrix as follows.

	predicting	terminal	predicted	initial
I	+	-	-	
R	-		+	-
F	-		-	
R/I	+	-	+	-

The intention of Coulthard and Brazil's definitions is clearly that I is +initial, and F is -initial, but these features do not necessarily follow from their definitions. So, for example, exchanges such as ?⟨F⟩ and ?⟨I R I R⟩ are not explicitly ruled out. Several structures are ruled out, however, including *⟨I F⟩ and *⟨I R/I⟩.

A further possible anomaly is that both R and R/I are defined as +predicted. If R/I occurs then it is in response to a preceding I. But it need not occur. The choice is between R on its own or both R/I and R.

Possible exchanges include:

⟨I R (F)⟩

⟨I R/I R (F)⟩

As it is defined, F is optional, and the round brackets are redundant, but I will continue to use them for clarity.

As I noted above, Sinclair and Coulthard (1975) analyse three-part teacher–pupil exchanges as ⟨I R F⟩. But F is now defined as -predicted and therefore optional. A better analysis for such exchanges, with an obligatory third move, would be ⟨I R/I R⟩. Coulthard and Brazil (in this volume, p. 98) propose such an analysis for exchanges such as

T: can anyone tell me what this means	I
P: does it mean 'danger men at work'	R/I
T: yes	R

It is tempting to analyse the pupil's utterance in this particular case as R/I, because it both answers the question and explicitly requests a response. But a third move is predicted from the beginning of the exchange, irrespective of the form of P's utterance. The correct analysis would seem to be to regard the pupil's syntactic choices as being largely neutralised in such exchanges, so that interrogative, declarative and moodless items are all equivalent as R/I moves. Forms such as

does it mean 'danger'
it means 'danger'
danger

differ in the certainty versus tentativeness they convey, but they all expect a following R.

Such exchanges can therefore be distinguished from the following which begins with a genuine request for information.

A: what time does this period end is it ten	I
B: quarter past	R
A: quarter past oh that's all right then	F

These two exchanges are intuitively different: the first begins with a test question to which the teacher already knows the answer; the second begins with a genuine question. This difference is captured in two distinct structures. Note also that it is at R in each case that the piece of information conveyed is given, as it were, its stamp of authority. (Cf. Berry, in this volume, for a detailed discussion of this issue.)

Another problem arises since the definitions of moves rule out four-part exchanges with the structure

$$*\overrightarrow{I}\ \overleftarrow{R}\ \overleftrightarrow{R/I}\ \overleftarrow{R}$$

since R/I is defined as predicted, but the prediction of I is already fulfilled by R which makes no further predictions. It is easy, however, to find data which seem to require some such four-part structure. For example,

A:	can you tell me where the Savoy Cinema is	I
B:	ooh yeah it's only round the corner here	R
A:	is it	?
B:	it's not far like	R
A:	cheers thanks very much ta	

An alternative would be to analyse this as two exchanges $\overline{[I\ R]}\ \overline{[I\ R]}$. But this would fail to account for the coherence of the interchange. Also, A's 'is it?' is intuitively non-initial (cf. below).

A solution to some of these problems would be to specify +initial separately from +predicting and +predicted. (Tests for +initial are given below.)

	predicting	terminal	predicted	initial
1 I	+	(−)	−	+
2 R	−		+	(−)
3 F	−		−	−
4 R/I	+	(−)	+	(−)

The features in brackets are redundant, being entailed by other features, but are left in for clarity. I is now explicitly defined as +initial, and F as −initial.

If we add +initial to the feature specifications, this gives in turn four further possibilities for combining features:

	predicting	terminal	predicted	initial
5 *	+	(−)	+	+
6 *	−		+	+
7 Inf	−		−	+
8 Ir	+	(−)	−	−

Possibilities 5 and 6 are logically contradictory: an utterance cannot be both initial and predicted. Possibility 7 could define an inform, as in lecturing, where no R is expected: this would allow one-part, non-interactive exchanges. Possibility 8 could define a non-initial initiation: Ir for re-initiation.

Let us see more systematically what other exchange structures the matrix generates. It may be that they are mere artefacts of the model, but they may turn out to have explanatory value.

The model allows one one-part exchange:

$$\overline{[Inf]}$$

This was ruled out by the initial informal definition of exchange above, which regarded $\overline{[I\ R]}$ as the minimal exchange. But it would

seem intuitively acceptable for, say, moves in a lecture where no
response is required or expected.   The model allows the two-part
exchange:

[Inf F]

Feedback may be provided by a lecture audience, therefore [Inf F]
seems intuitively acceptable.   Inf is at least potentially interactive.
But as we have noted, F is optional; therefore:

[Inf (F)]

Even in casual conversation, it is arguable that one finds
sequences of Infs, with only some acknowledged.   In this data fragment, a twelve-year-old boy is talking about the area of Edinburgh
where he lives:

G: there's quite a lot of they old fishermen's houses –	Inf
I used to go along there when I was much younger	Inf
but they've demolished most of the Haveners	Inf
M: aye	F

Inevitably there will be problems in distinguishing Inf and I: that is,
in distinguishing utterances which do or do not expect a follow-up
utterance.   But it is possible to distinguish F and R on formal
grounds.   F can be restricted to a closed class of items including:
low pitch 'yes' or 'no' (depending on the polarity of the preceding
utterance), 'uhuh', and so on.   That is, I and Inf differ both in
terms of whether they predict following items and in the form of the
items.

Taking again the example of moves in a lecture: there seems no
constraint on two feedback moves after an inform.   The model will,
in fact, allow Inf followed by any number of Fs, therefore:

[Inf (F^n)]

Similarly, it will allow [I R] or [I R/I R] followed by any number of
Fs:

[I R (F^n)]

[I R/I R (F^n)]

The move R/I is itself recursive, therefore:

[I R/I^n R (F^n)]

Re-initiations, Ir, which are non-initial and predicting, but not
predicted, can occur after [Inf ...], [I R ...] or [I R/I R ...],
for example:

[Inf Ir R]

[I R Ir R]

[I R/I R Ir R]

Finally, [... Ir R ...] is recursive.

The basic exchange structures generated are therefore:

[Inf], [I R] and [I R/I R].

Each of these may be followed by any number of Ir R pairs and/or
any number of Fs.

The method I have proposed in this section is to follow the formalism as far as it leads.   We may decide that it leads, in some cases,

to unacceptable conclusions: this is the only way of testing the
initial concepts which were the starting point.

So far I have looked only at some structures which appear to
follow automatically from the initial definitions of basic discourse
categories.   These structures do not seem to be merely artefacts
of the model, as I have shown from a few illustrative examples.
However, in order to motivate the proposed exchange structures,
we would have to show that they can account for naturally occurring
data.   We could also attempt to elicit informants' intuitions about
discourse sequences and see whether they correspond with the
model.   The rest of the paper will indicate briefly how we might go
about this.

Analysis of complete interchange

First, let us see what complications arise if we try to account for
the coherence of a short but complete interchange.   The data cited
below comprise the whole of a short speech event between two
neighbours, A and B, calling to each other between their allotments.
B could not see A, but recognised the voice.   The data were not
audio-recorded, but were noted down verbatim immediately after the
event.   It can be assumed that the interchange was recorded word
perfectly.   It was impossible to recall the intonation contours used,
but utterances printed on separate lines and numbered will be
assumed to have been spoken as one separate tone group each.

The interchange is, on the face of it, rather banal.   But it is
highly structured in some fairly obvious ways, and although it is
simple enough to allow different analyses to be proposed and compared, it is rather more complex than may be apparent at first sight.

A: John	(1)
have you got your watch on you	(2)
B: yes	(3)
A: what time is it	(4)
B: five fifteen	(5)
A: is it	(6)
B: yes	(7)
A: thanks	(8)
B: ok	(9)

My intuitions would allow various combinations of utterances to be
deleted and still leave a well-formed interchange.   For example,
(4-5-8) and (4-5-6-7) seem well-formed, but *(2-6) does not.   My
intuitions would allow over forty well-formed combinations.   However, the superficial banality also allows the possibility of comparison with other very similar interchanges.

The main aim of an analysis of such an interchange must be to
account for its perceived coherence: it occurred as a complete
speech event, and an analysis should make explicit that it is a well-
formed, complete unit.   Also, any structural claims should be as
powerful as possible and make interesting predictions about other
data.   And, of course, the analysis, which may well turn out to be

wrong in detail, should at least be specific enough to allow counter-examples to be found.

Tests for +initial

The definitions of I, R, R/I and so on above are based entirely on logical distinctions. We require also some tests for the defining criteria. A test for +initial is as follows. An utterance is −initial if its lexis or surface syntax requires to be expanded from preceding utterances, and could not otherwise be understood in isolation. Thus, in the data, (3) can be expanded into (3a) but not (3b):

(3a) yes I have got my watch on me
(3b) *yes I'd like a drink

Similarly (5) can be expanded into (5a) not not (5b):

(5a) it is five fifteen
(5b) *the train arrives at five fifteen

Similarly (8) can be expanded into (8a) but not (8b):

(8a) thanks for telling me the time
(8b) *thanks for the lift

On the other hand, (1), (2) and (4) cannot be expanded in this way, and are therefore +initial. Utterance (9) has no obvious expansion, and it may be best to treat it as a boundary marker for this reason. In this case a closing boundary, although 'ok' can also be an opening. Such boundary markers cannot be expanded since they have no lexical content which can be regarded as having been deleted: they are not 'about' anything, but function purely to mark units in the discourse.

I am making the assumption that the expansion of such elliptical utterances is uncontroversial. Of course, such expansion is open-ended. For example, (4) might be expanded as

(4a) I ask you what time it is
(4b) do you know what time it is

and so on. But then any utterance may be expanded with explicit performative verbs in this way. (Cf. Labov and Fanshel, 1977, and McTear, 1979, for a discussion of problems in the open-ended expansion of utterances.)

This definition of +initial suggests a way of defining the exchange as an information unit, in which major information is introduced and then supported by elliptical syntax in the rest of the exchange. There is no room to discuss this further in the present paper. (See Berry, in this volume.)

Some candidate analyses

Let us now consider various analyses of the data and their advantages and disadvantages.
1 (1) could be regarded as an I which is realised by a summons, and which gets no R. This would leave us with an ill-formed exchange *[I], but no deviance appears to be recognised by the participants.

It also leaves us with two exchanges over the first three utterances, and no account of the relation between them: ⌈I⌉ ⌈I R⌉.

2 Alternatively, (3) could be regarded as both the answer to the summons and the response to (2). We now have one item as an element of structure in two different exchanges, one of which is discontinuous.

3 Alternatively, (1) could be regarded as a summons which gets pushed down to an O(pening) by (2), giving a single exchange: ⌈O I R⌉. This introduces a new move: O. It also introduces a new concept of a push-down mechanism, where a move is interpreted, then re-interpreted in the light of what follows. Such a concept could, however, be motivated from other data. For example, teachers often ask strings of questions, but pupils only answer the last one: the first questions could be regarded as pushed down to openings (Sinclair and Coulthard, 1975, p. 35).

4 Various analyses of (4-9) suggest themselves. The simplest might appear to be ⌈I R⌉ ⌈I R⌉ ⌈I R⌉. But (6) and (8) are non-initial. And this analysis would leave us with three unrelated exchanges, whose coherence would have to be accounted for in some other way, for example, by grammatical cohesion.

5 Alternatively, since (6-7) appear to be deletable as a unit, leaving (4-5-8-9) as well-formed discourse, we might propose ⌈I R ⌈I R⌋ F F⌋. This would give one exchange embedded within another. Again (6) is coded as I, but is non-initial.

6 Alternatively, we might propose ⌈I R Ir R F F⌋, which accounts for the coherence of (4-9) by analysing them as a single exchange. As I suggested above (9) might more appropriately be regarded as a C(lose).

A candidate analysis is therefore:
   ⌈O I R⌉ ⌈I R Ir R F C⌋
This is compatible with the exchange structures proposed above. But, as we would expect, an attempt at an analysis of a whole speech event, even such a short one, has introduced further complications.

We would further have to account for the relation between the two exchanges. Note here simply that a question such as 'have you got your watch on you' is predictably heard as a preparatory to a following question.

Eliciting informants' intuitions on discourse

As I have noted above, intuitions about discourse sequences are unreliable. However, it is possible to place some control on informants' intuitions, by starting from a real piece of data and manipulating it in various ways. One experiment which was tried with the data above was to print the numbered utterances on separate pieces of card (without information about who was speaking), shuffle the pieces and give them to about thirty informants with the following instructions:

1 Try to reconstruct the conversation from the pieces of the jigsaw. (A piece of paper does not necessarily represent the

whole of a contribution to the conversation. There are no long pauses in the middle of the conversation.) Copy out your conversation and label it 'FIRST VERSION'.

2 Can you put the conversation together in any <u>other</u> way? Copy out and label 'SECOND VERSION'.

3 Which bits of the conversation would you regard as essential? Copy out and label 'ESSENTIAL ELEMENTS OF CONVERSATION'.

4 Is there any order of the bits of the conversation which you would regard as impossible? Copy out and label 'IMPOSSIBLE VERSION'. Can you say why?

First, none of the informants appeared to have any difficulty in following the instructions, and produced both plausible and impossible versions. In other words, they appeared to have strong intuitions about the data. Versions proposed as impossible, for example, included:

A: what time is it
B: *yes/*is it/*thanks

A: John
B: *is it?

Second, all the informants, in attempting to reconstruct the original order, produced versions identical or very close to the original. Versions with minor differences were due to: (1) and (2) being reversed, which makes no difference to the turn-taking; (8) and (9) being attributed to one speaker as 'ok, thanks', and the order being given as (1), (3), (2), i.e.

A: John
B: yes

which involves a change at the end. This gives some weight to an analysis which treats (1) 'John' as an I which could be followed by R, but is not, and is therefore pushed down to O.

Consider the following sub-problem in exchanges such as:

A: what time is it
B: five fifteen
A: thanks

Is the 'thanks' obligatory? That is, should this be analysed as an obligatorily three-part exchange $[$I R/I R$]$, or as an optionally two- or three-part exchange $[$I R (F)$]$? The questionnaire data were ambiguous. In answering question 3, most informants allowed two-part exchanges, but a few gave three- or four-part exchanges including an obligatory 'thanks'. Observational data were therefore collected. Students and colleagues collected naturally occurring instances of people asking the time: examples of speakers asking them, or examples overheard. And they noted down a brief description of who the speakers were and the situation. The findings were quite clear-cut: two-part exchanges occurred only between family or friends. But three-part exchanges occurred between both friends and strangers. (Only strangers were offered a 'thanks', but friends were offered other acknowledgments.) With strangers the structure is $[$I R/I R$]$: with family or friends it is $[$I R (F

In this way, emerging theory can be made to control data-collection.   That is, once our emerging concepts have given us precise questions to answer, we can use theoretical sampling to collect the data to answer them (Glaser and Strauss, 1967).   A next obvious step is to collect data in broadly comparable situations: for example, adult strangers asking each other for well-defined pieces of information in the street and other public places.   The analysis of such data is currently under way.

Concluding comments

I will end here with a brief note on a problem which is often raised in connection with the kind of model of exchange structure proposed above: how widely applicable is such a model?   It is often argued that not all discourse is as highly structured as this paper may seem to have proposed and that the concept of exchange is primarily applicable to relatively formal social situations in which a central aim is to formulate and transmit pieces of information.   Such situations would include teacher-pupil interaction, doctor-patient consultations, asking strangers for directions and service encounters in shops.   The concept is not so obviously applicable to casual conversation between social equals, where the general function of much of the discourse may be phatic and social, rather than to transmit information.

One way in which this objection may be answered is to regard the exchange structures proposed above as a relatively restricted set of possibilities which are generated by a more general exchange structure which has fewer constraints.   One such more general exchange structure applicable to casual conversation is proposed by Burton (in this volume).

Often statements about conversational structure are formulated too loosely to allow different descriptions to be compared with any precision.   A central aim of discourse analysis should be the development of a formalism which will allow such comparisons.

Acknowledgments

I am grateful to Margaret Berry, Deirdre Burton, Malcolm Coulthard and Mike McTear for useful comments on previous drafts of this paper; and to Brian Poole and Douglas Smyth for permission to use some data which I have quoted.

Chapter 6

Systemic linguistics and discourse analysis: a multi-layered approach to exchange structure*

Margaret Berry

Two considerations have led me to write this chapter. Firstly, in Burton (1978b), Coulthard and Brazil (1979) and Stubbs (1979) there have recently been published three accounts of exchange structure which develop the original account given in Sinclair and Coulthard (1975). Each of these accounts seems to me to be very interesting and insightful, both from the point of view of describing texts and from the point of view of constructing a general theory of discourse. But they are very different. The three more recent accounts differ very greatly from each other and each differs in some measure from the original Sinclair and Coulthard account, the differences not being wholly explicable in terms of a concern with different types of data. Are we to be forced to choose between these four accounts or are they compatible? The main purpose of this chapter is to attempt to bring together within the same general framework what seem to me to be the most essential features of the four different approaches.**

Secondly, I was surprised when I first read in Sinclair and Coulthard the last sentence of the following passage:

Halliday insists that without an examination of grammar there is no reason for making any particular classification of language uses, unless one uses 'external' psychological or sociological generalisations about the uses of language. He finds in the structure of the clause three functions: (1) the 'ideational' - expressing content; (2) the 'interpersonal' - maintaining social relations; and

---

* This chapter is a revised version of a paper read to the Sixth Systemic Workshop at Cardiff, 19 September 1979. A longer version of the paper can be found in Berry (1980a). In particular this longer version deals more fully with the third layer of structure outlined here.

** The accounts of exchange structure of Burton, Coulthard and Brazil and Stubbs are all represented by chapters in this present volume. Wherever possible, references to these accounts will be to the versions which appear herewith rather than to the original versions, even though it was the original versions that provided the starting-point for this chapter.

(3) the 'textual' - enabling links to be made with the situation and cohesive texts to be constructed. <u>This approach to function did not provide us with a useful starting point.</u> (Sinclair and Coulthard, 1975, p. 12. My underlining. The reference which Sinclair and Coulthard give for Halliday is Halliday, 1970.)

I have always thought that Halliday's approach to function was eminently suitable for application to discourse analysis and I have recently been encouraged in this view by Burton who does herself begin to use this approach:

> The Discourse Framework set up by an initiating Move has two aspects, which, loosely following Halliday 1971 I shall label: 1. Ideational + Textual; 2. Interpersonal (Burton, 1978b, p. 147).

Following Halliday closely (I hope) rather than loosely, I shall suggest that the discourse framework set up by an initiating move in an exchange has three aspects, which I shall label: 1 Interpersonal; 2 Textual; 3 Ideational. I hope that this approach will enable me to provide a solution to the problem outlined in the previous paragraph; I hope, that is, that it will allow me to have the best of a number of different worlds.

The case for more than one layer of structure

An attempt to motivate a form of analysis before outlining that form of analysis is not likely to be very successful. However it is perhaps necessary to say a little under this heading at this point. I shall first state the case in very general terms and then give a specific example.

I assume that the aims of discourse are twofold: to describe texts in such a way as to be able to say something worthwhile about the individual texts and groups of texts; to work towards a theory of discourse.

In connection with the first aim I take it that when one is describing texts one wishes to be able to compare the texts or bits of the texts in such a way as to be able to show similarities and differences. Further, I take it that one wishes to be able to show as many similarities and differences as possible. If describing a literary text this would be in order to pin-point exactly what was special about that text and to relate the special features to one's literary intuitions. If describing classroom discourse it might be in order to relate differences in discourse structure to differences in teaching technique. An account of discourse structure based on a single linear structure for each unit just does not, as far as I can see, allow one to take account of enough similarities and differences. When coding, one finds oneself forced to code in the same way things which one intuitively feels to be different and to code as different things which one intuitively feels to be the same. What one really wants to be able to say is that they are alike and different, alike in one way, different in another. Different patterns of organisation are observable in the discourse at the same time.

In connection with the second aim, I take it that when one is constructing a theory of discourse one of one's main aims is to predict the distribution of surface forms, to generate 'grammatical' forms of discourse and to block 'ungrammatical' forms. Again an approach based on a single linear structure seems to me to be too limited and limiting to enable one to carry out this aim successfully. A major defect is that an element of structure has to be labelled as either obligatory or optional. There is no way of showing that it may be obligatory under certain circumstances, optional under others, still less of specifying the relevant circumstances. In these cases the element is usually shown as optional since this captures the greater degree of generality. However, this means that incomplete, and hence 'ungrammatical', forms may be generated in those circumstances in which the presence of the element is obligatory.

As one example of the above general points I take the case of feedback. It has always seemed to me one of the most interesting of Sinclair and Coulthard's observations that there are, in discourse, tripartite structures, structures with three obligatory elements, and that these exist even in classroom discourse alongside bipartite structures, structures with two obligatory elements which may or may not be followed by a third, optional element (Sinclair and Coulthard, 1975, pp. 51-3).

This observation, though made clear informally, is not properly formalised by Sinclair and Coulthard. Their coding scheme does not capture the difference between obligatory feedback and optional feedback. One is thus forced to code the following examples in exactly the same way – as IRF – regardless of the fact that in (1) the feedback is obligatory while in (2) it is optional.

(1) Quizmaster: in England, which cathedral has the tallest
                  spire
     Contestant: Salisbury
     Quizmaster: yes

(2) Son: which English cathedral has the tallest spire
     Father: Salisbury
     Son: oh (good now I can finish my crossword)

(Example (1) is real data taken from a television quiz programme. Example (2) and other variations that follow are hypothetical and introspective data.)

This is an instance in which one is forced to code in the same way things which one intuitively feels to be different. The third move in (1) seems to have a different function from that of the third move in (2). One's intuitions are supported by the very fact that the third move in (1) is obligatory while the third move in (2) is optional. Further support comes from the fact that the two are not interchangeable: 'Oh' would not be an appropriate realisation of feedback in (1); 'Yes' would not be an appropriate realisation of feedback in (2) (not, at least, if the intonation patterns were held constant).

So far I have been discussing Sinclair and Coulthard's account of feedback from the point of view of describing texts. I now turn to the point of view of constructing a theory of discourse. (The two

are of course linked and in my view should always go hand in hand.)
Presumably Sinclair and Coulthard's Summary of the System of
Analysis (1975, pp. 24-7) is intended to be an explicit model of discourse. Here the feedback is shown as always optional. This
means that it would be possible to generate:

 *(3) Quizmaster: in England, which cathedral has the tallest
        spire
    Contestant: Salisbury

which would surely have drawn protests not only from the contes-
tants but also from the viewers. (See Sinclair and Coulthard's own
remarks on what happens if obligatory feedback is withheld in classroom discourse. (1975, p. 51.) From this point of view also, we
need to distinguish between obligatory and optional feedback, in
order to prevent such forms from being generated.

 Burton dispenses with feedback altogether (Burton, 1978b, p. 139)
on the grounds that it hardly ever occurs outside the classroom.
She is surely wrong about this. My own observations suggest that
optional feedback occurs very frequently in non-classroom forms of
discourse. Most of the conversations in which I have engaged
recently have included instances of optional feedback. And even
obligatory feedback occurs more often than one might at first think –
not only in such obviously likely forms of discourse as radio and
television quiz programmes, but also in adult leisure conversations.
For instance, as in a family crossword solving session, when A gets
the answer before B and C and, in order not to spoil their fun by
telling them the answer straightaway but unable to keep quiet
altogether, leads them to the solution by a series of questions to
which A already knows the answer. Parties too usually seem to
include puzzle-solving sessions at some stage in the proceedings,
with consequent appearance of obligatory feedback – informal dinner
parties as well as more organised occasions. This is perhaps a
third reason for distinguishing between obligatory and optional feedback, that they appear to differ in their distribution in terms of
different types of discourse.

 Coulthard and Brazil appear to ignore obligatory feedback in
favour of optional feedback or, as they prefer to call it, 'follow-up'.
(Coulthard and Brazil, 1979, pp. 39-40.) They characterise follow-
up as not predicting and not predicted. This is a fair enough description of optional follow-up, but obligatory follow-up is surely
predicted. (I am again agreeing with Sinclair and Coulthard's
firmly stated observations rather than with their formalisation of
these observations (1975, p. 51).) It is predicted, though, by the
initiating move rather than by the immediately preceding move.
Coulthard and Brazil only take account of prediction relations which
hold between immediately adjacent moves.

 Stubbs (Chapter 5, pp. 112-14) indicates the possibility of an alternative approach to obligatory feedbacks. These would now be coded
as responses on the grounds that, like other responses, they are
–predicting, +predicted, –initial. This is a welcome break with the
tradition of lumping together obligatory and optional feedback. It
captures the difference between obligatory and optional feedback and

it marks the similarity between obligatory feedback and responses. However it loses sight of the similarity between obligatory and optional feedback, that both typically occur in third place, and of the difference between obligatory feedback and responses.

Although Stubbs distinguishes between a structure with three obligatory elements and a structure with two obligatory elements, he has no way of specifying the circumstances under which each would occur. He has no way of distinguishing between an I move which predicts two following moves and an I move which only predicts one. This means that it would still be possible to generate an incomplete exchange in circumstances in which two following moves are obligatory.

The point of this discussion of feedback has been to show the limitations of an approach based on a single linear structure. If we are to be able to use discourse analysis as a sufficiently sharp tool for the description of texts, and if we are to be able successfully to predict the distribution of surface forms, we need both to say with Stubbs that obligatory feedbacks are like responses and unlike optional feedbacks and also to say with Sinclair and Coulthard that obligatory feedbacks are like optional feedbacks and unlike responses. We must not, as at present, be forced to choose between them. We need an approach which will allow us to account for newly observed patterns of organisation in discourse alongside those which have already been accounted for.

New patterns of organisation in language is a recurring theme in Sinclair and Coulthard. This is of course why they proposed a level of discourse in the first place (1975, p. 23) and they also discuss the way in which the discovery of new kinds of patterning leads them to set up new ranks of unit (ibid., p. 20). Since I am not proposing either a new level or a new rank of unit, I should perhaps say what criteria I use for distinguishing the kind of new patterning which warrants a new layer of structure from other kinds of new patterning.

If I were to draw up a set of working rules (after the manner of Sinclair and Coulthard's working rules for the setting up of new units (ibid., pp. 122-3)), they would be as follows:

1 In order to motivate the setting up of a new anything - level, rank, or layer of structure - it is of course necessary to show that the new kind of pattern one is observing is independently variable from the kinds of pattern already accounted for. (I shall show below what I understand by 'independently variable' in connection with layers of structure.) The expectations set up on the basis of the new pattern must be, to use Burton's phrase (1978b, p. 147), differently retrievable from the expectations set up on the basis of the other patterns.

2 If the new, independently variable pattern relates to stretches of language which are not coterminous with the stretches of language to which other patterns relate, then it is necessary to set up a new level. To take an elementary and well-known example, it is possible for a morpheme to extend across a syllable boundary as in squirrels and for a syllable to extend across a morpheme boundary

as in I'm. Morphemes and syllables are not coterminous. They
and the patterns into which they enter must be handled at different
levels.

3 If the pattern relates to stretches of language which are coterminous but not co-extensive with the stretches of language to which
other patterns relate, then it is not necessary to set up a new level
but it is necessary to set up a new rank. For instance the pattern
coded in systemic grammar as SPCA as in The pattern observed
necessitates a new rank immediately and the pattern coded as mhq as
in The pattern observed are coterminous in that the mhq pattern can
never extend across the boundary of a stretch of language which
carries the SPCA pattern. However the stretch of language which
carries the mhq pattern and the stretch of language which carries
the SPCA pattern are not co-extensive. Normally a stretch of
language which carries the SPCA pattern will be larger than a
stretch of language which carries the mhq pattern and the former
will include the latter within it. This is of course part of the
motivation for setting up the clause and the group as separate ranks
of unit. (For the sake of simplicity I have slightly misrepresented
the facts here. I discuss this point more fully in the longer version
of this chapter.)

4 It is when the new pattern relates to stretches of language which
are both coterminous and co-extensive with the stretches to which
other patterns relate that it is necessary to set up a new layer of
structure. Halliday has demonstrated this most clearly in relation
to the clause, where he has shown that there are independently
variable patterns – e.g. agent+process+goal; modal+propositional;
theme+rheme – all relating to the same extent of stretch of language.

In order to account for the new kinds of patterning which I claim
are observable in discourse, I propose to adopt Halliday's approach
with its layers of simultaneous structures each consisting of a configuration of micro-functions. This is discussed fully in Halliday
(1970) and nicely summarised and exemplified in Halliday (1973, pp.
38-44). For my own point of view on micro-functions and their
place in the overall systemic model, which differs minimally from
Halliday's, see Berry (1977, pp. 4-6 and 28-35).

For reasons of space I am confining myself in this paper to discussion of exchange structure. However the approach would I consider be equally applicable to the other ranks of discourse unit.

Also for reasons of space I am only going to be able to discuss
inform and elicit exchanges. I am confident however that it would
be possible to discuss along similar lines direct exchanges and
boundary exchanges, particularly now that Burton has stressed the
interactive nature of the latter (1978b, p. 150).

1 THE INTERPERSONAL LAYER

1.1 The functions

Coulthard and Brazil make the interesting suggestion that 'the
exchange is the unit concerned with negotiating the transmission of
information' (Chapter 4, p.101). Let us consider informally what is
involved in the transmission of information.

Firstly, there must be someone who already knows the information. I shall call this person the 'primary knower'. The primary
knower may not necessarily be the first person to speak. In
example (4) the first person to speak, the only person to speak,
certainly is the primary knower. But in example (2) (repeated here
for ease of reference) the son, the first person to speak, has cast
his father, the second person to speak, in the role of primary
knower.

(4) Guide (conducting party round cathedral): Salisbury is the
                 English cathedral with the tallest spire

(2) Son: which English cathedral has the tallest spire
     Father: Salisbury
     Son: oh

Secondly, there must be someone to whom the information is
imparted. I shall call this person the 'secondary knower'. The
role of secondary knower may be filled by one person, as in (2), or
by a number of people, as in (4). For the sake of simplicity
however I shall for the moment speak of the secondary knower as if
he were always singular.

The primary knower must make a contribution to the discourse if
an inform or an elicit exchange is to exist at all. There must be a
slot in the exchange where the primary knower indicates that he
knows the information and where he consequently confers upon the
information a kind of stamp of authority. In (4) the first slot has
this function; in (2) the function is carried out by the second slot.
I shall call this function k1.

As shown by (4) it is not always necessary for the secondary
knower to make a contribution to the discourse. It is necessary
under certain circumstances however, as in (2) where the first
speaker is not the primary knower. (To put this in commonsense
terms, if one wants to be in possession of certain information and
one does not know it oneself, one is obviously going to have to make
a contribution to the discourse in order to persuade someone else
who does have the information to give it to one. Like most linguists
I have no objection to stating the obvious provided that I then go on
to attempt to formalise it.) In such circumstances there must be a
slot in which the secondary knower indicates the state of his own
knowledge in relation to the information. In (2) the first slot has
this function. I shall later show that it can occur elsewhere. I
shall call this function k2.

If the first speaker is the primary knower, he has the option of
straightaway declaring his knowledge of the information, as in (4),

or of delaying his admission that he knows the information in order
to find out whether the secondary knower also knows the information,
as in (1).

  (1) Quizmaster: in England, which cathedral has the tallest
                          spire
         Contestant: Salisbury
         Quizmaster: yes

Here $k1$, the admission of knowledge of the information by the
primary knower and the consequent stamping of the information with
primary knower's authority, does not occur until slot 3.   And $k2$,
the indication by the secondary knower of his own state of knowledge
in relation to the information, occurs in slot 2.   In slot 1 we have
an additional function, that of delaying $k1$ in order to elicit $k2$.
I shall call this additional function $dk1$.

    In example (2) there is a third slot, 'Oh', to which I have not yet
ascribed a function.   The secondary knower has the option of making
a contribution to the discourse which is not actually demanded of
him.   If he has not already been called upon to indicate the state of
his knowledge, he may do so voluntarily, as in (5).

  (5) Father: Salisbury is the English cathedral which has
                        the tallest spire
       Son: oh

(I am assuming that 'Oh' here means 'That's news to me'.   The son
could alternatively have said 'Yes' which would have meant 'That
accords with what is already my understanding of the situation'.)

    Even if the secondary knower has already indicated the state of
his knowledge, he may reinforce this indication, as in (2) and as in
(6).

  (6) Quizmaster: in England, which cathedral has the tallest
                          spire
         Contestant: is it Salisbury
         Quizmaster: yes
         Contestant: oh

(Sinclair and Coulthard make no provision for structures of this
kind, but they do occur – in university teaching situations and very
frequently in certain types of radio and television quiz programme.)
This optional function I shall call $k2f$ (f standing for follow-up).

  (Note: It is important to distinguish between a role, such as
primary knower, and the function of a slot occupied by the speaker
who plays this role.   I discuss this point more fully in the longer
version of this paper.)

    I am, then, proposing four functions:

    $dk1$ $k2$ $k1$ $k2f$

I have arrived at these through commonsense reasoning and I have
given them notional labels.   However I claim that the functions are
also identifiable on formal grounds.

1 $k1$, obligatory itself, marks the point in the exchange after
which all further contributions become optional.   This is true
regardless of whether it occurs in slot 1, as in (4), in slot 2, as in
(2), or in slot 3, as in (1).   This does suggest that I of an inform
exchange, R of a pupil-elicit exchange, and F of a teacher-elicit

exchange do have something formally in common even though they have not as far as I know been given the same coding in any previous account of exchange structure. (As indicated above, Stubbs would give the last two of these the same coding.)

2 The four functions are sequentially ordered. This means that k2, dk1 and k2f can be identified by their position in sequence relative to k1 and to each other. When k2 occurs, it always comes before k1. When dk1 occurs, it always comes before k2. When k2 occurs, it always comes after k1.

3 The four functions are also ordered in terms of obligatoriness. They can thus be identified on the basis of the dependency relations which hold between them. k1 is obligatory under all circumstances. The other functions all depend on k1 in the sense that none of them can occur if k1 is not present: dk1 and k2 predict k1, and k2f presupposes it. k2f is optional under all circumstances. In between come dk1 and k2, which are obligatory under certain circumstances. Of these middle two, k2 is more obligatory than dk1 in the sense that k2 must occur if dk1 occurs. The reverse is not true. (When I say 'none of them can occur', 'must occur', I mean of course if the discourse is to be well-formed. As has been observed, in discourse as elsewhere, anything can happen and frequently does.)

4 The four functions have different ranges of possible realisations. For instance 'Oh' can be used to realise k2f but not to realise any of the other functions. (Further remarks about possible and impossible realisations are made in the longer version of this chapter.)

5 Another way of formally identifying a function is to show that it marks the point at which a particular set of options becomes available, which is different from the sets of options available at other points. Or, if the same set of options is available at different points, then that the options are differently constrained at this particular point. Superficially similar sets of options are available at k1, k2 and k2f, but the options are differently constrained at these three points. These options are not available at all at dk1. Some of the options in question will be discussed below; others are discussed in the longer version of this chapter.

1.2 The interpersonal layer of structure

Since the functions are sequentially ordered they can be said to form a layer of structure:

  dk1   k2   k1   (k2f)

As usual in a representation of a structure I have attempted to give, as well as information about the sequential ordering, information about obligatoriness. I have used underlining to indicate that k1 is obligatory under all circumstances. I have used the usual brackets to indicate that k2f is optional under all circumstances. I have left unmarked the functions which are only obligatory under certain circumstances.

  It is not necessary to be more explicit at this stage about the obligatoriness of dk1 and k2 since it will always happen that when they are obligatory they will be mapped onto functions from other layers which are obligatory under all circumstances. Thus the realisation statements which map the layers of structure onto each other will predict the obligatoriness of dk1 and k2 in the relevant circumstances.

I would claim that each of the four functions can occur only once in an exchange. Any recurrence of a function should be taken as indicating at least a new bound exchange, if not a new free exchange. (I discuss this point more fully in the longer version of this chapter. See also Berry, 1980b.)

1.3 Options available at places in the interpersonal structure

1.31 System at k2

I have said that k2 is the indication by the secondary knower of the state of his knowledge in relation to the information which is the subject matter of the exchange. This indication may be positive or negative: the secondary knower may indicate that he is fairly confident that he does know the information already or that he is not so confident. This would appear to be the difference between k2 in (1) and k2 in (7).

(1) Quizmaster: in England, which cathedral has the tallest
                           spire
      Contestant: Salisbury
      Quizmaster: yes

(7) Quizmaster: in England, which cathedral has the tallest
                           spire
      Contestant: is it Salisbury
      Quizmaster: yes

We thus have a system at k2:

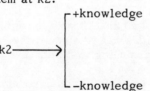

(Throughout this chapter I am using standard systemic notation for systems and system networks. See, for example, Halliday, 1973, p. 47.)

Examples (1) and (7) provide instances of these options when k2 is in slot 2. If the set of options really is to be taken as a distinguishing feature of k2, as claimed above, it must be shown to be available at k2 no matter in what slot k2 appears. Examples (8) and (9) show that the options are also available when k2 is in slot 1.

(8) Son: which English cathedral did you say had the
                          the tallest spire
      Father: Salisbury

(9) Son: you said that Salisbury was the English
                     cathedral with the tallest spire
     Father: yes

In (9) the son is fairly confident that he knows the information already.   In (8) he is not.

(9) is of course an example of A making a statement about a B event, which is heard as a request for confirmation (Labov, 1972a, p. 124).   This can now be shown to be part of a general pattern. It can now be seen exactly why a statement about a B event is heard as a request for confirmation.   The first speaker cannot fill the k1 slot since he is not the primary knower.   But k1 is obligatory. Therefore the second speaker is constrained to provide it.

1.32 System at k1
A superficially similar but differently constrained set of options is available at k1.   (This is discussed in the longer version of this chapter.)

1.33 System at k2f
Again, a superficially similar set of options is available at k2f.

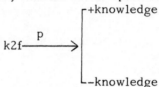

(5) has –knowledge at k2f, (10) has +knowledge.

(5) Father: Salisbury is the English cathedral which has
                     the tallest spire
     Son: oh
(10) Father: Salisbury is the English cathedral which has
                     the tallest spire
     Son: yes

(I am assuming that 'Oh' means 'That's news to me' and that 'Yes' means 'That accords with what is already my understanding of the situation'.   I am also assuming that both are spoken with non–contrastive intonation.)

However, the choice from this system is constrained by the choice which has been made from the system at k2.   I would predict that the choice of –knowledge would not be made by a secondary knower who had already indicated that he was reasonably confident that he did know.   Thus for me (5) would be well–formed, as would (2) and (6), but (11) would not.

*(11) Quizmaster: in England, which cathedral has the tallest
                     spire
      Contestant: Salisbury
      Quizmaster: yes
      Contestant: oh

(Still assuming non–contrastive intonation.)

Since the system at k2 does seem to constrain the choice of option from the system at k2f, it would be necessary to have a pre–

selection realisation statement linking the two – hence the p over the arrow above.

One more option at k2f is perhaps worth mentioning briefly. So far the options discussed have related to the indication given by the secondary knower of his state of knowledge before the exchange begins. It is also open to him in the k2f slot to indicate the state of his knowledge at the end of the exchange – 'I see' for example can be used as the realisation of this. It is surprising how seldom this option is actually taken up. It seems to be much more relevant to the discourse for the secondary knower to indicate the initial state of his knowledge than for him to indicate that the information being transmitted has been successfully received!

2 THE TEXTUAL LAYER

2.1 The functions

I began my discussion of the interpersonal layer by quoting Coulthard and Brazil's definition of an exchange. I begin the discussion of the textual layer by suggesting that, as well as being the unit which negotiates the transmission of information, the exchange is also the unit within which turn–taking is predictable. The opening of an exchange sets up an expectation that turns will be taken until the information has been successfully transmitted. It is only at an exchange boundary that a speaker can take two turns following or can miss a turn without disrupting the normal course of the conversation. If either of these two events occurred before the information had been successfully transmitted, it would presumably be regarded by Burton as a challenge. (1978a, p. 148.) The importance of turn–taking in conversation has of course been very much stressed by the ethnomethodologists (e.g. Schegloff and Sacks, 1973). It has perhaps however been underemphasised by the Birmingham discourse analysts, though it has been partially resurrected by Burton.

My interpersonal layer was intended to reflect the view of discourse as knowers transmitting and receiving information. The textual layer is intended to reflect the view of discourse as speakers taking turns. As before I shall follow Burton's example in first conceptualising in a commonsense sort of way and then proceeding to formalisation.

There must of course be at least one speaker and this speaker must make at least one contribution to the exchange. Otherwise we have no language. I shall call the first contribution of the first speaker ai and I shall underline it to show that it is obligatory for all exchanges.

The first contribution of the second speaker I shall call bi. (For the moment for the sake of simplicity I am confining my remarks to two–participant discourse situations, though bearing in mind, as Sinclair and Coulthard show, that a number of people can collectively act as one participant.) I do not regard bi as obligatory in all circumstances. One–move exchanges manifestly occur –

Sinclair and Coulthard, Burton and Stubbs have all found it necessary to make provision for them in their coding schemes (though
apparently not Coulthard and Brazil (Chapter 4, p.   )).   Nor do I
think they are confined to monologue situations.   An argument sometimes used against my view here is that in a discourse situation even
an informative (term used as in Sinclair and Coulthard (1975, p. 41))
must be followed by a response of some kind or the exchange is ill-
formed, this being shown by disputes which occur.   The disputes
apparently take the following form: A makes a remark, B feeling
that there is no need to answer it does not do so, A complains, an
argument ensues as to whether B should have answered or not.
The very fact that A and B seem to have different intuitions on this
point and that an argument is possible seems to me to suggest that
an informative without an acknowledge is not ill-formed in the way
that an elicitation without a reply is ill-formed.   If B had been
accused of failing to reply to an elicitation he would have had no
option but to admit that he had been remiss, apologise, and remedy
the deficiency, unless of course he were being deliberately deviant
and disruptive.   (It is of course possible to be 'grammatical' without necessarily being sociable.   Maybe we should distinguish
between practical discourse, discourse designed to convey information or to accomplish specific purposes of other kinds, and sociable
discourse, in which the participants are interacting for the sake of
interacting.   For sociable discourse we could have a rule over-
riding other rules to the effect that the bare minimum is seldom
sufficient.   For this kind of discourse it would be 'grammatical' but
unacceptable to leave an informative unacknowledged.   Similarly
one would be expected not just to reply to elicitations but also to
initiate exchanges of one's own.   I suspect that the disputes referred to above are really disputes about which kind of discourse is
being engaged in.)

The contributions ai and bi would be followed by further contributions from the two speakers in turn – aii, bii, aiii, biii, etc.

The number of functions in this layer is theoretically infinite, but
in practice constrained by the structures at the other layers, since
each function from another layer must be mapped onto a function
from the textual layer and no function from the textual layer can
occur unless a function from another layer is mapped onto it.
Thus, apart from ai, which is obligatory under all circumstances,
the presence of the functions from this layer will be predicted by the
realisation statements which provide for the mapping of the layers
onto each other.

The formal features of the functions are as follows:

1 They are again sequentially ordered, this time by definition.
It is perhaps worth noting that the sequential ordering for this
layer is in absolute, not just relative, terms.   It is not just that ai
always occurs before bi; ai always occurs in first position, bi
always in second position, etc.

2 They are again ordered also in obligatoriness.   There is an
implicational scale such that if biii is present this presupposes that
aiii must have occurred, and aiii in turn presupposes that bii must

have occurred, etc.   Or putting it another way, the absence of aii
predicts the absence of bii, aiii, biii, etc.

3 The realisations of these functions are determined to some extent
by the functions from other layers which have been mapped onto
them.   However there are some constraints on realisation which are
statable in terms of functions from this layer.   For instance, elliptical forms such as 'Yes' and 'No' cannot realise any function which
has been mapped onto ai.

4 As far as systems are concerned, ai will be found to have a set of
systems all its own, the choices from which will set up expectations
of different kinds for the rest of the exchange.   (ai is my equivalent
of the initiating or opening move in earlier accounts of exchange
structure.)   At primary delicacy the functions which follow ai will
all be found to have a system in common.   The availability of more
delicate systems however will vary according to (i) whether the
function is an a or a b; (ii) the absolute position in sequence of the
function; (iii) what other functions have been mapped onto the function.   There will not be room in this paper for a full treatment of
these more delicate systems.

2.2 The textual layer of structure

Thus the layer of structure I am proposing under the textual heading
is:

ai   bi   aii   bii   ...   an   bn

To justify my setting up of this layer as a separate layer from the
first layer, I must show that the two layers are independently variable.   The two layers must be mappable onto each other in different
ways in different circumstances.   This is in fact the case for these
two layers.   The general rule is:

If the information inaugurated at ai is an A event (Labov, 1972b,
p. 124), map functions from the interpersonal layer which have 1's
in their labels onto functions from the textual layer which have as in
their labels (first 1 onto first a, second 1 onto second a, etc.), and
similarly map functions from the interpersonal layer which have 2's
in their labels onto functions from the textual layer which have bs in
their labels.

If the information inaugurated at ai is a B event, do the reverse:
map functions from the interpersonal layer which have 2's in their
labels onto functions from the textual layer which have as in their
labels, and map functions from the interpersonal layer which have 1's
in their labels onto functions from the textual layer which have b's in
their labels.

Bearing in mind the restrictions placed on the individual layers by
the sequential ordering of the functions and the ordering in obligatoriness of the functions, this mapping rule yields just six basic
structures:

1 (dk1 / ai) (k2 / bi) (k1 / aii) (k2f / bii)   e.g. example (6)

2 (dk1 / ai) (k2 / bi) (k1 / aii)   e.g. example (1)

3 (k2 / ai) (k1 / bi) (k2f / aii)   e.g. example (2)

4 (k2 / ai) (k1 / bi)   e.g. example (8)

5 (k1 / ai) (k2f / bi)   e.g. example (5)

6 (k1 / ai)   e.g. example (4)

Each bundle of functions is an element of structure. If an element includes within its bundle a function which is obligatory under all circumstances (shown by underlining), then the element of structure is obligatory. According to my own intuitions as to what is well formed, I have successfully predicted the obligatoriness of the obligatory elements of structure, except in two cases. After outlining my third layer of structure I shall also be able to predict the obligatoriness of these two elements of structure.

2.3 Options available at places in the textual layer of structure

2.31 Systems at ai
Most of the options available at ai have already been discussed informally. They can now be formalised and explicit realisation statements attached to them.

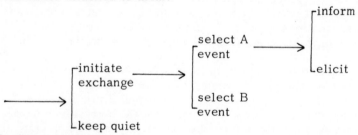

Realisation statements:
initiate exchange: include k1 and ai.
select B event: include k2 and bi; conflate k2 and ai;
                   conflate k1 and bi.
inform: conflate k1 and ai.
elicit: include dk1 and k2, bi and aii;
                   conflate dk1 and ai; conflate k2 and bi;
                   conflate k1 and aii.

2.32   Systems at places after ai
Burton says:

> given an Opening Move by speaker A, B has the choice of politely
> agreeing, complying, supporting the discourse presuppositions in
> that Move, and behaving in a tidy, appropriate way in his choice
> of Move and Acts, or he has the choice of not agreeing, not sup-
> porting, not complying with those presuppositions, possibly
> counter-proposing, ignoring, telling A that his Opening was mis-
> guided, badly designed, etc.   This range of possibilities open to
> B (and of course subsequently to A, then to B and even to C, D
> and E) seemed to cluster under two types of conversational behav-
> iour which for mnemonic convenience I labelled 'Supporting' and
> 'Challenging' Moves (1978b, p. 140).

This is an extremely valuable contribution to the field of discourse
analysis.   When attempting to code data in Sinclair and Coulthard
terms it was never long before one was confronted with the problem
of data which conflicted with what Burton calls 'the polite consensus-
collaborative model'.   This was true even of classroom data when
the classrooms were less formal than those investigated by Sinclair
and Coulthard themselves.   It is Burton's innovations that I am
attempting to build into my model at this point.

I assume with Burton that a speaker has the choice of supporting
or challenging and I assume that this choice would be available at
each place in structure after ai.

The support option would be negatively realised.   The realisation
statements attached to the options at ai would simply be allowed to
proceed unhindered.   This would make it unnecessary to distinguish
between different types of support at this point in the model, as the
appropriate form of response would already have been specified.

The main way of making a challenge would be by producing an ill-
formed exchange, particularly an exchange which was ill formed
through the withholding of a function which was obligatory under all
circumstances.   Effectively, since ai would already have occurred,
this would mean the withholding of k1 or the obligatory function
which I shall be introducing as part of the third layer, or both.
There would thus have to be attached to the challenge option a
realisation statement cancelling the inclusion of k1 and/or the
obligatory function from the third layer (and whichever of the textual
functions was the last to be included, since the number of functions
at this layer depends on the number of functions at the other layers).

As well as withholding k1 and/or the obligatory function from the
third layer, the challenger might initiate a new exchange.   In this
case however he would simply select from the usual options available
at ai, with the usual consequences in terms of realisation statements.
It would not be necessary to make special provision in the model.
This would I think cater for all the types of challenge in Burton's
first and third groups (1978b, pp. 148-9).   (It must be remembered
that I am at present only concerned with these challenges in so far
as they affect the structure of exchanges.)

Burton's second group of challenges seem to me to be rather different from the other two groups.   They may delay the appearance

of an obligatory function, but they do not prevent its occurrence
altogether. They only conflict with the expectations set up by the
initiating move in a relatively trivial way. The resulting structures would not, I think, be regarded by most speakers as ill
formed. To cater for these less serious challenges, I propose a
third term in the system. I shall call this 'query'.

$$\text{each place in textual layer} \longrightarrow \left[\begin{array}{l} \text{support} \\ \text{query} \\ \text{challenge} \end{array} \right.$$

each place in
textual layer
after ai

2.33 Queries

Some sort of query is possible at each of the places after ai.
Further investigation would be necessary before it would be possible to specify exactly which sorts of query were possible at which
places, and before it would be possible to formulate explicit realisation statements.

Preliminary investigation suggests that many different kinds of
query can be distinguished – distinguished not only in notional terms,
but also in terms of (i) the types of structure to which they give rise
and (ii) their lexical and syntactic realisations. (Queries tend to
have very stereotyped forms of realisation.) The distribution of
these different kinds of query is predictable in terms of the functions from my three layers of structure. To account for the distribution of all possible kinds of query it would be necessary to refer
to all the functions from all three of the layers – the constraints on
the occurrence of some kinds of query are so complex that it would
be necessary to provide a kind of 'grid reference' composed of loca-
tions in each of the three layers. I discuss here by way of exemplification just two kinds of query, whose distribution is predictable
in terms of the two layers which I have so far introduced.

Query 1: qk2. Notionally this kind of query is a query about the
state of knowledge which the secondary knower has indicated for himself. Formally it gives rise to a tripartite structure: the qk2 itself
is effectively equivalent to dk1, since it predicts the occurrence of a
following k2 and k1. An optional k2f is also possible. The realisation of qk2 takes the form of the lexical item 'Well', followed by
the auxiliary verb which has been most recently used in the exchange
and a pronoun, these last two being in interrogative order.

The distribution of this kind of query is predictable on the basis
of a grid reference in terms of layers 1 and 2. It is available in a
potential k1 slot, a slot in which k1 has been predicted to occur,
provided that the slot is not also an ai slot. The query is in fact
substituted for the k1 which has been predicted, thereby delaying the
occurrence of this k1. The k1 does eventually occur, but not until
two moves later than originally predicted.

Examples of this kind of query, together with the analyses which
I would propose, are:

(12) Quizmaster: in England, which cathedral has the tallest
                     spire
     Contestant: is it Salisbury

Quizmaster: well, is it   (implication: you're supposed to
know, not ask me)
Contestant: yes
Quizmaster: that's right
dk1   k2   ~~k1~~
          dk1   k2   k1
ai   bi   aii   bii   aiii

(13) Son: is Salisbury the English cathedral with the
tallest spire
Father   (who considers son should really know the answer
already):
well, is it
Son: yes
Father: that's right
k2   ~~k1~~
          dk1   k2   k1
ai⁻   bi   aii   bii

(The notation ~~k1~~ indicates that this is a potential k1 slot in that k1
was what was predicted, but that the k1 was not actually allowed to
occur in that slot, the query being substituted for it.)   (For reasons
which I discuss in the longer version of this chapter, I would in
each case regard the query and the two moves which follow it as
forming a bound exchange.   See also Berry, 1980b.)

These two examples show that this kind of query is available at a
potential k1 slot, regardless of whether this is slot 2 or slot 3.
This could not be predicted by any model which fails to show a similarity between obligatory feedback and response in a pupil-elicit
type of exchange.   My k1 does show this similarity.   Of course to
demonstrate that I had made the correct prediction about the distribution of qk2, I would have to show that it was not available in slots
other than potential k1 slots.   This is quite definitely demonstrable,
though I shall not have room to demonstrate it in full in this paper.
When I have introduced the second kind of query, I shall go part
way to demonstrating it in that I shall show that the two kinds of
query are not reversible; they cannot occur in each other's slots.

Query 2: qk1.   Notionally this kind of query is a query about the
state of knowledge which the primary knower has indicated for himself.   Formally it gives rise to a bipartite structure, with the
optional addition of 2kf: the qk1 itself is effectively equivalent to k2,
since it predicts the occurrence of a following k1.   The realisation
of qk1 takes the form of the auxiliary verb which has most recently
been used in the exchange and a pronoun, these being in interrogative order.   (In other words it is like the realisation of qk2, but
without the 'Well'.)

qk1 is available in a potential k2f slot, and nowhere else.
Examples, together with analyses, are:
(14) Quizmaster: in England, which cathedral has the tallest
spire
Contestant: is it Salisbury
Quizmaster: yes

```
Contestant:   is it
Quizmaster:   yes
dkl       k2        kl       ~~k2f~~
                             k2        kl
ai        bi        aii      bii       aiii
```

(15) Son: is Salisbury the English cathedral with the
                    tallest spire
      Father: yes
      Son: is it
      Father: yes

```
k2        kl        ~~k2f~~
                    k2        kl
ai        bi        aii       bii
```

(16) Father: Salisbury is the English cathedral with the
                    tallest spire
      Son: is it
      Father: yes

```
kl        ~~k2f~~
          k2        kl
ai        bi        aii
```

These examples show that qkl is available in all possible k2f slots.
Again, to show that I had made a correct prediction it would be
necessary to demonstrate that qkl could not occur in any slot that
was not a k2f slot.   Again this is demonstrable, but again there will
be room in this chapter only to show that it is not reversible with
qk2.

That qk2 and qkl cannot occur in each other's slots is, I think,
shown by the following five examples, all of which for me are ill
formed.

*(17) Quizmaster: in England, which cathedral has the tallest
                    spire
       Contestant: is it Salisbury
       Quizmaster: yes
       Contestant: well, is it
       Quizmaster: yes
       Contestant: that's right

(I am assuming the same intonation, etc. here as the query would
have in the well-formed examples given previously.)

*(18) Son: is Salisbury the English cathedral with the
                    tallest spire
       Father: yes
       Son: well, is it
       Father: yes
       Son: that's right

*(19) Father: Salisbury is the English cathedral with the
                    tallest spire
       Son: well, is it
       Father: yes
       Son: that's right

*(20)   Quizmaster: in England, which cathedral has the tallest
                       spire
         Contestant: is it Salisbury
         Quizmaster: is it
         Contestant: yes
         Quizmaster: ∅

*(21)   Son: is Salisbury the English cathedral with the
                       tallest spire
         Father: is it
         Son: yes
         Father: ∅

(I am assuming here that the son has not set himself up as a self-
appointed quizmaster.)

3 THE IDEATIONAL LAYER

3.1 The functions

At the beginning of this section I return again to Coulthard and
Brazil's definition of an exchange as 'the unit concerned with
negotiating the transmission of information'.   I have discussed the
knowers of the information and the speakers of the information.
The other essential ingredient for the transmission of information is
of course the information itself.

   Coulthard and Brazil do in effect propose a layer of structure
based on the distribution of information (see above, p. 101), which
they imply (p. 100) is independently variable from the exchange structure which they eventually propose (p. 98).   Their proposal is a very
exciting one, a major breakthrough in discourse analysis, and my own
proposal for a third layer of structure is heavily indebted to it.

   For reasons which I have discussed elsewhere, however (Berry,
1980b), my third layer of structure, though based on theirs, will
look rather different from theirs.

   I will once again begin by conceptualising in an informal way.

   I have said that information is an essential ingredient for an
exchange.   How much information is necessary?   I would suggest
that the minimum amount of information for an exchange is a completed proposition.   (For the sake of simplicity I shall for the
moment assume that the maximum amount of information for an
exchange is also one completed proposition.   However, in the
longer version of this paper I suggest that an exchange may transmit
more than one completed proposition.)

   The completed proposition may be presented straightaway, by the
first speaker, as in (5).

   (5) Father: Salisbury is the English cathedral which has
                       the tallest spire
        Son: oh

Or it may be left to the second speaker to complete the proposition,
as (1) and (2).

(1) Quizmaster: in England, which cathedral has the
                  tallest spire
     Contestant: Salisbury
     Quizmaster: yes

(2) Son: which English cathedral has the tallest
                  spire
     Father: Salisbury
     Son: oh

I shall call the function of completing the proposition pc, standing
for propositional completion.   I have underlined it to show that it is
obligatory for all exchanges.

Even if the first speaker leaves the second speaker to complete
the proposition, the first speaker still determines the form of the
completed proposition.   If the first speaker does not provide the
completed proposition himself, he still provides a basis for the
completed proposition by producing an utterance which predicts the
completed proposition.   It is important to note here that the prediction is not just a vague prediction that some sort of response will
follow.   It is a very precise prediction indeed.   It is a prediction
that one of a relatively small range of propositions will be conveyed
by the second speaker.

Thus, if the first speaker says 'Who stole three horses?', this
predicts that the completed proposition will be 'John stole three
horses', or 'Tom stole three horses', or 'Dick stole three horses',
or 'Harry stole three horses', or etc.   In other words the completed proposition must take the form 'X stole three horses'.   (I am
deliberately using Smith and Wilson's example here.   It is the work
of Wilson and Sperber, as reported by Smith and Wilson (1979, pp.
148-9), that makes possible the type of analysis of an exchange that
I am suggesting.)

If the first speaker says 'Is John coming?' this narrows the range
for the completed proposition even more markedly.   Only two propositions are now open to the second speaker: 'John is coming';
'John is not coming'.   (The second speaker need not of course
actually say 'John is coming' or 'John is not coming', but he must
make it possible for one of these completed propositions to be re-
coverable.   In the longer version of the paper I discuss the possible relationships between what is meant by the second speaker and
what is actually said.)

For this function of providing a basis for the completed proposition by predicting the form of the completed proposition I shall use
the term pb, standing for propositional base.

Once the proposition has been completed, either straightaway by
the first speaker or by the second speaker in response to the prediction of the first speaker, the proposition may then be supported
by the speaker who did not actually complete the proposition.   For
instance, in (1) the first speaker provides a base for the proposition, the second speaker actually completes the proposition and the
first speaker then supports the proposition.

(1)   Quizmaster: in England, which cathedral has the
                               tallest spire
       Contestant: Salisbury
       Quizmaster: yes

I shall call the function of supporting the proposition ps, standing for propositional support.

The function of supporting the proposition is usually conflated with a function from layer 1 to the extent that the two together can be realised by a single item.   In the third move of (1) the function of supporting the proposition is conflated with k1 from layer 1.   The 'Yes' simultaneously supports the truth of the proposition and stamps the information with primary knower's authority.   Similarly in the second move of (10) the function of supporting the proposition is conflated with k2f.   The 'Yes' simultaneously means 'I support the truth of that proposition' and 'I was already aware of that information'.

(10) Father: Salisbury is the English cathedral which has
                           the tallest spire
       Son: yes

The conflation here is so complete that it is really rather artificial to try to separate the meaning into two meanings.

However sometimes the conflation is not so complete.   In the Sinclair and Coulthard Analysed Texts (1975, p. 79) the teacher, in response to a pupil-inform says 'Oh yes.   You're right.   It is.' The 'Oh' presumably means that what the pupil has just said is news to the teacher – k2f.   'Yes.   You're right.   It is.' presumably means that even though she was not previously aware of it she now supports the truth of the proposition – ps.   k2f and ps have been conflated here to the extent that they appear in the same move. However, since they are represented by separate formal items it would seem reasonable to regard them as separate acts within this move.

I am, then, proposing three functions at this layer:

$$\text{pb} \quad \underline{\text{pc}} \quad \text{ps}$$

When all three are present they seem to represent three stages in a progression through the exchange.   This progression takes the form of a decrease in the range of propositions that are negotiable. At the slot occupied by pb there is an almost unlimited range of propositions that can be introduced.   The pb itself, however, narrows the range so that the range of propositions available for the pc slot is relatively limited.   The actual completion of the proposition narrows the range even further – to one; at the ps slot only one proposition is negotiable.   This one proposition may at this point be positively supported, as in (1), or negatively supported through a query, as in (22), or a denial, as in (23).

(22) Son: which is the English cathedral with the
                           tallest spire
       Father: Salisbury
       Son: is it
       Father: yes

(23)   Son: which is the English cathedral with the
                    tallest spire
       Father: Norwich
       Son: no, it's not   (I don't know which it is but I do
                    know it's not Norwich)
       Father: oh

The one proposition is still negotiable at this point but it is the only
proposition which is still negotiable.

(Although the query and the denial are the result of an option at a
point in a free exchange, I would regard the query and the denial
themselves as the initiating moves of bound exchanges.   This point is
discussed further in the longer version of this chapter and in Berry,
1980b.)

When all three functions are present they also seem to represent
three stages in another kind of progression through the exchange.
This second kind of progression takes the form of an increase in
ellipticity.   Normally the pc function will be realised by a move
which is more elliptical than the move which realises the pb function.
In turn the ps function will be realised by a move which is more
elliptical than the move which realises the pc function.   (Further
details of this progression in ellipticity can be found in the longer
version of this chapter and in Berry, 1980b.   The proposals in the
longer paper and in 1980b are based on an idea of Stubbs (Chapter 5,
p. 116).

To summarise the formal features of the functions at this layer:

1 They are again sequentially ordered, though again in relative
terms like the functions of the first layer rather than in absolute
terms like the functions of the second layer: pb, when it occurs,
always comes before pc; ps, when it occurs, always comes after pc.

2 They are again ordered in terms of obligatoriness: pc is obligatory under all circumstances; pb is obligatory if pc is not to be conflated with ai; ps is obligatory if kl has not occurred by the time the
proposition has been completed; in these circumstances ps must be
conflated with kl.   In other circumstances ps is optional; pb predicts pc and ps presupposes pc.

3 The realisations of these functions can be specified in terms of the
opposition between declarative syntax and interrogative syntax and in
terms of degree of ellipticity.   (Details are given in the longer version of this chapter, and see also Berry, 1980b.)

4 Each of the functions has a distinctive set of systems.   (The systems are discussed in the longer version of this chapter.)

3.2 The ideational layer of structure

Thus the layer of structure I am proposing under the ideational
heading is:

                        pb   <u>pc</u>   ps

I claim that each of these functions can occur only once in an
exchange.   Each, when it does occur, must be mapped onto a function from the textual layer and onto a function from the interpersonal
layer.

Once again, in order to justify my setting up of the ideational layer of structure as a separate layer from the other layers, I must show that it is independently variable from the other layers, that it is mappable onto the other layers in different ways in different circumstances.

That it is independently variable can be seen fairly easily if we consider the positions relative to the other layers that can be occupied by pc. It can be mapped onto ai as in (5) or onto bi as in (1). It is thus variable in relation to the functions of the textual layer. It can be mapped onto k1 as in (2) or onto k2 as in (1). It is thus variable also in relation to the functions from the interpersonal layer. Furthermore it can be said that the variation in relation to one layer is not an automatic consequence of the variation in relation to the other layer. It is true that if we move from example (5) to example (1), we find that pc moves from ai to bi and simultaneously moves from k1 to k2. But if we move from example (2) to example (1), although pc moves from k1 to k2, it remains at bi. And if we move from example (5) to example (2), although pc moves from ai to bi, it remains at k1. Movement in relation to one layer is independent of movement in relation to the other layer.

When pb and ps occur they move in step with pc: pb slots in to the left of it wherever it happens to be; ps slots in to the right of it wherever it happens to be.

(In the longer version of this chapter I provide explicit mapping rules for the ideational layer. I also discuss revisions to the system network and realisation statements given in Section 2.31. These are now necessary in the light of the account which has been given of the ideational layer.)

When the three layers have been conflated in all the permissible ways, the following ten structures result:

1   (dk1 / pb / ai) (k2 / pc / bi) (k1 / ps / aii) (k2f / bii)   e.g. example (6)

2   (dk1 / pb / ai) (k2 / pc / bi) (k1 / ps / aii)   e.g. examples (1) and (7)

3   (k2 / pb / ai) (k1 / pc / bi) (k2f / ps / aii)

4   (k2 / pb / ai) (k1 / pc / bi) (k2f / aii)   e.g. example (2)

5   (k2 / pb / ai) (k1 / pc / bi)   e.g. example (8)

6   (k2 / pc / ai)   (k1 / ps / bi)   (k2f / aii)

7   (k2 / pc / ai)   (k1 / ps / bi)   e.g. example (9)

8   (k1 / pc / ai)   (k2f / ps / bi)   e.g. example (10)

9   (k1 / pc / ai)   (k2f / bi)   e.g. example (5)

10 (k1 / pc / ai)   e.g. example (4)

Structures 3 and 6 have not yet been exemplified.   (24) would be an
example of 3.   (25) would be an example of 6.

(24) Son: which English cathedral has the tallest
                 spire
     Father: Salisbury
     Son: oh   yes it must be

(25) Son: you said that Salisbury was the English
                 cathedral with the tallest spire
     Father: yes
     Son: I thought so

I have now come some way towards accomplishing the two tasks I
set myself in the introductory section of this chapter.

1   From the point of view of coding texts I can now show more similarities and more differences between the exchanges of the texts than
would have been possible with an approach based on a single linear
structure.   Furthermore, I can show the similarities and the differences at the same time.   I am no longer forced to say either that
example (1) is like example (2) or that it is different from example (2).
I can now say that the two examples are alike in some ways, different
in others.

(1) Quizmaster: in England, which cathedral has the tallest
                   spire   dk1   k2   k1
    Contestant: Salisbury   pb   pc   ps
    Quizmaster: yes   ai   bi   aii

(2) Son: which English cathedral has the tallest
                   spire   k2   k1   k2f
    Father: Salisbury   pb   pc
    Son: oh   ai   bi   aii

The two examples are alike in having three elements of structure (shown by the ai bi aii structure of the textual layer), but different in that the third element of (1) is obligatory while the third element of (2) is optional (shown by the fact that the third element of (1) includes the obligatory kl among its functions, while the third element of (2) only has k2f). The examples are alike in that the first element of each is a question (I define a question as an initiating move which does not include pc among its functions and which, since pc is obligatory, consequently predicts pc), but different in that in (1) the proposition when complete is supported, while the proposition in (2) is not. The examples are alike in that the first element of each is an elicitation (I define an elicitation as an initiating move which does not include kl among its functions and which, since kl is obligatory, consequently predicts kl), but different in that the first element of (1) is an A event elicitation (defined as an initiating move which includes dkl among its functions), while the first element of (2) is a B event elicitation (defined as an initiating move which includes k2 among its functions). This difference in type of elicitation also results in a further difference: that in (1) pc is mapped onto k2, while in (2) pc is mapped onto kl.

2 From the point of view of constructing a theory of discourse, I can now predict the obligatoriness of all the elements which must occur if an exchange is to be well formed. The second move in structure 1 (e.g. example (6)) and the second move in structure 2 (e.g. example (1)), the two moves whose obligatoriness I could not predict on the basis of just the first two layers of structure, can now be shown to be obligatory owing to the inclusion in their bundles of pc, the obligatory function from layer 3.

The obligatoriness of elements can be shown to be predictable on the basis of just three obligatory functions. In every exchange, the verbal interaction must be initiated – ai; a proposition must be completed – pc; and the information in the proposition must be stamped with the authority of someone who knows – kl. If any of these do not occur in the first move they are predicted. They continue to be predicted until they do occur.

As a bonus I am now also in a position to suggest criteria for the assignment of exchange boundaries and to predict the distribution of surface forms such as interrogative syntax, ellipticity, various types of query, and certain formal items such as 'yes', 'no' and 'oh'. (These points are discussed in the longer version of this chapter.)

An approach such as I am suggesting will not of course solve all problems. However, the applicability of Halliday's notion of simultaneous structures to discourse analysis does at least seem worth investigating.

Acknowledgments

I am grateful to friends with whom I have discussed exchange structure and who have given me comments on the first draft of this paper, particularly Michael Stubbs, Christopher Butler, Ronald Carter, Malcolm Coulthard and David Young.

Chapter 7

The place of intonation in a discourse model

David Brazil

In Chapter 1, Section 4, we outlined a description of the intonation
system of English that took as its starting point the need to determine how the speaker-options it provides affect the communicative
value of the constituents of interactive discourse. The result, as
we suggested there, was a new view of how we can best conceptualise what intonation contributes to the meaning of an utterance. To
elaborate this view, and to strengthen its claims to be taken ser-
iously, we have thought it proper to pursue the investigation to the
point where the description could be said to approach comprehen-
siveness in its own terms: that is to say, until the full set of
systemic variables the method of analysis postulates are related to
the meaning system and, via the meaning system, to each other.
This aim has no doubt deflected us from our original purpose. It
could fairly be said that in our concern to show that intonation is
most satisfactorily approached from a discourse perspective, we
have failed to be explicit about how we see intonation fitting into the
model set up to handle the structure of discourse. References to
intonation are frequent elsewhere in this book, but the principles on
which its criterial status is determined are not discussed. Having
demonstrated, then, how consideration of the pattern of verbal interaction helps us to understand intonation, it remains to ask how important a consideration of intonation is for an appreciation of this
pattern.

The question has pressing practical as well as theoretical implications. The phenomenon of verbal interaction is attracting wide-
spread and growing attention both inside and outside linguistics.
Researchers and others who have a linguistically oriented interest
in the matter are by no means to be identified with those who have
either the training or the inclination to make detailed intonation
transcripts. In neighbouring disciplines, where the same data may
be illuminated by the application of different conceptual frameworks,
the requisite expertise and interest are even less likely to be available. At some point it becomes necessary to ask whether the former
type of investigator must add this extra skill to the others he brings
to his task. It is no less necessary to ask whether, by seeming to
make the linguistic enquiry more esoteric than it need be, we are

reducing the likelihood of fruitful cross-disciplinary dialogue.
Clearly, there is need to encourage such dialogue among the various
disciplines that take verbal communication as a focus of study;
grafting on to a linguistic model of discourse the elaborate, and
possibly gratuitous, paraphernalia of an explicit theory of intonation
could certainly be seen as a hindrance to the development of an
interdisciplinary approach.

It seems hardly necessary to insist that intonation is correlated
with discourse functions in various ways.   What needs to be demonstrated, however, is that it is, in a considerable number of cases,
the sole realisation of a distinction that the discourse analyst cannot
afford to overlook.   Given the high degree of redundancy of almost
any situated act of speech, it is just conceivable that no analytical
decisions depend upon intonation alone.   Or it could be that only in
a clearly delimitable set of circumstances is intonation to be regarded as criterial: reference to the 'high fall' in connection with
frames in Sinclair and Coulthard (1975) exemplifies a kind of selective appeal to intonation, and might be taken as suggesting possible
further ad hoc references, to be brought into the description when
setting up realisation rules for particular discourse categories.   A
further possibility is that such rules can be formulated successfully
only on the basis of a thoroughgoing examination, tone unit by tone
unit, of how intonation contributes to the communicative value of each
and every constituent of the discourse under scrutiny.   This assumption is made in the exploratory exercise with which we end the
present chapter.   We cannot, however, rule out the possibility that
the ultimate outcome of such explorations will be to demonstrate the
adequacy of something less demanding.

Much work needs to be done before we can begin to account systematically for the relationship between discourse functions and the
formal categories that realise them.   There is, to take a very
obvious example, the apparent but far from predictable connection
between eliciting function and interrogative grammar, a connection
which could well be thought, in its seeming waywardness, to provide
the pattern for all form/function relationships.   If linguistic form,
viewed globally as an interrelated set of systems, is in so problematic a relationship to function, it may seem premature and potentially
misleading to single out those formal categories that happen to be
realised by intonation and try to associate them with events at the
level of discourse in a way that isolates them from the effects of co-
occurring formal categories of other kinds.

Our contention that such a course is justifiable is based on the
firm claim we make about the relation between intonation and other
forms of linguistic patterning and the place it consequently occupies
in the topology of the operational model.   Linguists have commonly
assumed that a descriptive apparatus which accounts satisfyingly for
the observable regularities of syntax will be made capable, by some
simple process of extension, of accommodating intonation.   Although
many have recognised its central importance as a meaningful variable,
few have thought it necessary to take it into account ab initio when
doing their model-building.   What generally goes for a tacitly

assumed truth in the transformational generative tradition is stated
explicitly by Halliday: intonation is a department of phonology, the
contrasts it makes available being exploited as realisations of grammatical systems similar to those realised by non-intonational means,
like tense, number and mood (Halliday, 1967, p. 10). Thus Halliday
regards a given intonational opposition – for instance that between
tone 1 and tone 4 – as realising a number of different grammatical
systems, precisely which one depending on the grammatical environment as this is determined by choices in other systems. The
Firthian-type model, modified to represent Discourse as a functional
level, represents this view as:

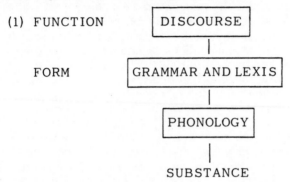

(1) FUNCTION

         DISCOURSE

     FORM

         GRAMMAR AND LEXIS

         PHONOLOGY

         SUBSTANCE

An interesting, though easily overlooked, feature of Halliday's
description is that labels like tone 1 and tone 4 are, in effect, both
formal and phonological labels. The terms of a system whose realisations are tones 1 and 4 are always realised by the same abstraction from the phonetic data. This contrasts markedly with the way
non-intonational systems are realised. The traditional argument for
setting up a separate level of phonology has two aspects: plural
number, for instance, is not always realised by the phoneme /s/;
neither does the phoneme /s/ always realise plural number. The
fact that such a condition of double articulation does not hold for
intonation is one reason for further modifying the model to:

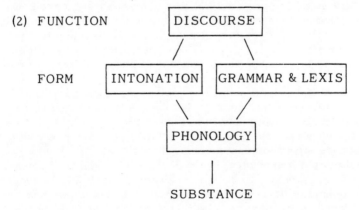

(2) FUNCTION

         DISCOURSE

     FORM   INTONATION   GRAMMAR & LEXIS

              PHONOLOGY

              SUBSTANCE

In (2) we represent the proposal that the meaning of intonation is best captured by postulating a set of formal options, to which the label 'intonation' is applied, alongside those labelled 'lexis and grammar'. Intonation contrasts are conceived of as existing at the same level of abstraction as such relations as 'subject of ...' and 'object of ...'. The argument for setting up the description as two parallel channels linking function and substance is based partly, as we have said, upon the observation that there is significantly less opacity in the intonation channel: the theoretical apparatus necessary to deal with the chain that connects sound to sense is less elaborate than that needed to deal with syntax. In addition, the two modes of formal patterning can be associated with two distinct aspects of the act of communication. While the meanings of contrasts that are realised lexically and grammatically are stated in terms of stable and publicly available categorisations of experience, what the speaker encodes intonationally is a set of distinctions that apply only at the moment of utterance and in the semi-private world that the parties to the interaction share.

In Chapter 4 the structure of the exchange is represented as:
I (R/I) R (F) (F)
The moves that realise elements in its structure are:

e_1 eliciting move which seeks major information and polarity;

e_2 eliciting move which seeks polarity information;

i_1 informing move which asserts polarity information;

i_2 informing move which asserts major information and polarity;

a acknowledging move.

Recognising the exchange as the carrier of a single piece of information and its polarity leads us to note the following constraints upon the occurrence of eliciting and informing moves: they occur only in the order $e_1 i_1 e_2 i_2$, and no sub-class is represented more than once in any exchange. Below, we examine a sample of the exchange types that this description generates in order to demonstrate how intonation choices interact with other variables in a number of instances. To simplify the presentation, we have considered only exchanges in which moves realising the element of structure I have grammatical specifications as follows:

e_1 wh- theme

e_2 interrogative mood

i_2 declarative mood

In Part I, another variable is kept constant by assuming mid key in the initiation. The effects of tone selection (referring or proclaiming) and of internal choices of key are then examined.

In Part II, we are concerned with the relationship between the exchange and the pitch sequence.

I(i)

Exchange with initiation realised by e_2
   STRUCTURE: I   R   (F)
   (1a)   I   //r are YOU mister <u>ROB</u>inson//
          R   //p <u>YES</u> //
         (F)   //p i <u>SEE</u> //...

         I   ...//r in <u>THAT</u> case//p i HAVE a <u>MES</u>sage for you//

   (1b)   I   //r DO you <u>LIKE</u> indian food//
          R   //p OF <u>COURSE</u> //
         (F)   //p <u>GOOD</u> // ...

         I   ... //p i THOUGHT we might go to a CURry house
                 i know//

Referring tone occurs in cases like this where the speaker is
checking the truth of an assumption before introducing some business
or other. Because the elicitation asks only for confirmation of what
is taken to be common ground, it is heard as preparing the way for
another exchange which will modify the state of speaker/hearer convergence. Conversations which merely reinforce the status quo
are rare. The examples can be compared with:
   (2)   I   //p IS it a <u>LIV</u>ing animal //
        R   //p <u>NO</u> //
       (F)   //p <u>NO</u> // ...

       I   ... //p CAN you <u>EAT</u> it//

When the elicitation has proclaiming tone, and is duly responded to,
the exchange does constitute a step forward towards greater convergence. The fact that this type of eliciting move is most often used
conversationally to check that the truth of a proposition can be taken
as agreed in what will follow seems to be one reason why it is often
said that there is a special relationship between 'rising tunes' and
'polar questions'. Seeking polar information as an end in itself is
fairly uncommon outside a limited number of situations of which
guessing games like Twenty Questions are typical.
   The event prepared for need not be verbal:
   (3)   I   //r is THIS the <u>SHEF</u>field train//
       R   //p <u>YES</u> //
       (F)   //p <u>THANKS</u> //
In such a case, the speaker may continue 'I shall get on it then', but
he is more likely simply to do so. Generally, however, the tone
choice in the eliciting move affects expectations about what verbal
activity will come after the exchange, and so is one of the ways in
which the relationship between exchanges can be differentiated
intonationally.
   When the response also has referring tone only, neither speaker
makes any move towards convergence.

(4) I   //r is THAT ARTHur over there ///
⎧ R   //r it COULD be //
⎨ (F)   ∅
⎪
⎩ R   //r it COULD be //p YES //
   (F) //pp MM //....

Both speakers here confine themselves to articulating an assumption the other is already disposed to find acceptable. Since there is no exchange of information, there would seem to be nothing for the initiator to acknowledge. Nor is he likely to introduce any business he is trying to prepare the way for. The addition of a proclaimed YES alters the situation and may well lead to

   (F) //p MM //...
   I .../ /p i THINK i shall go and have a WORD with him//

A response having only referring tone can, indeed, be heard as indicating that the second speaker has anticipated the impending business, and is deliberately heading the first speaker off:

(5) I   //r ARE you BUSy tonight //
     R   //r well NO //
     (F)   ∅

In all cases with mid termination, the expectation is that the respondent will agree with the polarity the initiator has in mind – in (5), for instance, 'no' – with a mid-key response. With high termination, the respondent is asked to supply polar information – for instance 'Are you, or are you not Mr Robinson?' – with a high-key response:

(6a) I   //r are YOU mister $\overline{\text{ROBinson}}$ //

(6b) I.   //r DO you $\overline{\text{LIKE}}$ indian food //

(6c) I   //r is THAT $\overline{\text{ARTHur}}$ over there //

(6d) I   //r ARE you $\overline{\text{BUSy}}$ tonight//

High termination in a second utterance works differently:

(7) I   ///r is THAT ARTHur over there //

   I   //p i THINK it $\overline{\text{MUST}}$ be //
   R   //p $\overline{\text{YES}}$ //p so do I //
   (F) //p MM //

Here, there is a prediction of a high-key YES or NO rejoinder to 'I think it must be' (What do you think?). It therefore constitutes a further eliciting move seeking polar information, and since the structural description does not permit two in the same exchange, it is analysed as a new initiation. The justification for this is that it sets up the same predictions and possibilities of continuance as (6a to d) above.

Note that the first exchange is similarly truncated when a speaker responds minimally to an utterance having high termination:

(8a) I   //r are YOU mister $\overline{\text{ROBinson}}$ //

   I   //p $\overline{\text{YES}}$ //

To say that the second speaker was here seeking a YES or NO
answer would be to accuse him of anomalous behaviour: it would be
very odd for the first speaker to be asked for a polar decision that
he has just asked the second speaker to make for him.   The explanation of the oddity lies in the general rule that moves having the
formal properties of e_2, when used in self-evidently inappropriate
circumstances, are interpreted as belonging to sub-class e_1
(seeking major information).   A comparable example having the
grammatical appearance of an e_2 is:

'are you still here'
'I thought I'd wait till Tom comes back'

where, since 'Yes' would be a statement of the obvious the respondent interprets it as 'Why are you still here?'.   The new exchange
in (8a) might continue

I   //p $\underline{\text{YES}}$ // (= 'why do you ask')

R   //p ^{OH} // p because i HAVE a $\underline{\text{MES}}$sage for you//
F   //p i $\underline{\text{SEE}}$ //

In practice, the 'Yes' would usually be followed by an information-
ally redundant item which removes the expectation of a high-key
response:

(8b)   I   //r are YOU mister $\underline{\text{ROBinson}}$//

R   //p $\underline{\text{YES}}$ //r THAT'S $\underline{\text{RIGHT}}$ //
(F)   //p $\underline{\text{GOOD}}$ //...

Mid termination in a response anticipates nothing more than an
acknowledgment and does not, therefore, mark the beginning of a
new exchange.

When the second speaker initiates a new exchange by means of
interrogative mood he has a choice of tones:

(9a)   I   //r is THAT $\underline{\text{ARTH}}$ur over there //

I   //r do you mean the MAN in the $\underline{\text{RAIN}}$coat //
R   //p $\underline{\text{YES}}$ //

I   //p no ARTHur never $\underline{\text{WEARS}}$ that kind of coat //

(9b)   I   //r is THAT $\underline{\text{ARTH}}$ur over there //

I   //p OVer $\underline{\text{WHERE}}$ //
R   //p beHI$\underline{\text{ND}}$ the $\underline{\text{B}}$AR //

I   //r i DON'T $\underline{\text{THINK}}$ //p he still $\underline{\text{WORKS}}$ here //

In (9a) the second speaker seeks clarification by saying what he
takes the first initiation to mean and asking for it to be confirmed.
In (9b) he does so by asking for further information.   Although our
description, as it stands, does not distinguish these structurally,
this does not seem to be an unimportant difference.

I(ii)

Exchanges with initiation realised by i_1
    STRUCTURE: I R (F)
    (10a) I   //p we shall HAVE to <u>GO</u> //r because of <u>HIM</u> //
        R   //p <u>YES</u> // (I agree, that is the conclusion)
       (F) //p <u>MM</u> //

    (10b) I   //r we shall HAVE to <u>GO</u> //p because of <u>HIM</u> //
        R   //p <u>YES</u> // (I agree, that is the cause)
       (F) //p <u>MM</u> //
It is the proclaimed portion of the initiation to which the second
speaker responds. Because, in the context of any conversation,
the proclaimed part of the initiating move is so clear, respondents
hardly ever have to make explicit what they are agreeing with. In

    'He'll be seventeen in August'
    'Yes'

the response will be unproblematically characterised as 'Yes, that's
how old he will be' or as 'Yes, that's when his birthday is', in
almost any case.
    Note, however, that high termination in the last tone unit would
result in the initiating move being classified as an e_2 whichever
order the referring proclaiming tones occurred in, since the expectation would then be of a high-key <u>yes</u> or <u>no</u> response.
    STRUCTURE: I R/I R (F)
    (11) I   //p we shall HAVE to <u>GO</u> //r because of <u>HIM</u> //
               ⎡//r HAVE TO GO //
               ⎢//r HAVE to /⎺
       R/I⎨//r <u>be</u>CAUSE of <u>HIM</u> //
               ⎣//r YES //
       R //p <u>YES</u> //   (F) //p <u>YES</u> //
When any part of the initiation (including its polarity) is repeated
with referring tone, it seeks confirmation that this part is now to be
regarded as common ground. (The proclaimed portion, once it has
been proclaimed, can now be regarded as conversationally in play in
the same way as the referring portion.) We may say that it is
because the second speaker does not provide the sought-for response
that the expectations set up by the initiation remain operative and the
second move is predictive as well as predicted. Any of the part
repetitions in (11) would, if spoken with proclaiming tone, be heard
as a simple response which set up no predictions, unless, of
course, it had high termination:
    (12) I   //p we shall HAVE to <u>GO</u> //
       R/I //p HAVE to <u>GO</u> //
       R //p <u>YES</u> // p i'm a<u>FRAID</u> so //
      (F) //p <u>YES</u> //
Here the second speaker treats the truth of the proposition as open
to question until it has been reiterated by the first speaker. As we
said in connection with (8a), however, speakers sometimes make
what appear to be requests for polar information in circumstances

where polarity is not really in doubt, and the move is then interpreted as an e_j. The structural description can be crucially affected by this interpreting procedure:

(13a) I   //p i had a TIGHT pain doctor //p in my $\overline{\text{CHEST}}$ //

     R/I //p a $\overline{\text{TIGHT}}$ pain //

     R   //p $\overline{\text{YES}}$ //r THAT'S RIGHT //   (F) //p YES //

(13b) I   //p i had a TIGHT pain doctor //p in my $\overline{\text{CHEST}}$ //

     I   //p a $\overline{\text{TIGHT}}$ pain // (='what do you mean?')
     R   //p $\overline{\text{WELL}}$ //p it was just TIGHT //p in my CHEST //
    (F) //p YES //

If the doctor merely questions the truth of what he has heard, 'A tight pain' falls within the sequence permitted in one exchange. If it is heard as a request for clarification it constitutes an initiating e_1 in a new exchange. The onus of interpretation falls, of course, upon the patient: unless there is a possibility of the doctor's mishearing, it seems unlikely that the first interpretation would be made.

I(iii)

Exchanges with initiating move realised by e_1
  STRUCTURE: I R (F)
(14a) I   //p WHOSE in CHARGE here //
     R   //p ARTHur //
    (F) //p $\overline{\text{OH}}$ //

(14b) I   //r WHOSE in CHARGE here //
     R   //p ARTHur //

     I   //p i THINK ill go and have a WORD with him //

The alternation of p and r tone in I is similar in effect to the alternation in e_2 moves which realise I. With proclaiming tone the speaker seeks new information. With referring tone, the implication is usually that he is checking an already made assumption, before proceeding with business. There may be a suggestion of intimacy of the 'a word in your ear' kind, often insinuated by referring tones, but the most interesting structural consequence is the fact that asking about something as if it were known is strongly predictive of real business to follow.

The effect of alternating tones in the response can be seen in
(15a) I   //p WHEN are you LEAVing //
     R   //p on FRIday //
    (F) //p YES //

(15b) I   //p WHEN are you LEAVing //
     R   //r on FRIday //
    (F) //p OH yes //

Whereas (15a) straightforwardly supplies the information sought, there is an implication in (15b) that the first speaker already knows when: the response is presented as a reminder, which does not add anything to his present knowledge. The latter example can be interestingly compared with the one following:

STRUCTURE: I R/I R (F)

(16a) I   //p WHERE have they put my BRIEFcase //
       R/I //r IN the OFfice //
       R   ⎡//p NO //r it ISn't THERE //
            ⎣//p OH yes //p THANKS //

Here, too, the second speaker's contribution has the character of a reminder, or perhaps of a suggestion about where it would be sensible to look. The reason this can be interpreted by the other speaker as an R/I lies evidently in ongoing assumptions about how knowledge is distributed: in (16a) it would be reasonable to substitute

//r have you LOOKED in the OFfice //

but in (15) we should scarcely expect

//r am i GOing on FRIday //

Once again there is an alternative way of making the move predictive: the version

(16b) R/I //p IN the $\frac{OFfice}{}$ //

expects a YES or NO response. Both patterns occur in the kind of exchange we have now come to recognise as specially characteristic of classroom discourse:

(17a) I   //p WHATs the capital of FRANCE //
       R/I //r PARis sir //
       R   //p YES //p PARis //

II

An example of an exchange which is coterminous with a pitch sequence is:

(18) I   //p ^{HOW} OFten //p do you GET these pains //
      R   //p EVery few DAYS doctor //
      F   //p EVery few $_{DAYS}$ //

We can consider the effect of three kinds of variation from this pattern:

(i)   The exchange may not end with low termination
(ii)   The exchange may not begin with high termination
(iii) There may be pitch sequence boundaries within the exchange.

II(i)

The effect of ending an exchange with low termination is normally to reserve to the speaker the opportunity of making the next initiation:

(18b) F   //.p EVery few <u>DAYS</u> //

    I   //p have you ^{HAD} anything like this _{be}<u>FORE</u> //

If the F-move ends with mid termination, there is a possibility of a
further F-move from the other party:

(18c) F   //p EVery few <u>DAYS</u> //
        F   //p <u>YES</u> //

In the following example, two closely related exchanges are
included in one pitch sequence:

(18d) I   //p ^{HOW} OFten //p do you <u>GET</u> these pains //
      R   //p EVery few <u>DAYS</u> //

    I   //p and HOW long do they <u>LAST</u> //
   R   //p about HALF an <u>HOUR</u> //
   F   //p HALF an _{<u>HOUR</u>} //

Note that when this happens, the first response is not likely to be
acknowledged. A third and subsequent initiations could have been
included in the same pitch sequence. This is one of a number of
ways in which relationships can be established intonationally between
consecutive exchanges in a series. We have already seen that
choice of a referring tone in some initiating moves is another
(p.

II(ii)

A third way is by choice of sequence-initial key choice. Consider:

(18e) I   //p ^{HOW} OFten //p do you <u>GET</u> these pains //
     R   //p EVery few <u>DAYS</u> //
     F   //p EVery few _{<u>DAYS</u>} //

      ⎡a //p have you ^{HAD} anything like this ^{be}<u>FORE</u> //
  I⎢b //p and HOW long do they <u>LAST</u> //
      ⎣c //p you GET them as frequently as ^{<u>THAT</u>} //

Having terminated the first exchange, the doctor can exploit the
contrastive, additive or equative significance of key to indicate a
relationship between the exchange that is beginning and the immediately preceding one. Ia indicates that this is an unrelated
exchange, that is to say structurally contrastive. Ib indicates an
additive relationship: the information sought is an enlargement of
that just obtained. Ic initiates an exchange which will result in a
further presentation of the same information.

II(iii)

Within a pitch sequence, every utterance–final termination choice constrains the next speaker to begin with a matching key choice. When an utterance ends at the same time as a pitch sequence, there are no such constraints.

(19) I //p well <u>TELL</u> me mister smith //p HOW are you feeling <u>NOW</u>//

Pitch sequence closure at the end of an eliciting move like this serves often as an invitation to reply at length precisely because the addressee is free to begin as he likes. In other kinds of discourse the pitch level pattern is frequently associated with questions set up for discussion rather than questions intended to be answered summarily.

Closing the pitch sequence in a response has a rather different effect. Any subsequent move will then be an acknowledgment, and politeness usually requires that we exhibit concern about how our responses are received. In example (20) this concern is markedly absent.

(20) I //p ^{HOW} OFten //p do you <u>GET</u> these pains //
      R //p EVery few <u>DAYS</u> //

Because there is no built-in expectation that the response will be acknowledged in any particular way – or even that it will be acknowledged at all – it carries evident overtones of brusqueness or sullenness.

Chapter 8

Kinesics in discourse

John Gosling

'We speak with our vocal organs, but we converse with our entire bodies; conversation consists of much more than a simple inter-change of spoken words.' (Abercrombie, 1968)

Kinesics in the sense used here is intended to cover certain aspects of non-vocal communicative behaviour between participants in a dis-course. What follows is a theoretical account of such behaviour, closely based on analysed data, which is deliberately 'powerful' in its hypothesisation. First, however, some initial justification must be given for considering kinesics as an essential and integral part of the linguistic analysis of face-to-face discourse.

In a previous paper (Gosling, 1977), attention was drawn to the fact that the original model for discourse presented by Sinclair and Coulthard in 1975 depended fairly heavily on an unstructured notion of situation, and that this presented major theoretical difficulties for its development and use in areas of linguistic interaction where the situational constraints were more complex and less clear-cut than in those speech-situations which had already been examined, namely, formal classroom teaching, broadcast interviews, and doctor-patient consultations.

It was suggested then that the analysis of discourse needed to be supported by some systematic description of the relevant but often implicit metalinguistic knowledge which participants utilised as the contextualising basis for their everyday linguistic interactions. Following Goffman's (1964) definition of a social situation as 'an environment of mutual monitoring possibilities', and Hymes's (1971) notion of 'communicative competence', it seemed reasonable to sug-gest that for any particular situation there were sociolinguistic con-ventions, or 'rules of use' to which participants were expected to conform. Thus, for instance, certain choices of discourse function might be acceptable in one situation but not in another, even between the same participants. An example might be provided by the dis-course options taken up by a tutor and a student discussing an essay, compared with those employed by the same two people when involved in a teaching practice session in a classroom with pupils present. A systematic formulation of such rules of use, it was thought, might enable a more general model of discourse to be constructed, which would have greater predictive power across widely differing situations. Unfortunately, this seemed to necessitate postulating a separate level of 'situational analysis', whose integration within a properly linguistic framework would prove extremely difficult, if not impossible.

An alternative and more promising way forward was to show that it was not necessary to go so far from immediately observable communicative behaviour in order to solve the 'problem of situation' in relation to a more generalisable theory of discourse. After all, even on first acquaintance, we are usually able, with minimal help, to acquire and mobilise at least an adequate amount of information about co-conversationalists in order to initiate and sustain a reasonable level of interaction, and this is in principle describable in linguistic terms. People manage themselves before others on the basis of a combination of whatever relevant previous knowledge they have, plus the internalisation and interpretation of various kinds of signals from the other. This is a complex, and not necessarily fully conscious series of interrelated activities. The actual nature of the participant's relevant previous knowledge is not of course directly accessible to linguistic description, but the way he uses that knowledge, in terms of its interactive outcomes, very well may be, as may be the ways in which he receives and processes more immediately available signals from the other which are important for the tactical organisation of subsequent interaction.

Given this, then one possible way out of the need to invoke an unstructured notion of situation is to increase one's descriptive and analytic power to the point where one is able to handle all the observable variables which contribute significantly to the meaningfulness of the interaction for the participants. Since 1975, considerable progress has been made in this direction, much of it documented in previous chapters. The contributions made to the organisation of discourse by syntax, clause relations and cohesion, as well as some aspects of lexical choice, are now much better understood. The role of intonation has proved to be particularly illuminating in the development of a more generalisable account of exchange structure.

If, however, one looks at the linguistic variables available to a speaker, elements of which he chooses in the framing of his discourse in face-to-face interaction, there is one important area which has so far received little or no attention in ways which are directly relevant for the enterprise of discourse analysis, and this is the area of non-vocal communication. What is required is a principled approach, a properly linguistic account, which, like the description of other levels, accords with the guidelines laid down in Halliday's Categories of the Theory of Grammar (1961).

It will be argued here that without some principled way of handling the role of kinesics in discourse, any attempt at a full description and analysis of the significant linguistic data in face-to-face interaction will necessarily be incomplete in a number of important respects, particularly where multi-party discourse with widely shared speaking rights is being examined.

On the other hand, given the present state of the art, it does seem true to say that all communicatively significant outputs in face-to-face interaction will, in principle at least, be covered by a description of a speech-event which includes a treatment of phonology, lexis, grammar and kinesics as formal realisations of various kinds of interactive functions, of which discourse is a major component. Parallel descriptions of a speech-event in terms of these four levels would enable increasingly powerful statements to be made about how discourse functions are realised at various formal levels, which in turn would contribute very greatly to the explanatory power of the model of analysis as a whole.

The very nature of the enterprise however, would preclude the treatment of very long texts, because of the sheer amount of analysis required. This limitation would not necessarily invalidate the findings, since linguistic observations do not require further validation by statistical methods. Rather, a body of appropriate data is analysed and hypothesised upon, and the conclusions are tested by applying the techniques developed in the first data sample to a further body of data, and so on. The data-base for this chapter is a number of video-taped seminar discussions in British higher education, and initially, an attempt was made to analyse the material in terms of the Sinclair-Coulthard 1975 model.

Seminars are multi-party communicative events, in which a great emphasis is placed upon the vocal elements of interaction. Even so, it became evident very early on that an audio-tape alone does not provide sufficient retrievable data for a functional analysis of communicative behaviour to be undertaken, even given a sophisticated approach to intonation, and observational notes made at the same time as the recording. If visual data are unavailable, a great deal is lost: who is addressing whom, who is visibly attending to whom and at what points, and often whether someone is attempting to enter the discussion. Attitudinal information can also be carried by non-vocal means, as are responses to speakers: nods are a good example. The inadequacies of a purely audio approach are further highlighted where speaking rights are fairly democratic, and thus have to be extensively negotiated. Indeed, if a video-recording is obtained of such a speech-event, and the sound is turned down, it is surprising how much discourse-functional information can still be obtained.

At this point, a very obvious, but none the less important observation is worth making, namely that non-vocal communication seems to be of great significance in managing the mechanics, or interpersonal aspects, of interaction when the vocal channels are not available since they are already in use. One very early expectation was that a salient aspect of non-vocally-realised discourse function would be prospective, and relate closely to turn-taking and speaker-nomination.

Kinesics as a level of linguistic form

The kinds of interactive function which seem to be realised by non-vocal communicative behaviour suggest that it has more in common with phonology than with the other two formal levels of grammar and lexis. It seems useful to think in terms of two kinds of 'contextual information': one of them is affective, or attitudinal, and at the present time, linguistics has no way of categorising or classifying this type of information. The other kind of information is dis-course-functional. That is, it has to do with the management of those aspects of the interpersonal which have to do with the organi-sation of discourse. Here a lot more can and has been said: recent work on intonation is a good example – see Brazil (pp. 146–57) The same seems broadly true of non-vocal behaviour: there is a great deal one cannot yet handle linguistically which may be of great communicative significance for participants, but on the other hand, there are a number of recurrent features of non-vocal behaviour which do seem to be realisations of discourse function, and it is these which form the major focus of attention here.

It has been assumed above that the non-verbal realm can be broken down into the 'vocal' on the one hand, and the 'non-vocal' on the other. In some ways, the dividing line between the two is difficult to draw, particularly from the physiological point of view since, for example, a highly stressed syllable will be accompanied by associa-ted muscular tension in other areas. None the less, it is descrip tively useful to make a distinction between that behaviour which is directly concerned with phonation, and that which is not, and to call the former vocal, and the latter non-vocal.

The underlying rationale for the approach taken in relating an investigation of non-vocal behaviour to intonation in the first instance, was firstly, that if, following Laver's (1970) view that the 'tone group' or 'tone unit' was the typical stretch of language which involved some kind of neurolinguistic pre-assembly on the part of the speaker, then it was likely that it would provide a useful base-line for the systematic study of discourse-related non-vocal behav-iour. Secondly, there seemed to be a more immediate relationship between the non-vocal and intonation than between it and other levels such as grammar or lexis. In particular, both intonation and non-vocal behaviour seemed more closely related to a participant's view of the 'other' in terms of his discourse orientation (e.g. selection of referring and proclaiming tones), and his use of key to signify, among other things, contrastive- or equative-ness, and the possible continuation or ending of an utterance, by a progressive step down to low termination of a tone-unit which was sequence-final, for instance. Indeed, the very notion of intonation sequence seemed related in some ways to initial observations undertaken of non-vocal behaviour involving change of speaker, which made them worth pur-suing further. Thirdly, there seemed to be something of a bridge between some aspects of the non-vocal and intonation provided by Kendon's (1972b) report of Lenneberg's 1968 Pittsburgh paper in which he stated that a subject was asked to tap his finger on a table

in a comfortably fast rhythm and then, after about 10 seconds, to
begin speaking.   It was found that in his first tone group, the tonic
syllable coincided with a finger-tap.   This was replicated informally, and found to work.   There was also additional work which suggested that, quite often at least, the rhythmicality of an utterance
was supported by simultaneous kinetic movement (Ekman and
Friesen, 1972), and it seemed reasonable to suspect that the locus
for this in the tone unit would be those syllables showing major
prominence, and particularly, perhaps, the tonic.   How significant
these latter items are for discourse-functional aspects of the non-
vocal is questionable;   they do, however, help to make the case for
relating it closely to intonation.

That there are connections between the two areas seems highly
probable, but it also seems evident that, in its own right, non-vocal
behaviour is very important in the human communication of meaning
of various kinds.   In multi-party discourse, especially where
speakers may address themselves to any participant or participants,
it is immediately clear from a consideration of sound-track alone
that any attempt to establish addressor-addressee relations is nuga-
tory without reference to visual cues of some kind.   This in itself
provides a justification for the enterprise of discourse kinesics in
such speech situations, which do of course constitute the majority of
human conversational interactions.

At the present time, discourse functions are seen as realised by
three formal levels: grammar, lexis, and intonation choices.   The
term 'formal level' is taken from Halliday (1961), and here phonology
was seen as an 'inter-level' connecting phonic substance with form.
Halliday's original framework of levels, was, however, designed to
explicate the internal organisation of spoken and written text, and
text starts by being an essentially verbal notion.   If one includes
human interactiveness as a component of text, and if, in particular,
one includes discourse function as a salient element in the exchange
of meanings between participants in face-to-face interaction, then
there is a case for expanding what is contained within the general
level of form.   A crucial element remains, however, namely that
form is characterised by recurrent linguistic patterning which in
various ways realises language functions.   This is the burden of
Halliday's later work, exemplified in the following quotations:

> Whatever we are using language for, we need to make some refer-
> ence to the categories of our experience;   we need to take on some
> role in the interpersonal situation;   and we need to embody these
> in the form of text (Halliday, 1976).

> An utterance must be about something;   it must express the
> speaker's stake in the matter;   and it must be operational in its
> own context, either in the 'here and now' or in some second-order
> context created by the language.   These conditions would seem to
> determine a significant part of the properties of the language
> system (ibid.).

It therefore seems reasonable, while keeping Halliday's model in
Categories of the Theory of Grammar as a basis, to expand the

specific levels of form in order to embrace all those areas which
systematically realise discourse function. Hence, discourse intonation is seen as a formal level, and it is proposed here that a new
level be created, called KINESICS, which includes all those meaningful gestures or sequences of gestures which realise interactive
functions in face-to-face communicative situations.

As a starting point, one could perhaps describe some general interactive functions of the kinesic level as making available information
about the participants' involvement, or 'states of play' at particular
points within the speech-event. One of the more interesting specific
uses of gesture is to provide non-vocal surrogates for discourse
functions: for an accept, a nod is as good as a 'yes' – it serves as a
minimum engage item (Sinclair, 1977). So far as Halliday's 1961
framework is concerned, perhaps kinesics can best be seen as help-
ing to relate discourse functions in various ways to the extra-textual
features of situation, where situation here is seen as the ongoing
dynamic relations between the participants as well as its more usual
sense of the fairly static state of affairs within which the text has its
being. As well as providing alternative realisations for existing
discourse functions as exemplified above, it will also be shown that
the study of kinesics reveals a number of new functions which have so
far not been identified in realisations at other formal levels.

An example of a very early piece of research which suggests that
it is profitable to regard the non-vocal as an independent level of
form along the lines outlined above, is the work done by Pfungst
(1911) on 'Clever Hans', a performing horse. Hans could 'solve'
mathematical problems written on a blackboard, communicating his
answers by tapping his forefeet on the ground the appropriate number
of times, taking his cues from the non-vocal behaviour of the
audience (Farb, 1973). In terms of discourse, the 'Clever Hans
Phenomenon' suggests quite strongly that both vocal and non-vocal
communicative behaviour can be influenced very materially by exclusively non-vocal outputs from the other – in this case, the audience.
That is, meaning of some kind is being transmitted, whether inten-
tionally or not, and is being picked up by the 'speaker', who uses it,
in this case, to terminate his part of the discourse. For Hans, the
meaning of the audience's non-vocal behaviour was 'end your turn'.

The example also demonstrates rather nicely that to be useful, and
to tie in with existing discourse analysis theory and method, any
descriptive framework for non-vocal interactive behaviour should,
at least in the first instance, be functional, rather than immediately
semantic in its emphasis. Exactly this functional approach is taken
by Saussure in his insistence that 'tout revient à la différence', and
is succinctly stated by Brazil (1975) in respect of intonation:

> Once the functionally contrastive features have been identified and
> related to each other in a way which properly recognises the
> various dimensions of function involved – once, that is, we have
> established just what is in contrast with what – it is possible to
> provide a consistent characterisation of the 'meaning' of each
> feature. Such characterisation is not tied to lexically-derived
> notions like 'expectancy' and 'surprise', nor to grammatically-

derived concepts like 'interrogative' and 'declarative'. Instead it makes direct reference to the interactive process which I take to be implicit in every spoken utterance. Centrally, the reference is to the speaker's moment-by-moment assessment of the state of convergence at the time and place of speaking. Establishing kinesics as a separate formal level is important as a

heuristic device, quite apart from other more theoretical considerations. In this respect, there is support from Coulthard and Brazil's (1979) approach to intonation:

> Intonation choices are seen as making separate and distinctive contributions to the discourse functions of the utterance, capable of being described at an appropriate level of abstraction without reference to co-occurring lexical and grammatical choices.

Despite this, however, there are, in practice, limits to how far one can go in isolating formal realisations of discourse function, especially when investigating a new level, without seeking some explicatory relations elsewhere. It is thus necessary to engage in Hallidayan 'shunting' across levels in the search for interactive functions of various kinds realised by kinesics. One reason for positing the notion of discourse function in the first place was that the topmost elements of structure in grammar were overloaded (Sinclair and Coulthard, 1975), and within classroom discourse, whether an act in a follow-up move is coded as evaluate or accept may depend on its intonation: a high-key p+ 'YES' is evaluative, whereas a mid-key p realisation would be an accept (Coulthard and Brazil, 1979). In establishing the boundaries of tone units too, there do seem to be occasions when this is helped quite a lot by a look at the grammar, and it seems reasonable to assert this without in any way denying the separate and distinctive contribution of intonation to discourse function. For the participants, a speech-event is in many ways a unified item in terms of communicative behaviour, and it is the analyst who erects divisions in order to explicate the functional role of its various components.

Although it is beyond doubt that rigorous separation has been very productive, none the less it is also true that, by now, with recent work by Montgomery (1976), Burton (1978a and b) and Richardson (1978), to name but three, it is becoming increasingly possible to look at the management of discourse in terms of the co-occurrence or otherwise of boundaries of different units within different formal levels. For example, in any discourse, 'points of completion' (or potential completion) in an utterance/turn are, or may be, characterised by completions in various formal levels, of which kinesics seems to be one. For instance, to end a 'turn' really decisively, one would expect to find a clause boundary, no more outstanding clause-relational or cohesive ties, low termination, and unfocused gaze (possibly followed by eye nomination, or gaze inviting it, but this would be coded as a subsequent item), with hands folded or at rest. Such a major co-occurrence of boundaries in a seminar would probably be followed by a considerable silence before the next speaker spoke, and there might be quite a lot of non-vocal behaviour before that, perhaps of a fairly major kind. If there were a 'residual speaker' (someone with preferential speaking rights – a seminar 'leader' say), there might be an attempt to force him into action. This hypothetical example is one pole of what seems to be a cline: more usually, there would be less complete co-occurrence of boundaries, with some of them absent.

There is an analogy here with stylistics, where, in poetry, it is often observed that there either is or is not a good 'fit' between phonological units such as stanza and line, and grammatical units like sentence and clause (Sinclair, 1966), and that this has implications for meaning and/or 'significance' (Leech, 1969). So far as kinesics is concerned, additional notions which are potentially useful from other areas of linguistics include lexical sets and collocations, 'bound' and 'free' (as of clauses), the phoneme and allophones (including free variation and complementary distribution), cohesion (both lexical and grammatical, and including clause-relations), deep and surface structure plus additional ideas from stylistics, such as deviation from a norm, parallelism, etc.

A further reason for considering kinesics as a formal level of realisation for discourse function is that it seems possible to use non-vocal behaviour to maintain a speaking turn (i.e. continue speaking rights), even though in terms of realisations at other levels the turn should really have come to an end. The perceived status of participants and their consequent rights to speak and be interrupted are also involved here, but it is anticipated that much of this too is explicable in kinesic terms. In other words, that people, as part of their socialisation, learn, among other things, to recognise kinesic signals of dominance from others, and react accordingly, producing realisations at various points in various levels. There is, however, no necessary relationship between the linguistic level of a perceived input item and its position on, say, a hierarchy of units on the one hand, and the level and position of a corresponding subsequent output response, judged as appropriate, on the other. For instance, though outside the scope of this present chapter, raised eyebrows and intent gaze in the hearer might impel a speaker who perceives them to choose his subsequent lexical items with more care than he had beforehand, particularly if the status relations are as symmetrical in favour of the hearer. A future task might well be to look at this kind of thing, to see whether any consistent statements can be made about behaviour across levels of realisation: that is, whether any patterns exist which consistently tally with pre-existing social relations obtaining in an interaction.

Returning to turn-taking, however: suppose a point of possible completion has been arrived at in a discourse. At this point, in theory, there are several possibilities: another speaker may take over at length; there may be an 'awkward pause', and the original speaker may continue; the silence may become 'stony' (three seconds is a very long time indeed), or it may be preceded and punctuated by minimum-engage 'mms' or nods. A really adequate theory of discourse ought, ultimately, to be able to make some fairly hard predictions about what is likely to happen next, and why. That is, it ought to be able to predict the form of subsequent interaction, though not of course the content. To do this, though, involves an extension of existing theory to take account of realisations across levels in a principled way. To do this for turn-taking requires kinesics to be regarded as a formal level in its own right.

It is, for instance, fairly well known that if, at the end or towards the end of his turn, a speaker manages to establish eye-contact with another member of the group, then that person is under considerable pressure to speak next. The greater the status of the first speaker, the more pressure on the person concerned. Use of eye-contact to influence the selection of next speaker seems to be a general characteristic of face-to-face linguistic interaction in Western culture. If one avoids eye-contact, then one is under no obligation to speak. Eye-contact (or 'eye-nomination') is a tactical device used a great deal by tutors to students in this way. It can be 'forced' by recourse to the verbal channel: in small groups, it is very difficult to deny eye-contact if a tutor has called one's name, for instance. To do so may be interpreted as a major challenge, and cause embarrassment all round. Verbally forced eye-contact in such a situation is a fairly brutal device and needs heavy subsequent verbal mitigation, but it does show that there is a relation across levels of some kind here. Participants wishing to speak actively seek eye-contact, and orient their gaze accordingly to the speaker, who then has the option to actualise it, if he so wishes. In those undergraduate seminars where the status relations between tutor and students are perceived as highly asymmetrical, many students seem aware of the need to support their peers and avoid embarrassment by getting them 'off the hook' of eye-contact with the tutor through offering another contribution, which may not have received prior kinesic elicitation from the latter. Incidentally, such a contribution, because of its origin, seems to be allowed topical differentiation from the previous contribution, and hence influence the directions of the topic of subsequent discussion. Clearly, there is a great deal here which needs to be untangled before observations of this kind, interesting and important as they may be, can be properly incorporated into an enlarged theory of discourse.

Some relevant considerations from the literature

In 1927, Edward Sapir noted the systematic communicative value of gesture as follows:

> we respond to gestures with an extreme alertness and, one might almost say, in accordance with an elaborate and secret code that is written nowhere, known by none, and understood by all (emphasis ours, RB).

Birdwhistell used this as a starting point for much of his work, brought together in 'Kinesics in Context' (1970), whose major premise is that there is 'a set of necessary and formal body motion behaviours which are tied directly to linguistic structure'. Unfortunately, his model of language does not seem to involve a separation into formal linguistic levels, combining in various ways to realise discourse functions, and this is a major disadvantage. However, his work with Hockett and McQuown on interaction yields the important insight that kinesic (or in his terms, 'parakinesic') and phonological data are 'but aspects of more comprehensive units, which somehow combine the behaviour of both channels'.

Birdwhistell sees his 'parakinesic' signals as cross-referencing outputs from other channels of interaction in two distinct ways, the second of which is particularly relevant to the present approach:

These cross-referencing signals amplify, emphasise, or modify the formal constructions and/or they make statements about the context of the message situation. In the latter instance, they help to define the context of the interaction by identifying the actor or his audience, and, furthermore, they usually convey information about the larger context in which the interaction takes place.

His tentative conclusion is that kinesic (i.e. his 'parakinesic') elements appear in interactional streams 'both concurrent with and apparently independent of the flow of speech':

We know something about the shape of spoken sentences and about the shape of intricately constructed kinesic strings, but we have only begun to envision the shape of communicative blocks.
Certainly, everything that we have come to know about utterances and conversations indicates that communicational behaviour is multilinear in time, but observational conventions screen much of the dynamics of this process from analytic view.

Significantly, Birdwhistell has a gloss on 'meaning', which again reinforces the approach taken here. The question 'What does X mean?' in the context of kinesic research, should be rephrased as 'How do you know the place of this phenomenon in that larger pattern which you are describing?' He concludes this section of his work with a major caveat:

From the seminal insight that kinesic activity constitutes an infra-communicational system is derived a plethora of data which, unless explicitly and methodically ordered, drowns the investigator in myriad shapes and sizes and orders of behavioural pieces.

In view of this, it seems more than ever important to restrict initial investigations to those kinesic elements which appear to be discourse-functional. A small beginning has been made along these lines by Coulthard and Montgomery (1976) in connection with lecture monologue, and Coulthard and Brazil (1976) have identified 'at least six parameters which must be taken into account in any discussion of turn-taking: tone, termination, intensity, eye-contact, syntactic and semantic completeness.'

Adam Kendon has produced several papers which attempt to systematise different aspects of non-vocal behaviour in terms of their functional role in communication. His work with Ferber (1973) on human greetings, for instance, suggests a basic four-phase 'transaction', which in its elaboration of approach is the closest yet found in the literature to existing formulations in discourse analysis:

we have drawn a distinction between the structure of the greeting as an interpersonal transaction, and the specific gestures and other actions that comprise its various stages....

Thus we suggested that greetings would have a pre-phase of sighting and announcement, a distance salutation, an approach phase and a close salutation; that the close salutation has a distinct location, and the participants as they engage in it orient themselves to each other in a way that is distinctive. Each of these components of the greeting transaction can be thought of as a spot in a programme where one of a number of different actions can be performed. We expect that for each of these spots there will be a restricted class of actions that will be 'selected' from.

Precisely which 'selections' are made at each 'phase' of the 'greeting transaction' depends on factors such as 'relative dominance, friendliness, familiarity and identity' and 'on what occasion the greeting occurs, and how long ago it was that the participants last met, if they have met before'.

In the seminars considered here, unlike greetings, there is a large contextual constraint: all the participants are seated round a high table. The visible non-vocal behaviour is thus restricted to the upper parts of the seated body. This does not mean, of course, that the relative positions of those bodies is communicatively irrelevant: research in 'group dynamics' deals with this in great detail (e.g. Lott and Sommer, 1967). Position also affects specific gestures: which way a participant turns his head when attending to a co-conversationalist will depend on the relative positions of the two participants, and the distance between them is also important gesturally. None the less, whatever motivates participants to select the chairs they do, it will still be something of a fait accompli once the interaction has started, or as Turner (1972) puts it, once 'starting' has been 'done'. In fact, in seminars, as in almost all the other speech-events so far investigated in discourse analysis, 'starting' has to be 'done', and a precondition for it is a seated company. Interestingly, though, in formal classroom teaching and lecture monologue, the person with the greatest speaking rights (the teacher or lecturer), also has the greatest positional freedom: he can stand up and walk around, and this may enable a greater repertoire of gestures to be deployed.

Goffman (1963), discussing conversation, describes the arrangement of participants as an 'eye-to-eye ecological huddle [which] tends to be carefully maintained', and Kendon (1974) develops this by reference to an individual's 'transactional segment', which he defines as

a space extending in front of a person which is the space he is currently using in whatever his current activity may be.... It is the space into which he looks and speaks, into which he reaches to handle objects. He will endeavour to maintain this space, in the face of any intrusion, so long as he is engaged on the particular line of activity which requires it. As a rule, others respect this space, not entering it or crossing it.

When there is a change of activity, the transactional segment is also seen to be modified by various types of change in non-vocal behaviour.

Where two or more persons interact, their transactional segments overlap and they thus co-produce a 'facing formation', which 'provides a circumstance for the exchange of utterances, glances and gestures of which conversations are constituted'. In some situations, the 'frame for joint business' which the facing formation provides, is seen as taken over by the furniture, and this is true of seminars. None the less, the concepts of 'facing formation', and, especially, 'transactional segment' are very suggestive for discourse, since they imply that part of turn-taking behaviour may involve the achievement of transactional segment overlap, and hence facing formation, as a precondition for successful change of speaker. Significantly, Kendon and Ferber (1973) reported that greeting behaviour entailed the co-production of a distinctive spatial-orientational 'frame' and once the salutation was completed,

> the two greeters always stepped away from their respective
> locations and orientations, to form a new and different arrange-
> ment as they embarked upon the task that followed. A change of
> arrangement here occurred, thus, as the participants changed
> from one kind of interaction to another.

By analogy one might expect, in seminars, that a potential next speaker would perhaps need to engage in something similar to greeting behaviour as a precondition for making a successful contribution to the discourse, and that such non-vocal behaviour would be differentiated from other, in-turn, behaviour.

Kendon's work demonstrates clear parallels between the systematics of some aspects of non-vocal behaviour which do seem discourse-functional, and existing work in discourse, particularly at the ranks of exchange and transaction. A further example may clarify this. In any work-place, a routine minimal greeting is performed by mutuality of gaze plus raised eyebrows. If one participant raises eyebrows, the other participant will do the same (or violate rules of politeness – at least in Western culture). This may be seen as a kinesic exchange – possible indeed a transaction-initial boundary exchange – and, potentially, it may be exactly paralleled by realisations at vocal levels: if one participant produces a mid-key proclaimed 'Hi', the other will do the same. Interestingly, although vocalisation may not occur, and the greeting may be entirely realised at the kinesic level, none the less a precondition for vocalisation here is appropriate kinesic behaviour.

One may add that, as in spoken discourse, it seems entirely possible to apply Grice's (1975) notion of 'overbuilding' to such a kinesic exchange: the interactants' definition of the situation, their degree of commitment and so on – as partially specified by Kendon above – will affect their choice of realisation at the kinesic level. Here, the previous distinction between general interactive function and specific discourse function is useful: a greeting is still a greeting discoursally, even though it may be overlayed by realisations stemming from other factors, such as affective state, which are important in terms of interaction, but are not yet systematisable, and do not fall within the purview of specifically discourse function as defined here.

Limitations on discourse-functional kinesic description

The enterprise of discourse kinesics involves isolating and describing those consistently patterned non-vocal behaviours which systematically realise interactive, and particularly discoursal functions. Thus, it is not a useful approach to seek immediately and intrinsically 'meaningful' gestural items, nor, initially, to regard as important those occurrences of non-vocal behaviour which are merely supportive, or illustrative of a verbalised proposition, along the lines suggested by Riley (1975). Rather, it seems more fruitful, and less confusing, to see kinesics in terms of a pretty restricted number of choices between items realising discourse function, whose communicative role is dictated by their place in a system. Further ascription of meanings is a second-stage operation, involving a description of the co-occurrence of observable interactive behaviour at various formal levels in the total speech-event and at particular places within it. Stipulations of this kind immediately rule out a great deal of literature and research findings in the general area of non-verbal behaviour as irrelevant to the approach as projected. At most, much of this material provides clues to an approach and relevant examples of behaviour, rather than a useful theoretical framework.

In setting up a kinesics model, it is useful to identify and discuss some examples of non-vocal communicative behaviour which are not discourse-functional, so that they may be eliminated from further consideration. This is not to say, however, that in the wider context of interactive function generally they will turn out to be unimportant or unmeaningful. There is a precedent in Birdwhistell for this approach, and in his 1972a review of 'Kinesics in Context', Kendon writes that Birdwhistell

> seems to shunt to one side those elaborate demonstrative or pictorial movements that people use when they describe something: a man describing how he played and landed a trout, for example. Birdwhistell says 'At the moment I am inclined to regard such behaviour as examples of derived communicational systems. As such, they are not the primary subject of kinesics at present' (p. 126). Birdwhistell thus implies that kinesics deals with only a part of communicatively significant body-motion phenomena. However, he never makes clear, in so many words, what this is. Presumably this would become apparent as the study of the whole system of communicative behaviour progresses'.

Following Birdwhistell here, there are two kinds of gestures which it is easy to exclude immediately from a discourse-functional kinesics, namely 'emblems' and 'mimetic' items. An emblem is a ritualised gesture which has an overt and well-established meaning or cluster of meanings within a particular culture (e.g. a 'V' sign; 'hour-glass' with both hands to denote an attractive woman, and so on). More common in seminars are mimetic items in which a speaker 'draws pictures' in the air. These are not necessarily representational. A good example was provided in the data by a speaker talking about 'leadership in education', where, during the utterance of the words 'leaders of the same type and leaders of complementary types at different levels in the school', he disengaged from both arms folded to extended right hand with pen, and produced a three-place horizontal movement, followed immediately by a three-place vertical movement. Emblems and mimetic items are both seen as in some sense superimposed on the basic communicative gestures which realise discourse function.

Other features from the data which do have important implications for interactive, but not necessarily discourse function, are those which involve certain kinds of postural and/or gestural change resulting from co-participants' behaviour at particular points in the conversation. A good example is a frown, which is popularly held to indicate a potential disagreement with what has just been said (or possibly done). Furthermore, there are several instances between participants of very marked similarities of postural and gestural change, both temporally, and in terms of the specific type of posture or gesture adopted. This accords with some aspects of non-vocal 'response-matching' reported by Argyle (1969), and more particularly with Scheflen's (1964) notion of 'postural congruence'. Such behaviour seems to realise two distinct interactive functions: its similarity between participants suggests solidarity in the sense employed by Brown and Gilman (1960), and in addition, it appears possible to use it to indicate agreement or challenge. Participants thus seem able to employ non-vocal means to demonstrate solidarity in opposing or assenting to what they have just heard. It is institutionalised as a show of hands when a vote is taken at a meeting. Such a possible agreement/challenge distinction in the non-vocal realm has interesting parallels in other areas of linguistics: Giles's (1971) work on accent convergence/divergence and Burton's (1978b) model for casual conversation being two of them. It seems too, that what appear to be non-vocal 'disagreements' are more likely to precede subsequent attempts to obtain speaking rights than is the case with apparent 'agreement' behaviour, though this is a very tentative observation. It does, however, accord loosely with Burton's (1978) notion of discourse framework, which is an enabling device for establishing exchange structure in drama texts.

The interpretation of this kind of non-vocal behaviour does entail recourse to intentionality, however, and it has no obvious and necessary outcomes in the subsequent communicative behaviour of co-conversationalists. It should not therefore be seen as realising discourse function, even though it is undoubtedly a very important component of non-vocal interaction.

It has been noted above (p. 161) that one reason for using phonological patterning as a base-line for the investigation of kinesics was that the rhythmicality of an utterance was sometimes accompanied by complementary rhythmicality in non-vocal behaviour. The very beginning of one video-recording gave an excellent example of such data, where speaker M, replying to speaker S's 'Have we started?' produces the following item, which, incidentally, seems to fit Burton's description of a 'challenging move':

//r+ you ALways get on the beGINning //p of EVery FILM //r+ saying THAT

At each asterisked (*) point in the transcript, she makes a right-hand finger-point with simultaneous up and down arm-movement, and this arm-movement coincides exactly with the articulation of the tonic syllable in the first two tone units.   Rhythmical behaviour of this kind is very common in many speech situations (thumping the table while speaking in committee meetings is another example), and one of its interactive functions seems to be emphatic.   Again, though, it does not seem to realise specifically discourse function, and so is excluded from further consideration here.   However, whilst rhythmicality itself is discounted, the fact that such apparently emphatic behaviour does seem to occur on tonic syllables is significant, and suggests that this is a useful place from which to commence the investigation of discourse kinesics.

Preliminary data-based observations

A first very obvious point is that participants have the choice of two possible roles: speaker and non-speaker, and a major concern here is to investigate how these roles are negotiated kinesically.   Kinesic behaviour however, by its very nature, enables one to communicate without speaking, and this has important implications for its systematic investigation.   The tidy linearity of vocal analysis cannot be taken fro granted, and unlike in the highly disciplined speech of academic seminars, where no contribution is ignored and participants speak one at a time (Rogers, 1972), the associated kinesic behaviour only becomes potentially discourse-functional if it involves mutuality at some point.   Negotiation of speaking rights is essentially co-operative in this data, so far as its kinesic manifestations are concerned.

Another associated difficulty is deciding precisely which aspects of non-vocal behaviour are significant as realisations of discourse functions, and which are not, even given the preliminary exclusions noted above.   In the case of seminars, the largest observable item is a person sitting on a chair drawn up at a table, and although one is not suggesting a rank scale of kinesic units here, it is none the less useful to think in terms of basic posture.   In some respects, posture is akin to Birdwhistell's notion of 'stance', and this primary bodily configuration itself provides a 'context of situation' for other gestural possibilities, such as movements of arm, hand, head and eyes.   There are various ways of propping a body in a seminar with a table in front of one: it is partly a question of physics - people sitting down have to do it without falling over.   Resting the elbows on the table, for instance, probably entails hands touching and/or chin touching when 'at rest', or when being attentive.   Nodding, for example, involves a modification of, or detachment from this basic triangulation.   A problem of timing is thus involved: gross bodily movements take longer to perform, and it seems probable that a desire or readiness to speak is 'telegraphed' in this way.   Some people tend to sit well back, with their hands in their laps, and there are many other possible variations.   It may be possible to infer things from this basic posture (e.g. tiredness, degree of involvement), but that is not the immediate concern here. What seems significant, and indicative of a discourse function realised kinesically, is a postural change, but even here, only sometimes perhaps: a person may have cramp, or a local itch. Even so, it does seem as though the point at which things are rectified tends to coincide with a perceived discourse boundary, or indicates a desire for one (e.g. change of speaker).

During a turn, a non-speaker may often quite suddenly change his posture and gaze intently at the speaker: this is thought to have something to do with his degree of engagement with the matter just articulated, and it may be a very early-realised component of a discourse function, namely a desire to speak, or a turn-claim. Following Kendon and Ferber (1973) one might expect such a turn-claim to have several distinct 'phases', that is, for its kinesic realisation to be assembled over time, starting with an early gross bodily movement if necessary, possibly with associated gestures such as raised arm or even vocalisation (e.g. 'bid' in classroom discourse), all of which service the achievement of mutuality of gaze, which in turn culminates with eye-contact with existing speaker, and hence possible speaker change. 'Catching the Speaker's eye' is an important parliamentary tactic, and small children who wish to claim the gaze of adults in order to speak to them, quite frequently pull their garments: in large gatherings, an adult will sometimes touch another on the shoulder for the same purpose – but usually here only if other early kinesic components of a turn-claim are not possible owing to the prevailing circumstances.

Quite apart from the possible contributions to discourse function of overall postural change, the basic posture itself also influences the realisation of other discoursally important gestures. The way a speaker uses his arms and hands, for instance, seems to be affected by their role in overall body posture. For example, one participant rests her elbows on the table most of the time while speaking, and her arm/hand gestures are therefore rather minimal, because constrained by her elbows; none the less they are still very significant.

In terms of basic posture in relation to speaker role, it seems that the primary gestures associated with a 'speaking turn' (where 'turn' is a very elastic notion, similar to 'sentence' in grammar) are:

(a) a movement of body posture towards a mid-upright position, with head fairly raised at the start, oriented towards previous speaker;

(b) some movement of the dominant hand at some stage, either immediately prior to, or fairly soon after the start of the 'turn'.

(c) If the 'turn' is of some length, and becomes positively expository in nature, rather than being an extended reaction, there is a tendency to the formation of a 'box' with both hands (possibly associated with neutralisation of gaze, or loss of eye contact). It also seems a fairly strong rule that dominant hand gestures precede both-hands 'box' in any turn. Towards the end of a natural turn (i.e. one that is not interrupted), the 'box', if there is one, tends to disappear, and hands move towards an 'at rest' position.

(d) Associated with (a) above is the intake of breath, either before phonation, or very soon afterwards.

A number of caveats and further observations are needed, however. Firstly, everything can be over-ridden by basic posture. A person already holding a mid-upright raised head posture may not alter it perceptibly, although there may still be an increase in non-vocal muscular tension immediately before and during a speaking turn, even though this is not always directly observable. Basic posture may initially inhibit hand and forearm movement – sitting on one's hands is an extreme example of this. Whether a person is right-handed or not seems important, and whether one hand is involved in another activity: one participant for instance, holds his spectacles in his left hand while speaking, and this seems to inhibit 'box-formation', as does his general posture. The establishment of an accurate point of time for referring gross body movements of this kind to other levels of language was found to be a difficulty at this stage, and it was complicated by the kinds of postural inhibitions mentioned above.

Turning now to gaze and eye-contact, one is in much faster-operating kinesic territory. The limitations of the early video-recordings precluded uniformly consistent observations, but an attempt was made to encode directionality of gaze wherever possible, and it was found that a typical speaker tends to start his turn subsequent to mutuality of gaze with the previous speaker. After this he seems to look away, then 'panning' his gaze around the group, fixing briefly on individual members, and occasionally looking downwards, or gazing into space in what seems to be an unfocused way.

It is believed that a further discourse function – which might perhaps be termed feedback request – is realised by frequent in-turn redirection of gaze, and it may be that such behaviour is characteristic of democratic discussion. It may also relate to a desired mandate for continued speaking rights: if eye-contact is establishing with a speaker, then speaker-change may occur. If the speaker offers eye-contact, and it is taken up, but the other party does not produce a 'syntactic contribution' (in Richardson's (1978) sense), then the original speaker feels permitted to continue. In fact, if eye-contact is established by a speaker in this way, then it does elicit some kind of minimal 'engage' or response (e.g. a 'non-syntactic' 'mm', or a nod) more often than not. Precisely who, at any point in a turn, is the recipient of gaze may also be related to the speaker's ideas about the gazee's status, or his authority in respect to the speaker's content, or both. It was also found that speech directed at one member in particular is characterised by more constant direction of gaze. A speaker will then only seek confirmation from other group members with very rapid eye-movement, perhaps only involving peripheral vision. This kind of fixed gaze-direction seems associated with some kind of 'challenging' behaviour (which also involves a higher degree of concentration and muscular tension, and is characteristic of other animals too). In addition, a person who does not direct his gaze to others, by definition cannot establish eye-contact, and this seems to be a major factor in retaining his speaking turn.   Other factors are important too of course, like aspects of clause-relatedness, lexical and grammatical cohesion, and various kinds of intonational choice.   It seems, however, as though all of these can potentially be over-ridden by kinesic factors such as directionality of gaze and eye-contact, though this would be very unusual in seminars.   It can happen in classrooms: being 'silenced with a glance' is not infrequent, as every pupil knows.

Much more typical in the data however, was a general tendency on the part of speakers towards the ends of turns either to attempt eye-nomination of one person, or more than one - in which latter case it is thought that speaking rights are felt by the speaker to be more open than in the former.

In addition however, attempts at eye-nomination may go on until a potential next speaker is found, and this by definition, will occur last in the series, so far as existing speaker is concerned.   (He may be mistaken about this though, and it can have interesting kinesic implications - to be considered later.)   There is support for this view in classroom discourse, where there is a 'push-down mecha-nism, whereby an apparent <u>elicit</u> is recoded as a <u>starter</u> if it is followed by an immediately subsequent elicit.   It is the last item in a series which has functional significance for the exchange, and there seems to be an analogy here with eye-nomination, though it is less rigorously enforceable, particularly in democratic discussion.

Further data-analysis

The preliminary investigation was useful in showing the kind of material needed to facilitate further progress in discourse kinesics. A recording was made involving four students and their tutor, in which all visual data was retrieved using three cameras (see figure 8.1).*

A description of the tone units was undertaken according to the model developed by Brazil (1975, 1978a), which was then used as the basis for a description of what, following the previous discus-sion, appeared to be discoursally relevant kinesic behaviour for each participant.   Initial emphasis was placed on the tonic syllable of each tone unit as a provisional focus of attention.   It was very quickly discovered that, in those cases where they need to, hearers begin to orient themselves kinesically to the speaker at the <u>imme-diate onset</u> of the latter's first one unit, rather than waiting until the tonic syllable, and accordingly, such movement was coded where it occurred, as well as the behaviour at the moment of tonic syllable utterance.   The temporal occurrence of such activity means, of course, that most of the time hearers are looking at a new speaker

---

* For further details, see Gosling, J.N. (1981), 'Discourse Kine-sics', English Language Research Monographs, no. (X), University of Birmingham.

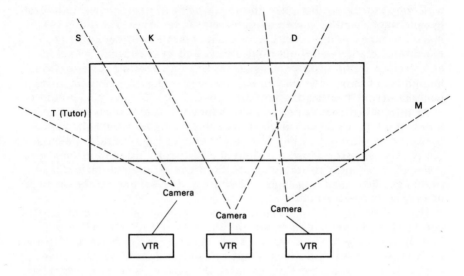

Figure 8.1

by the time he utters the first tonic syllable, unless it is the initial item in the tone unit, which is a fairly rare feature of the first tone unit in a turn which is part of the main discourse. It also suggests that, associated with the speech-onset of a new speaker, there is a kinesic structure apparent in hearers, which involves physical orientation to the speaker, in order to service direction of gaze to him and which is usually completed by the time the first tonic syllable is uttered. From the new speaker's point of view, he will already have sought to realise turn-claim by mutuality of gaze (and by inference, eye-contact) with the previous speaker, and it is hypothesised here that he will look away if necessary (for subsequent verbal planning purposes) only when he has perceived at least one of his hearers (preferably previous speaker) orient his gaze in his direction and achieved eye-contact with him. This will usually have been done by the time the first tonic syllable has been uttered. It is often a very fast process indeed, and requires very detailed analysis to illustrate it.

A further hypothesis is that a person deemed by participants to have preferential speaking rights – a tutor, for instance – may not conform as rigorously to this model, or be expected to by the others (though perhaps he should, so far as lies in his power, for optimally efficient interaction in terms of learning). This highlights an interesting point about tutor-student behaviour, in that, kinesically at any rate, it cannot be controlled by one person, since much of it is systematic in a mutual sense. This means that, with the best will in the world, a tutor cannot behave democratically if his students refuse to allow him to do so: he can provide opportunities for student-student interaction, by orienting his gaze appropriately, but he cannot actualise it by his own exclusive efforts.

Further support for the view that a speaker needs a kinesic

warrant from at least one of his hearers before he can look away, assured that he 'has the floor' and can therefore continue, is provided by several points in the data where two participants are speaking at once, both orienting their discourse primarily to T, and it does seem that he is able to legislate between them by gazing at one and not the other. When this happens, it is the recipient of continued gaze from T who maintains the turn.

At this point it is useful to return to a few more theoretical considerations involving some preliminary ideas about the relationship between kinesics and other levels of language. Starting with the 'wave-theory' of Condon and Ogston (1966, 1967), who suggest that there may be large kinesic 'ripples' with smaller, faster-moving ones inside them, it is tempting to think in terms of some kind of hierarchy of kinesic units for discourse. However, it is difficult to see how closely analogous it would be to, say, a rank-scale of grammatical units. One must be careful not to confuse anatomical (or even neurological) ordering of things with an abstract scale of communicatively functional units. There may not be a direct connection, but none the less there does seem to be some relationship derivable from the work of various researchers (especially Kendon), particularly in the case of changes of gaze, which do quite consistently seem to 'telegraph' a possible next speaker.

The problem may be somewhat overcome by positing a hierarchy of kinesic units, partly anatomically derived, but which combine in structural patterns over time in each individual as detailed above. These observable structures may then be seen as potentially available to serve as the necessary realisations in at least two individuals, which may then service kinesic states, which in their turn realise discourse function. It is these mutuality states, observed through their structural realisations in terms of kinesic rank-order, which may fit into a model of discourse of the kind recently developed mainly by various Birmingham ELR members, and which includes items like transactions, exchanges, moves and acts, with their accompanying intonational, grammatical and cohesive patterns.

One example of such a kinesic state has been provisionally termed a facing-formation state (ffs), following Kendon (1974) to some extent, but in relation to mutually-operating kinesic structures up to and including posture. A facing-formation state here is seen as a necessary precondition for speaking. Unlike in Kendon's use of a similar term, its major feature is mutuality of gaze, and very probably eye-contact, though this cannot be retrieved. It is of extremely brief duration, and once mutuality of gaze (and eye-contact) have been achieved, the state is immediately broken. It may of course be followed (and almost always is) by a further ffs towards the end of a turn (or move in exchange-structure terms), where mutuality of gaze is again sought and established between speaker and other participant in order to negotiate next speaker. Sometimes, more than one participant can produce facing-formation states with the speaker, in a linear sequence, obviously, and here it seems as though the last one has more speaking rights. If this is unobserved by a previous ffs participant, confusion can result, and does.

Legislation by gaze from previous speaker (or T), as described
above, is then invoked to help matters proceed.   During the course
of a speaking turn, other participants sometimes also create ffs
dyads, often with accompanying minimum-engage vocal items, and
this may have an effect on who speaks subsequently, but how exactly
this may operate has yet to be worked out.

Participants often seem to monitor the unfolding auditory and
visual channels, and if at any point they agree with what is being
said, or the way the interaction is going (whether in form or content,
or both), they 'stand down' their kinesics.   Otherwise, they maintain - or go into - a 'potential next speaker' mode in terms of their
own kinesic structure, with gaze on speaker, thus being ready to
fulfil their part of an ffs for instance, should it occur through matching speaker behaviour.

Sometimes, an ffs needs further kinesic support, or 'repair', if,
for some reason, things go wrong.   An example may be worth including here.   The participants are talking about assessment procedures, and a partial intonational transcript (ignoring key choice) is
as follows:

```
          "K      //p that's IT you see //*p afFORD to enJOY //
          *M     // i ... //
          D//p YEAH well //
          K (in-drawn breath/laugh)
simul-   ⌈M      // i do ... //
taneous  ⌊T      //p i mean in SOME ways //p . YEAH *
onset            (inaudible)//
          *M     //r sorry i was gonna say i don't KNOW//p cos i
                 was a bit WORried //r about the exAM //"
```

At the beginning of this extract, T is orienting his gaze to D and K
(who are sitting next to each other) sets up an ffs with D and becomes
next speaker.   But he has also heard M's attempted contribution,
and as tutor he has conflicting obligations to content on the one hand
and to interactional democracy on the other.   Just after ' ... SOME
ways//' - which interestingly is the end of the first tone unit, and
the place at which in an extended contribution he might be expected
to look away and do some verbal planning, having secured the floor
- he looks at M and establishes ffs with her.   Because however he
has started a move in an ongoing discourse unit of some kind, he
uses the vocal channel 'says 'YEAH' to M) AND lifts his right arm,
which is already extended on the table, with hand holding pen, and
does a right-arm-plus-pen point to M.   That is, he feels the need
here to reinforce his gaze and floor-conceding 'YEAH' by a hand-arm
gesture in addition.   M, for her part, in commencing a new discourse item, feels obliged to apologise for what has become a kind of
interruption (and an interruption of T at that!) by starting her contribution with a very rapidly delivered mitigatory 'sorry i was gonna
say ...'.   At this place in the speech-event, all the participants
seem heavily involved in the matter being discussed, and for this
reason are perhaps not attending as fully to the visually functional
aspects of the interaction as they were, say, at the beginning.   The
example does however illustrate very clearly the functional employ-

ment of at least one gesture involving arm-hand movement.   It is
used, together with vocalisation here, to reinforce the ffs, and all
three items serve to realise a successful turn-claim, resulting in M
as next speaker.

To summarise, it has been shown that at least two discourse functions, namely successful turn-claim and in-turn feedback request,
are realised by elements of kinesic structure which operate through
simultaneous co-production in two participants, resulting in mutuality
of gaze and eye-contact, producing subsequent vocalisation – or non-
vocal surrogate (e.g. nod in the case of feedback-request).   This
intrinsic mutuality seems to be an essential difference between
kinesic realisations of discourse functions and their realisations in
other levels of form.   Furthermore, there is considerable relationship across levels in the production of discourse: it has already
been shown that participants often produce a very quick kinesic
reaction to speech-onset, and minimal engage items such as nods are
frequently kinesic responses to exclusively auditory inputs.   That
is, it is possible to have a vocal-kinesic relationship in terms of the
realisation of discourse function.   K, for instance, is the least
kinesically operative member of the group, and nods frequently while
looking downwards, responding kinesically to an exclusively vocal
input.

So far as the relationship of kinesic behaviour with other discourse units is concerned, at this stage one can only be somewhat
speculative, for two main sets of reasons.   Firstly, much more
needs to be done in the investigation of discourse kinesics itself,
and secondly, it seems that, using audio data alone, even an approxi-
mate model for multi-party discourse has yet to be worked out, if
indeed it is possible, using existing approaches.   An early attempt
by Stubbs (1973) to describe industrial negotiations, using a variant
of the formal classroom model, met with great difficulties in establishing unambiguous exchange boundaries, and McKnight's (1976)
work on a group therapy meeting encountered similar problems.
Subsequent work in discourse has tended to concentrate exclusively
on two-party interaction.

It is probable, therefore, that whilst a discourse model for multi-
party conversations will contain items like transactions, exchanges
and moves, their exact and unambiguous definition will involve the
importation of desiderata from the levels of intonation and kinesics.
A consideration of intonation has already enabled a better account of
exchange structure to be made, and it may not be too early to begin
a similar effort to integrate what has already been learned about
kinesic behaviour into an enlarged model of discourse.

Towards a discourse-functional kinesic model

Given that discourse functions are seen as realised through various
formal levels, a first priority must be to establish how kinesics fits
into the existing framework.   It has already been argued that
kinesics may be regarded as a formal level in its own right, and that

discourse function is a major component of a larger general level, called interactive function, which, whatever its other functional components, must also realise them through the four formal levels of grammar, lexis, intonation and kinesics.

If kinesics is a level of form, it must exhibit meaning-bearing patterns, in a somewhat similar way to grammar, perhaps, either meaningful gestures, or meaningful sequences or combinations, of gestures. It seems a useful approach to regard non-vocal communicative behaviour as somewhat analogous to sound, and to see gestures, initially, as kinetic substance. One would then wish to discover significant configurations of kinetic substance which are identifiably patterned at the formal kinesic level, and which thus realise various interactive, and particularly discoursal, functions.

To demonstrate such kinesic patterning, it is necessary to 'shunt' backwards and forwards through the data, using as clues function-realising patterns at other levels. It has already been established that discourse functions can be realised by any (or all) of the three existing levels of grammar, lexis and intonation, and this can be used to obtain a purchase on kinesic patterning. For instance, these three levels can independently, but usually simultaneously, realise 'end of turn', and the evidence strongly suggests that kinesics plays an additional and vital role in this process, particularly in multi-party interaction. Diagrammatically, the argument so far can be put as follows (figure 8.2):

SUBSTANCE   FORM   INTERACTIVE FUNCTION
                                             |
                                       DISCOURSE FUNCTION

                      ⎧ grammar ⎫   ⎧ discourse structure choices
phonetic ———— ⎨ lexis   ⎬   ⎜ (acts, etc.)
                      ⎩ intonation ⎭   ⎨ information structure choices
kinetic ———————— kinesics ⎭   ⎜ (given/new, etc.)
                                       ⎜ turn-taking, feedback-request
                                       ⎩ choices and information, etc.

Figure 8.2

Other aspects of interactive function, apart from discourse function, have been omitted from the diagram, as they have yet to be systematised, but they might well include indexical information about speakers' affective states, realised by choices from kinesic systems yielding items like smiles, frowns, and so on. In addition, however, intonational, lexical and grammatical choices would also be involved.

Traditionally, a formal level has been seen as internally organised without reference to other formal levels, and this still holds. None the less, in terms of realisation of function, one would expect cross-cutting between levels to occur, particularly if it is expected that the model for discourse should eventually take full account of the interpersonal, ideational, and textual macro-functions of language (Halliday, 1973; Burton, 1978b). In these terms, quite a lot, but by no means all, of the 'interpersonal' macro-function in face-to-face interaction seems to be carried kinesically. At any event, so far as existing discourse function is concerned, it is clear that there is at least one class of act (namely the acknowledge - and possibly the accept too) which may be realised either vocally or kinesically. The non-vocal surrogate nod is useful as a minimal-engage item, because it can realise feedback-request without intrusion into the ongoing speech, and the same general point can be made about other kinesic behaviour, whose realisations of discourse function are however somewhat more complex.

It has been suggested that discourse functional kinesic realisations are produced from significant gestures which, to be operative, must contain an element of mutuality at some point, such as eye-contact. It is further argued that such mutuality is a state of affairs achieved by a progressive build-up from grosser to finer body movement over time, and that it is an essential precondition for several discourse functions, which may be realised either kinesically or vocally, or both. (The distinction becomes hard to maintain at progressively finer degrees of delicacy for reasons discussed above.) Such an enabling state of affairs has been called a facing-formation state (ffs). The following is an instanced example of an exclusively kinesic transaction in a seminar:

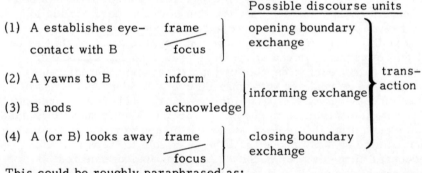

Possible discourse units

(1) A establishes eye-contact with B — frame / focus — opening boundary exchange

(2) A yawns to B — inform — informing exchange

(3) B nods — acknowledge — informing exchange

(4) A (or B) looks away — frame / focus — closing boundary exchange

trans-action

This could be roughly paraphrased as:
    A: I say, B.
    B: Yes, A.
    A: What a boring speaker this is.
    B: I agree.
    A: (or B) That's all.

A major interface of kinesic and vocal realisation is in the negotiation of speaker-change, or turn-taking, and the term turn-claim has been coined to describe discourse function in this area, realised, in the main, by kinesic behaviour. It seems to be a two-stage operation, culminating in ffs. The final stage is thus always eye-contact, but the first stage differs, depending on the situation. The first, or preliminary, stage, is orientational in function (Sinclair and Coulthard, 1975): that is, it has a 'telegraphing' or attention-getting job to do, and hence the kinesic behaviour associated with it is likely to be fairly gross, and will be grosser the larger the gathering and the further the participants are from each other. Thus, already-facing dyads telegraph by mutuality of gaze, then achieve eye-contact, followed by speaker-change. Members of small groups, on the other hand, may need to seek eye-contact by shifts in posture, more obviously intent gaze, and even audible intake of breath, 'ers' and other vocalisations. In still larger groups, such as school classes, pupils 'telegraph' by bid:

> realised by a closed class of verbal and non-verbal items - 'Sir', 'Miss', teacher's name, raised hand, heavy breathing, finger-clicking. Its function is to signal a desire to contribute to the discourse (Sinclair and Coulthard, 1975).

Here, one would wish to modify the functional description, and say that such behaviour is intended to produce eye-contact (i.e. it is part of achievement of ffs), as a precondition for speaker-change. In addition, one can also assert that the use of the term 'eye-nomination' is another way of talking about the achievement of ffs between teacher and pupil.

The timing of such kinesic realisations is of course to a great extent dependent on participants' interpretation of inputs at other formal levels as indications of potential points of completion, and non-attendance to these inputs usually results in non-achievement of ffs. If ffs is not achieved and/or, in terms of other levels, a point of completion has not been reached, but new-speaker vocalisation takes place none the less, the result is an interruption.

From the speaker's point of view, the co-production of ffs may be all that is required to end a turn and produce change of speaker. However, the model is capable of sophistication in that the same function can be realised with more intensity by additional forms of kinesic behaviour on the part of the speaker. (There is an analogy here with intonation, in the use of p+ tone, to signify more fully the status of information as new, so far as the speaker is concerned.) Thus, in the example above (p. 178), T is able to 'repair' M's unsuccessful turn-claim by recourse to intensified kinesic realisations, involving not only ffs but also arm and hand movement and accompanying vocalisation('p YEAH'). This example suggests that in kinesics, for any given discourse function, there is a series of possible realisations of differing degrees of intensity. It could also be said that here, T, in relinquishing his part in a new exchange in favour of M, is putting the interpersonal before the ideational and textual macro-functions, at least from his point of view.

Despite these remarks, much of what is involved in orienting one-self kinesically to the other remains problematic: facial expression, for instance, has not been dealt with except tentatively, in relation to indexical factors. It can be argued with some point, however, that a great deal of body movement generally is done simply to service gaze and eye-contact. One cannot establish eye-contact without gazing in the direction of the other, and this in turn may not be possible without head-movement and perhaps general postural change too. It is also true, however, that one's angles of vision are very wide indeed - even without including the possible role of peripheral vision. None the less, since kinesic orientation does seem very important in turn-taking, it could be that this may be 'over-built', containing considerable redundancy, especially in relation to points of potential speaker-change, in order to produce easily perceived and unambiguous kinesic signals to co-participants.

Looking more broadly at the overall shape of speech events, it seems that starting entails a crucial kinesic component. As every teacher knows, the effect of a well-performed framing element is to produce all-pupils gaze on T. In many classrooms this is formally held to be a requirement for doing starting, and it may be verbally explicit. ('All eyes on me!') In the seminar data under consideration, a general paradigm seems to involve T looking at participants, judging a moment as appropriate, perhaps having obtained some ffs, and then starting to speak. At this point however, he must obtain a p-gaze mandate for proceeding further, and certianly before producing a discoursally functional elicit. Elicits without ffs need to be recoded as initiations or glosses of some kind. A responding move, likewise, requires an ffs for its successful achievement.

So far as the role of kinesics in the delimitation of transactions is concerned, much detailed work still remains to be done. However, there does seem to be something of a kinesically observable relationship to discourse topic, and to the use by participants (particularly T in this material) of metadiscoursal terms like 'point', or 'thing' or 'question', to indicate some kind of conceptual unit in the discourse. It seems as though a typical cycle of elements is apparent, in which a series of exchanges occur, often, but not always, originally initiated by T, until a silence of some length ensues. At such places, participants tend to be using ∅-gaze, either looking downwards, or outwards in an up-participant-focused way. It seems a good general rule that under these conditions, T initiates verbally without prior ffs, but obtains it very quickly after vocal onset, in exactly the same way as when doing starting, and this could well indicate a transaction boundary.

In conclusion, it does seem fair to say that the work done so far in the area of discourse-functional kinesics, although it is comparatively little, nevertheless does seem to hold extremely promising implications for the clarification of important aspects of multi-party speech-events which have eluded systematic description for some years.

References

Abercrombie, D. (1968), Paralanguage, 'British Journal of Dis-
orders of Communication', vol. 3.
Argyle, M. (1969), 'Social Interaction', London, Methuen.
Argyle, M. and Dean, J. (1965), Eye contact, distance and affilia-
tion, 'Sociometry', 28, 289-304.
Austin, J.L. (1962), 'How to do things with words', Oxford,
Clarendon.
Barnes, D. (1969), Language in the secondary classroom, in:
D. Barnes, J. Britton ahd H. Rosen, 'Language, the Learner and
the School', Harmondsworth, Penguin.
Bellack, A.A., Kliebard, H.M., Hyman, R.T. and Smith, F.L.
(1966), 'The Language of the Classroom', New York, Teacher's
College Press.
Berry, M. (1977), 'An Introduction to Systemic Linguistics 2:
Levels and Links', London, Batsford.
Berry, M. (1980a), 'Layers of Exchange Structure', Discourse
Analysis Monographs, no. 7, University of Birmingham, English
Language Research.
Berry, M. (1980b), A note on Coulthard and Brazil's classes of
move, unpublished typescript.
Birdwhistell, R. (1970), 'Kinesics and Context: Essays on Body
Motion and Communication', Philadelphia, University of Pennsylvania
Press.
Bolinger, D.L. (1965), The atomisation of meaning, 'Language', 41,
555-73.
Brazil, D.C. (1973), Intonation, Working Papers in Discourse
Analysis, no. 2, mimeo, English Language Research, University of
Birmingham.
Brazil, D.C. (1975), 'Discourse Intonation', Discourse Analysis
Monographs, no. 1, University of Birmingham, English Language
Research.
Brazil, D.C. (1978a), 'Discourse Intonation II', Discourse Analy-
sis Monographs, no. 2, University of Birmingham, English
Language Research.
Brazil, D.C. (1978b), Discourse Intonation, unpublished PhD
thesis, University of Birmingham.

Brazil, D.C., Coulthard, R.M. and Johns, C.M. (1980), 'Discourse Intonation and Language Teaching', London, Longman.

Brown, R. and Gilman, A. (1960), The pronouns of power and solidarity, in: Sebeok, T.A. (ed.), 'Style in Language', Cambridge, Mass., MIT Press.

Burton, D. (1978a), Dialogue and conversation: a study of discourse analysis and modern drama dialogue, unpublished PhD thesis, University of Birmingham.

Burton, D. (1978b), Towards an analysis of casual conversation, 'Nottingham Linguistic Circular', 17, 2, 131-59.

Burton, D. (1980), 'Dialogue and Discourse: a sociolinguistic approach to modern drama dialogue and naturally-occurring conversation', London, Routledge & Kegan Paul.

Condon, W.S. and Ogston, W.D. (1966), Soundfilm analysis of normal and pathological behaviour patterns, 'Journal of Nervous and Mental Disorders', 143, 338-47.

Condon, W.S. and Ogston, W.D. (1967), A segmentation of behaviour, 'Journal of Psychiatric Research', 5, 221-35.

Coulthard, R.M. (1977), 'An Introduction to Discourse Analysis', London, Longman.

Coulthard, R.M. and Brazil, D.C. (1976), Aspects of discourse structure: a progress report, unpublished MS., University of Nancy.

Coulthard, R.M. and Brazil, D.C. (1979), 'Exchange Structure', Discourse Analysis Monographs, no. 5, University of Birmingham, English Language Research.

Coulthard, R.M. and Montgomery, M. (1976), KAAU ESP research project: the structure of lectures, final report, mimeo, University of Birmingham.

Ekman, P. and Friesen, W.V. (1972), Hand movements, 'Journal of Communication', 22, 353-74.

Evans, T.P. (1970), Flander's system of interaction analysis and science teacher effectiveness, paper presented to the 43rd annual meeting of the Association for Research in Science Teaching, Minneapolis.

Farb, P. (1973), 'Word Play', London, Jonathan Cape.

Flanders, N.A. (1965), 'Teacher Influence, Pupil Attitudes and Achievement', Co-operative Research Monographs, no. 12, US Office of Education, US Government Printing Office.

Flanders, N.A. (1970), 'Analysing Teaching Behaviour', Reading, Mass., Addison-Wesley.

Forsyth, I.J. (1971), Six studies on the language of the classroom, mimeo, English Language Research, University of Birmingham.

Galloway, C. (1968), Nonverbal communication, 'Theory into Practice', 7.

Giles, H. (1971), Our reactions to accent, 'New Society', 14 October.

Glaser, B.G. and Strauss, A.L. (1967), 'The Discovery of Grounded Theory', Chicago, Aldine.

Goffman, E. (1963), 'Behaviour in Public Places', New York, Free Press.

Goffman, E. (1964), The neglected situation, 'American Anthropologist', 66, 6, part 2, 133-6.

Goffman, E. (1971), 'Relations in Public: Microstudies of the Public Order', New York, Basic Books (reprinted Harmondsworth, Penguin).

Gosling, J.N. (1977), Some problems in discourse analysis: a working paper, 'MALS Journal', New Series, 2, 25-58.

Grice, H.P. (1975), Logic and conversation, in Cole, P. and Morgan, J.L. (eds), 'Syntax and Semantics III: Speech Acts', New York, Academic Press.

Halliday, M.A.K. (1961), Categories of the theory of grammar, 'Word', 17, 241-92.

Halliday, M.A.K. (1967), 'Intonation and Grammar in British English', The Hague, Mouton.

Halliday, M.A.K. (1970), Language structure and language function, in J. Lyons (ed.), 'New Horizons in Linguistics', Harmondsworth, Penguin.

Halliday, M.A.K. (1971), Linguistic function and literary style, in: 'Explorations in the Functions of Language', London, Edward Arnold, 103-38.

Halliday, M.A.K. (1973), 'Explorations in the Functions of Language', London, Arnold.

Halliday, M.A.K. (1976), The place of 'functional sentence perspective' in the system of linguistic description, in G. Kress (ed.), 'Halliday: System and Function in Language', London, Oxford University Press.

Halliday, M.A.K. and Hasan, R. (1976), 'Cohesion in English', London, Longman.

Hoey, M. (1979), 'Signalling in Discourse', Discourse Analysis Monographs, no. 6, University of Birmingham, English Language Research.

Hoey, M. (1981), 'On the Surface of Discourse', London, Allen & Unwin.

Hymes, D. (1971), 'On Communicative Competence', Philadelphia, Pennsylvania University Press.

Hymes, D. (1972), Models of the interaction of language and social life, in J.J. Gumperz and D. Hymes (eds), 'Directions in Sociolinguistics', New York, Holt, Reinhart & Winston, 269-85.

Jefferson, G. (1972), Side sequences, in D. Sudnow (ed.), 'Studies in Social Interaction', New York, Academic Press.

Jefferson, G. and Schenkein, J. (1978), Some sequential negotiations in conversation: unexpanded and expanded versions of projected action sequences, in J. Schenkein (ed.), 'Studies in the Organisation of Conversational Interaction', New York, Academic Press, 155-72.

Keenan, E.O. and Schieffelin, B. (1976), Topic as a discourse notion: a study of topic in the conversation of children and adults, in C. Li (ed.), 'Subject and Topic', New York, Academic Press.

Kendon, A. (1967), Some functions of gaze-direction in social interaction, 'Acta Psychologica', 26, 22-63.

Kendon, A. (1972a), Review of Birdwhistell's 'Kinesics and Context', 'American Journal of Psychology', 1972, 441-55.

Kendon, A. (1972b), Some relationships between body motion and speech – an analysis of an example, in A. Seigman and B. Pope (eds), 'Studies in Dyadic Communication', New York, Pergamon, 177–210.

Kendon, A. (1974), The facing formation system: spatial organisation in social encounters, mimeo, Australian National University, Canberra.

Kendon, A. and Ferber, A. (1973), A description of some human greetings, in P. Michael and J.H. Crooks (eds), 'Comparative Ecology and the Behaviour of Primates', London, Academic Press.

Kuhn, T. (1970), 'The Structure of Scientific Revolutions', 2nd edition, Chicago, University of Chicago Press.

Labov, W, (1970), The study of language in its social context, 'Studium Generale', 23, 66–84.

Labov, W. (1972a),.The study of language in its social context, revised version, in W. Labov, 'Sociolinguistic Patterns', Philadelphia, Pennsylvania University Press.

Labov, W. (1972b), Rules for ritual insults, in D. Sudnow (ed.), 'Studies in Social Interaction', New York, Free Press, 120–69.

Labov, W. and Fanshel, D. (1977), 'Therapeutic Discourse', New York, Academic Press.

Lakoff, R. (1972), Language in context, 'Language', 48, 4, 907–27.

Laver, J. (1970), The production of speech, in J. Lyons (ed.), 'New Horizons in Linguistics', Harmondsworth, Penguin.

Laver, J. and Hutcheson, S. (eds) (1972), 'Communication in Face-to-Face Interaction', Harmondsworth, Penguin.

Leech, G.N. (1969), 'A Linguistic Guide to English Poetry', London, Longman.

Lenneberg, E. (1968), The importance of temporal factors in behaviour: a discussion of a paper by Condon and Ogston, presented to the Conference on Speech Perception, Pittsburgh.

Lott, D.F. and Sommer, R. (1967), Seating arrangements and status, 'Journal of Personality and Social Psychology', 7, 90–5.

McKnight, K. (1976), Large group conversation: problems for discourse analysis, unpublished MA dissertation, University of Lancaster.

McTear, M. (1977), Starting to talk; how preschool children initiate conversational exchanges, unpublished mimeo, School of Communication Studies, Northern Ireland Polytechnic.

McTear, M.F. (1979), Review of Labov and Fanshel, 'Therapeutic Discourse', 'Nottingham Linguistic Circular', 8, 1.

Montgomery, M. (1977), The structure of lectures, unpublished MA thesis, University of Birmingham.

O'Connor, J.D. and Arnold, G.F. (1961), 'Intonation of Colloquial English', London, Longman.

Pfungst, O. (1911, 1965), 'Clever Hans', London and New York: Holt, Rinehart & Winston.

Richardson, K. (1978), Worthing Teachers' Centre, a case study in discourse analysis, unpublished MA thesis, University of Birmingham.

Riley, P. (1975), A model for the integration of kinesics in discourse analysis, Nancy, C.R.A.P.E.L.

Rogers, S. (1972), Language and the seminar, 'University of East Anglia Bulletin', 47-52.

Sacks, H. (1967-72), Unpublished lectures, University of California.

Sacks, H. (1972), On the analysability of children's stories, in J.J. Gumperz and D. Hymes (eds), 'Directions in Sociolinguistics: the Ethnography of Communication', New York, Holt Rinehart & Winston, 329-45.

Sacks, H. (ms), Aspects of The Sequential Organisation of Conversation.

Sacks, H., Schegloff, E.A. and Jefferson, G. (1974), A simplest systematics for the organisation of turn-taking in conversation, 'Language', 50, 4, 596-735.

Sapir, E. (1927), The unconscious patterning of behaviour in society, in D.G. Mandelbaum (ed.) (1949), 'Selected Writings of Edward Sapir in Language, Culture and Personality', University of California Press.

Scheflen, A.E. (1964), The significance of posture in communicational systems, 'Psychiatry', 27, 316-21.

Schegloff, E.A. (1968), Sequencing in conversational openings, 'American Anthropologist', 70, 1075-95.

Schegloff, E.A. (1972), Notes on a conversational practice: formulating place, in D. Sudrow (ed.), 'Studies in Social Interaction', New York, Free Press, 75-119.

Schegloff, E.A. and Sacks, H. (1973), Opening up closings, 'Semiotica', 8, 289-327.

Searle, J.R. (1969), 'Speech Acts', Cambridge, Cambridge University Press.

Sinclair, J. McH. (1966), Taking a poem to pieces, in R. Fowler (ed.), 'Essays on Style and Language', London, Routledge & Kegan Paul, 68-81.

Sinclair, J. McH. (1972), 'A Course in Spoken English: Grammar', London, Oxford University Press.

Sinclair, J. McH. (1973), Linguistics in Colleges of Education, 'Dudley Journal of Education', 17-25.

Sinclair, J. McH. (1977), A note on turn-taking, unpublished paper, University of Birmingham, English Language Research.

Sinclair, J. McH. and Coulthard, R.M. (1975), 'Towards an Analysis of Discourse', London, Oxford University Press.

Sinclair, J. McH., Forsyth, I.J., Coulthard, R.M. and Ashby, M.C. (1972), The English used by teachers and pupils, final report to SSRC, mimeo, University of Birmingham.

Smith, Neil and Wilson, Deirdre (1979), 'Modern Linguistics, The Results of Chomsky's Revolution', Harmondsworth, Penguin.

Stubbs, M. (1973), Some structural complexities of talk in meetings, Working Papers in Discourse Analysis, no, 5, University of Birmingham, English Language Research.

Stubbs, M. (1974), The discourse structure of informal committee talk, unpublished ms., University of Birmingham.

Stubbs, M. (1979), Review of Coulthard and Brazil, 'Exchange Structure', 'Nottingham Linguistic Circular', 8, 2.

Stubbs, M. (forthcoming), 'Discourse Analysis', London, Blackwells.

Stubbs, M. and Robinson, B. (1979), Analysing classroom language, in: M. Stubbs et al., 'Observing Classroom Language', PE 232, Language Development, Milton Keynes, Open University Press.

Turner, R. (1970), Words, Utterances and Activities, in J. Douglas (ed.), 'Understanding Everyday Life', New York, Aldine, 165-87.

Turner, R. (1972), Some formal properties of therapy talk, in D. Sudnow (ed.), 'Studies in Social Interaction', New York, Free Press, 367-96.

van Dijk, T.A. (1972), 'Some Aspects of Text Grammars', The Hague, Mouton.

Walker, R. (1971), unpublished MPhil thesis, University of London.

Widdowson, H.G. (1977), Approaches to discourse, in H.G. Widdowson, 'Explorations in Applied Linguistics', London, Oxford University Press, 1979.

Winter, E.O. (1977), A clause-relational approach to English texts: a study of some predictive lexical items in written discourse, special issue, 'Instructional Science', 6, 1.

Bibliography

The following bibliography lists work on discourse analysis written by members or associates of the English Language Research Group, University of Birmingham.

1972
* Coulthard, R.M., Sinclair, J.McH., Forsyth, I.J., Discourse in the classroom, mimeo London: CILT.
* Sinclair, J.McH., Forsyth, I.J., Coulthard, R.M., Ashby, M.C., The English used by teachers and pupils, final report to SSRC, mimeo, University of Birmingham.

1973
* Brazil, D.C., Intonation, 'Working Papers in Discourse Analysis', no. 2, mimeo, English Language Research.
* Coulthard, R.M., The analysis of classroom discourse, 'Preprints for the 1973 BAAL conference'.
* Coulthard, R.M. and Ashby, M.C., Doctor-patient interviews, 'Working Papers in Discourse Analysis', no. 1, mimeo, English Language Research.
* Pearce, R.D., The T.V. discussion programme, 'Working Papers in Discourse Analysis', no. 3, mimeo, English Language Research.
  Pearce, R.D., The structure of discourse in broadcast interviews, unpublished MA thesis, University of Birmingham.
  Sinclair, J.McH., Linguistics in Colleges of Education, 'Dudley Journal of Education', 17-25.
* Sinclair, J.McH., Practice and theory, 'Working Papers in Discourse Analysis', no. 4, mimeo, English Language Research.
* Stubbs, M., Some structural complexities of talk in meetings, 'Working Papers in Discourse Analysis', no. 5, mimeo, English Language Research.

1974
  Coulthard, R.M., Approaches to the analysis of classroom interaction, 'Educational Review', 229-40.
  Coulthard, R.M., The study of teacher-pupil talk, 'Cambridge Journal of Education', 2-13.
  Williams, S., A sociolinguistic analysis of the general practice interview, unpublished MA thesis, University of Birmingham.

1975
* Brazil, D.C., 'Discourse Intonation', Discourse Analysis Mono-
    graphs, no. 1, University of Birmingham, English Language
    Research.
  Burton, D. and Stubbs, M., On speaking terms: analysing
    conversational data, 'MALS Journal', 2, 1.
  Coulthard, R.M. and Ashby, M.C., Talking with the doctor,
    'Journal of Communication', 25, 3, 140-7.
  Coulthard, R.M., Discourse analysis in English: a review of the
    literature, 'Language and Linguistics Abstracts', 8, 1.
  Sinclair, J.McH. and Coulthard, R.M., 'Towards an Analysis of
    Discourse', London, Oxford University Press.
  Stubbs, M., Teaching and talking: a sociolinguistic approach to
    classroom interaction, in Channan, G. and Delamont, S.
    (eds), 'Frontiers of Classroom Research', Slough: National
    Federation for Educational Research.

1976
  Coulthard, R.M. and Ashby, M.C., A linguistic description of
    doctor-patient interviews, in Wadsworth, M. and Robinson,
    D. (eds), 'Studies in Everyday Medical Life', London, Martin
    Robertson.
  Stubbs, M., Keeping in touch: some functions of teacher-talk,
    in: Stubbs, M. and Delamont, S. (eds), 'Explorations in
    Classroom Observation', London, Wiley.

1977
  Burton, D., What's on the other channel: on channels of verbal
    interaction in the theatre, 'MALS Journal', 2, 1-19.
  Coulthard, R.M., 'An Introduction to Discourse Analysis',
    London, Longman.
  Montgomery, M.M., The structure of lectures, unpublished MA
    thesis, University of Birmingham.
  Pearce, R.D., 'Literary Texts', Discourse Analysis Monographs,
    no. 3, University of Birmingham, English Language Research.
  Roe, P., 'Scientific Text', Discourse Analysis Monographs, no.
    4, University of Birmingham, English Language Research.
  Willes, M., Early lessons learned too well, in: Adelman, C.
    (ed.), 'Uttering, Muttering', Reading, Bulmershe College.

1978
  Brazil, D.C., Discourse Intonation, unpublished PhD thesis,
    University of Birmingham.
  Brazil, D.C., 'Discourse Intonation II', Discourse Analysis
    Monographs, no. 2, University of Birmingham: English
    Language Research.
  Burton, D., Dialogue and discourse: a study of discourse
    analysis and modern drama dialogue, unpublished PhD thesis,
    University of Birmingham.
  Burton, D., Towards an analysis of casual conversation,
    'Nottingham Linguistic Circular', 7, 2, 131-64.

Richardson, K., Worthing Teachers Centre: a case study in discourse analysis, unpublished MA thesis, University of Birmingham.

1979

Berry, M., A note on Sinclair and Coulthard's classes of acts including a comment on comments, 'Nottingham Linguistic Circular', 8, 1, 49-59.

Coulthard, R.M. and Brazil, D.C. 'Exchange Structure', Discourse Analysis Monographs, no. 5, University of Birmingham, English Language Research.

Hoey, M., 'Signalling in Discourse', Discourse Analysis Monographs, no. 6, University of Birmingham, English Language Research.

Stubbs, M. and Robinson, B., Analysing classroom language, in Stubbs, M. et al., 'Observing Classroom Language', Block 5, P232, Open University.

Willes, M., Teaching explanations to five year old pupils, 'Language for Learning', 1, 2.

1980

Berry, M., 'Layers of Exchange Structure', Discourse Analysis Monographs, no. 7, University of Birmingham, English Language Research.

Brazil, D.C., Coulthard, R.M. and Johns, C.M., 'Discourse Intonation and Language Teaching', London, Longman.

Burton, D., 'Dialogue and Discourse', London, Routledge & Kegan Paul.

Willes, M., Learning to take part in classroom interaction, in French, P. and Maclure, M. (eds), 'Adult-child Conversation: Studies in Structure and Process', London, Croom Helm.

Index